THE CHERRYH ODYSSEY

THE CHERRYH ODYSSEY

EDITED BY EDWARD CARMIEN

I.O. Evans Studies
in the Philosophy and Criticism of Literature
ISSN 0271-9061

NUMBER TWENTY 25

Published in the United States by Borgo Press / Wildside Press
www.wildsidepress.com

I.O. Evans Studies in the
Philosophy and Criticism of Literature series: 25
(ISSN 0271-9061)

HB: 0-8095-1070-7
PB: 0-8095-1071-5

CONTENTS

PREFACE

Imagine it is the late 1970's. Imagine a small town in northern Michigan. Imagine a teenager with a strong taste for fantastic literature of all kinds—science fiction, fantasy, horror, even detective fiction—visiting a downtown bookstore. Horizon Books, in fact, the quintessential downtown bookstore packed to the gills with books of every description, and, luckily, a paperback section that includes science fiction and fantasy titles.

He visits on some dark wintry afternoon—if one is brave (or foolish) enough, one can ride a bicycle in the most outrageous conditions—and sees a distinctive yellow spine cover with black lettering, DAW's trademark book design scheme. *Well of Shiuan*. C.J. Cherryh. Who might he be? What might this be about?

He looks at the cover. Pictured is a woman on horseback (he loves horses and wishes he knew how to ride) with an eldritch-looking sword facing a half-clothed man with bound hands. Strangely, however, the back cover says "This is a novel of science fiction and fantasy . . . . " Careful examination proves that it is not an anthology—this lover of novels has been burned before—and that *Well of Shiuan* is in fact a sequel.

This bookstore sells new books. The teenager knows how to save a penny and heads for the downtown used bookstore and quickly finds *Gate of Ivrel*.

And so it began back some time during 1978. All I can recall about the month is that it was cold. It was several years before I learned C.J. Cherryh was not a man but a woman. Didn't matter to me in any case—being raised by a strong-minded woman tends to broaden one's sense of expectation. What began that cold day in Michigan was a life-long fascination with one of the science fiction and fantasy field's greatest and most prolific talents, a fascination and appreciation that ultimately has lead to what you hold in your hands at this moment.

What I didn't know on that day in 1978 would have filled a barn, and then some. I didn't know what kind of company DAW Books was, hadn't an idea who Donald A. Wollheim was, or how his contribution to the world of science fiction and fantasy was in one sense his publication of authors in the novel format, leapfrogging what had been the traditional path to publication at novel length, the strong magazine market of the day.

I didn't know that my strong preference for the novel form, shaped in my early reading days by a typical science-fiction library full of Asimov, Heinlein, Zimmer-Bradley, and others made me a different kind of reader than, say, the father of a high-school friend who possessed a large collection of magazines such as *The Magazine of Fantasy and Science Fiction* for whom the short form was the more common mode for science fiction and fantasy fiction. I remember reading some of this short fiction, and I remember missing the immersive wonder of a novel, the range of imagination required to really appreciate novel-length fantastic work.

Cherryh's work turned out to be compelling to a greater degree than anything I'd ever read. Her use of what she calls intense third person provides for a kind of immersion that can stun one's linguistic centers into new patterns if one isn't careful. Use of 80-word sentences that are nevertheless scalpel sharp and of starkly correct yet odd to the senses vocabulary are two symptoms one should watch out for.

For the next decade I haunted bookstores, checking to see, month after month, whether a new Cherryh book had hit the shelves. Dark Star in Yellow Springs, Ohio was to follow Traverse City's The Bookie Joint, and Bowling Green's "home of the strange change," Pauper's Paperbacks used bookstore, was one of the first amenities I investigated when I went to graduate school.

To fill the gaps between Cherryh releases I searched for authors who could engender the same sense of fascination and respect for craft as Cherryh did. Over the decades I've found a number, but there is always something lacking. Often it is sheer production—Cherryh to this day writes and publishes an amazing amount—and other times it proves to be consistency: one novel piques my interest, but the next by the same author doesn't quite have the same effect.

Robert Reed, John Crowley, Iain M. Banks, Sean Russell, Robin Hobb, James P. Hogan, and many others have caught my eye over the years. Steven Brust, Terry Pratchett, and Neal Stephenson in particular are authors I follow, along with Cherryh, from one book to the next. The works of Tony Hillerman and John D. McDonald are also particularly fascinating, though they don't write science fiction and fantasy (or at least not usually, in McDonald's case).

I make no claim of similarity between these authors and their texts beyond their ability to cause me to always wish to own and read their books when they arrive, fresh from the printer, on the shelves of bookstores.

Of all these authors, after all these years of reading books in the field and selling a dozen stories to science fiction and fantasy markets as a writer—why Cherryh? Why collect and edit the thoughts of a dozen people about this author? Beyond a continuing strong interest in her work, and beyond the several interviews I've been granted by Cherryh over the years for academic purposes, there was a growing sense that more needed to be done to recognize this prolific and influential science fiction and fantasy author. This sense crystallized after a Science Fiction Research Association conference at which Cherryh was the guest of honor.

I shared a few interesting conversations with Cherryh and another author at the conference, Jane Yolen, and listened with interest to Cherryh's keynote presentation that all but confirmed the gist of a paper I'd given earlier that day. Yet with all of this positive attention to Cherryh's literary life and career, as I drove home along the New York State Thruway it occurred to me that given Cherryh's intellectual and creative footprint in the world of the literary fantastic, more should be done to recognize her contributions to the field.

Someone, I said to myself, should write a bo—and then it happened, the lightbulb went off, my jaw sagged, and a sense of obligation settled onto my shoulders like a blanket. Not someone. I was the logical choice, or at least *a* logical choice for the task of bringing more attention to this important and prolific writer. The timing was right. While such a book was, commercially, not a worthwhile proposition, that's what life in academe can provide—support for important projects that don't necessarily have the promise of turning a sensible profit. And given the typical publication schedule, a book on Cherryh would come out close to the thirty-year mark of her remarkable career as a novelist.

As it happens, Wildside Press is nimble and quick, and *The Cherryh Odyssey* is hitting the streets ahead of that projected 30-year mark.

Why this title? Cherryh is a well-known traveler, like Odysseus of old. It came to be after some serious thought and seemed to make sense in many important metaphysical ways. Cherryh's writing career to date represents the skilled and focused attention of a very intelligent and creative person on the question of story telling. Her journey as a writer began, as she has frequently told the story, when at the age of ten her favorite television show went off the air and she had to resort to making up her own stories. Self-taught and highly motivated and inquisitive, she trained to become a classics teacher but has constantly sought out educational opportunities in many areas, including linguistics, anthropology, and archaeology to name but a few.

She has journeyed in many ways during the past decades, and looks ready to continue traveling for decades to come. Cherryh moved often as a child and while she's managed to spend lengthy periods in different places as an adult she remains a traveler, currently living in the northwestern United States. And while as the saying goes you can never go home again, she does revisit certain themes and ideas in her work as the years roll by, returning each time with greater skill and ability to craft a new view of something that echoes a past theme or concept but does not merely reproduce it.

Forge of Heaven, for example, tells a story of humanity living through a cataclysmic shift in the ecology, similar to a theme in *Well of Shiuan*. Of course there is little else in common between these texts, and one can enjoy each story fully without spoiling enjoyment of the other. As she travels, Cherryh, like any author worth her salt, learns and changes with time and experience.

Odysseus did not have an easy journey, and Cherryh does not, either. In fact, even traveling with Cherryh is a challenge, just as it was for Odysseus's crew of stalwarts. She does not choose the easy road when a difficult path may prove more rewarding. We readers must perforce follow along, unless we choose to jump ship. Some do. Many remain.

This text's primary purpose is to enrich the reader's experience of Cherryh's writing. To sit around the fire in the darkness with the eyed-ship pulled dry nearby and talk over the many important aspects of Cherryh's work is the journey this text represents. A dozen writers contributed to this project, and it is my hope you will find sympathetic voices here.

The design of this collection deserves mention, as this is not a text full of academic writing. Nor is it a book of essays only by fellow professionals. From the very beginning, perhaps with an excess of idealism, I set out to gather a wide array of voices together under one roof or if you will, around one campfire. I believe the collection of essays you now hold represents great success in this regard. Certainly, there are scholars, but they work in many fields, including languages, bibliography, and psychology. And there are fellow writers and editors, professionals who know first hand the science fiction and fantasy field, as well as Cherryh herself. No less diverse a body of contributors could possibly do justice to this subject.

In an ideal world there would also be the words of fans, people with no connection to the world of science fiction and fantasy beyond their love of it and their role as members of its audience. This proved to be impossible. However, the fans are indeed here—each and every contributor is in his or her own way a reader of Cherryh's works, and as they have contributed to this labor of intellectual love and attention, one can be sure their thoughts and ideas are well developed and well informed.

There are some practical consequences of this admixture of writers and perspectives. The more academic articles follow Modern Language Association (MLA) format and have a purpose in the world of ideas that is represented by formal citations. None are dry, however, and all are readable by non-academics. Other articles are less formal and do not use MLA format. Each essay has its own introduction: look there for cues about how the following material might best be digested and viewed.

Of all the items here, one stands out for being unreadable (in a traditional sense) and yet tremendously useful (mostly for academics). The selected bibliography of works by and about Cherryh will appear to non-academic eyes as a densely packed presentation of names and titles. Even non-academics may find this useful, however, for if you seek the answer to a question such as "how many books has Cherryh written?" or "I wonder if someone has written an article about my favorite Cherryh book?" this bibliography can be of great service.

Finally, one might ask if *The Cherryh Odyssey* answers a problem in the field. One reason the editing of this text recommended itself to me while driving on the New York State Thruway is, sadly, Cherryh's lack of sufficient (in my opinion) popular appeal and critical attention. I hold that there is no other more important writer active as of this writing that is less appreciated, understood, and read. Cherryh has a strong audience, and her work as a writer is not to my knowledge in jeopardy in an economic sense. However, at convention after convention, when contemporary authors are discussed by gatherings of fans and fellow professionals, Cherryh's contributions to the field, although demonstrable, are marginalized. Cherryh devotees form a semi-secret minority who happily meet and discuss her work, as at the 2003 BaltiCon or online at venues such as Shejidan. As Stan Szalewicz's "Selected Bibliography" shows, Cherryh has received a lot of critical attention over the years. Critics and academics are not the sole audience for this work, and it is hoped that this text will broaden the awareness of Cherryh's importance to the field among readers, new and old alike.

This does not represent a conscious effort on anyone's part to deny Cherryh her due. There are a number of factors that contribute to this atmosphere, however, and if *The Cherryh Odyssey* does nothing else but change this atmosphere, I will be a happy editor. Cherryh is commonly known as a hard read. This can be true but as I have argued in other venues, the effort is worth it, and indeed makes Cherryh's prose literary in stature. She has also published a number of books that are experimental. Being ahead of one's time is not always good for one's career. In particular, Cherryh's handling of languages has always been cutting edge, and she is much imitated—today. Contemporary writers have benefited from Cherryh's past experiments, not all of which, in the manner of experiments, proved to be successful. Cherryh, and DAW Books in particular, were brave enough to put pressure on science fiction and fantasy to evolve with such experiments—and the field has evolved, as any look at texts from 25 years ago will show.

In the end, a rational look at Cherryh's 60+ titles and her many, many contributions to the craft of writing will result in greater critical and popular recognition. I hope *The Cherryh Odyssey* provides a good way for readers to take such a look. I invite you to enjoy the following essays, and I hope they provoke further thought and discussion about Cherryh and her ongoing literary journey.

—Edward Carmien

ACKNOWLEDGEMENTS

There are many who deserve thanks for what you see before you. John Betancourt of Wildside Press deserves a nod for giving the green light to this project to a first-time editor. In no particular order, Karl Bates, Janet Deaver-Pack, Darrell Schweitzer, Craig Paulenich, Donald Hassler, Selina Rosen, Javier Martinez, Ernest Lilley, Beverly Hale, Sean Wallace, and many others have my thanks for advice and assistance. Organizations such as the SFWA, SFRA, and last year's BaltiCon organization have contributed venues for discussion of these subjects. My contributors deserve thanks, and thanks also go to those who supplied ideas and material to the project that proved impossible to use. Of particular note among the contributors stand Jane Fancher, who provided many key contacts and many other things, and Jan Stinson, who offered not only her contribution but also marketing and professional proofreading skills.

Thanks to the technical grace and 'drop-everything' effort of Igor Jonjic, Shane Smith, David Weise, and of Rider University's Office of Information Technology—Support Services, the bits and bytes of this project were protected during periods of hardware breakdown.

Finally, thanks must be accorded to Rider University, which supported a portion of the development of this project with a Summer Fellowship and a grant to cover certain office expenses.

Edward Carmien, Ph.D.
June, 2004
Princeton, New Jersey

ABOUT THE COVER

David A. Cherry

The cover for this book is one I had hoped would be used years back as the cover for the DAW Books edition of my sister's anthology, *Visible Light*. Since she had taken the unusual step of writing herself in as a character in the book, we felt it appropriate to have her portrait on the cover. As I worked up different ideas and treatments, I set aside a pencil portrait of Carolyn that I had done on tracing paper. As chance would have it, the paper landed on top of a page torn from a science digest. The image on the page was a colorful photograph of some sort of energy emission, and it was clearly visible through the tracing paper. It looked as though rays of [light, energy, thought?] were streaming from her. I loved it and determined that nothing else would do for the cover of that book. Unfortunately, the concept was not warmly received by the publisher and was shelved. Undeterred, I did the painting for it anyway. It was simply too fine an image to leave undone. Now, years later, I am pleased that I took the time to do it and even more pleased to know that it will finally achieve its destiny as a cover, if not for a book by her, then for a book about her, which I find even more satisfying. Kharma.

As I scanned the art for this cover in preparation for transfer to the publisher, I could not resist playing with it a bit in Photoshop, and I was very glad I did. I had always been slightly frustrated with the original. I could never find any way to make the acrylic paints achieve the vibrancy of the reference photo that had inspired the piece. Without that visual impact I was never sure that the painting accomplished its narrative purpose. Perhaps others only saw it as a woman with colored ribbons streaming from her head, not the bolts of energy I had meant to paint. So, it was with a real sense of fulfillment that, less than a full minute after I had the image fully scanned, I moved a "slider" in Photoshop and, whammo. The image was suddenly as I had always intended it to be. This was certainly a painting with a destiny of its own. Little did I know when I did it that so many years would pass before this particular project called for it at a time when I had the technology to finish it properly.

I wish I had time to write more for this book. I love my sister and owe her a great deal. There is so much I would like to say, so many stories to tell, like what it was like to have her as my Latin and Ancient History teacher in high school or what it was like to attend my first science fiction convention with her, watch as she received the Campbell Award for Best New Science Fiction Writer of the Year and afterwards meet such luminaries as Isaac Asimov, Marion Zimmer Bradley, and Robert Heinlein. In the limited time and space available I can, however, direct a message to her:

Thank you, Sis, for all that you have done for me. You gave me my appreciation of art, literature, history, and language. You gave me my basics in drawing and painting. You encouraged me to leave law and follow my heart to become an artist. Your greatest gift, however, has been your lifelong example of how to live with honor, integrity, and courage. I am always several steps behind you, but my eye is always on you as my guide.

Love always,
Little Brother

INTRODUCTION:
WHAT WE DO FOR LOVE

James Gunn

Science fiction started out as an old-boys club—old boys writing for young boys, no women need apply. The earliest female writers often used initials or sexually ambiguous first names, such as Francis Stevens, Leigh Brackett, C. L. Moore, Andre Norton, Wilmar Shiras, or later, U. K. Le Guin and the male pseudonym chosen by Alice Sheldon, James Tiptree, Jr. The barriers, if there were any, began to splinter in the 1940s, with writers such as Judith Merrill and Katherine MacLean. By the 1950s women were being published in the magazines with increasing frequency, although usually not in *Astounding*, considered the magazine for science and technology. Even if women could write SF, it was thought, it was a softer, literary kind tending toward fantasy.

That still was the situation when Carolyn Janice Cherry submitted her first novel to Donald A. Wollheim, publisher of DAW Books, in 1975. The novel was the fantasy *Gate of Ivrel,* and Wollheim persuaded Cherry to publish it using the initials C. J. and adding an "h" to her family name. It was an auspicious beginning for an author, even if her gender was obscured, and Cherryh soon became a full-time writer, first of fantasy trilogies, and then of science fiction, beginning with *Brothers of Earth* in 1976. And not only science fiction, but hard science fiction, and not only hard science fiction but Hugo Award-winning hard science fiction concerned with space flight and extra-planetary colonization and competition between space-faring cultures.

Cherryh became a successful freelance writer in what had been, until then, a male-dominated publishing world. It might all have seemed unlikely to the parents of the child born in 1942 in St. Louis. And still unlikely to the student who earned a B.A. in Latin from the University of Oklahoma in 1964 and an M.A. in classics from Johns Hopkins University the following year. And still unlikely when she taught Latin and classical history in Oklahoma City schools from 1965-1976. But not so unlikely when she was voted the John W. Campbell Award as the most promising new writer in 1977.

Since then, Cherryh has produced two books a year, and is still happily at work pleasing fans and critics while alternating between SF and fantasy. An early SF novel, *Downbelow Station*, won a Hugo Award for 1981, and her SF novel *Cyteen* won a Hugo Award for 1988. An earlier short story, "Cassandra," won a Hugo Award for 1978. Clearly she has been doing things right.

Of her own aspirations, Cherryh has written, "The reach for space and its resources is the make-or-break point for our species, and the appropriate use of technology and the adjustment of human viewpoint to a universe not limited to a blue sky overhead and the curvature of the horizon are absolutely critical to our survival." As to her methods, she has written science fiction ought to "create new symbologies and new understandings appropriate to the space age, not forgetting the traditions of our culture, but widening its viewpoints."

In another context I have suggested that SF operates by using one of two strategies: by estranging the familiar or by familiarizing the strange. Cherryh has specialized in the second strategy, in surrounding her fantastic concepts with such convincing detail that it makes us feel that we are experiencing reality, and that may be the reason why even her fantasy is different—it is solidly grounded in naturalistic detail.

That may have been what John Clute was describing, in the *Encyclopedia of Science Fiction*, as the "almost unfailingly creative tension . . . between argument and fantastication." He went on to suggestion that for Cherryh

"the Universe, and everything imaginable within its particoloured quad-
rants, is both evanescent and full of marvel, and that sentient species must
revere whatever habitats remain to them after the terrible years of species
growth and species destruction hinted at in . . . books set early in the
Universe."

It is time for the kind of critical consideration of Cherryh's remarkable
body of work that this book incorporates. Ed Carmien, a remarkable enthu-
siast, SF author and academic, has gathered together a group of equally
enthusiastic admirers of science fiction or of a particular SF author, to write
appreciatively and often perceptively about Cherryh's body of work: a business partner, an author, a critic, a publisher, a psychologist, a librarian and
gender-studies authority, another librarian and organist, and a handful of
literary scholars. Her brother, a professional artist, contributed the cover. It
raises an interesting and perhaps not obvious question: why do they do it?

That's been a question that has bedeviled science fiction almost since its
beginning. There has been little money in it for anyone—publishers, editors,
or authors, and now for scholars. Except for a favored few, and then only in
recent times, SF has been a choice that people made, or had made for them, in
spite of obvious rewards rather than because of them, and such financial
successes as there are, with a few exceptions, have come in recent years and
to those who worked on the periphery of the central core of SF.

Take Donald A. Wollheim, Cherryh's perceptive editor. A brilliant mind
and a publishing genius, he toiled for years in the editorial salt mines, first as
a magazine editor (originally at no salary), then as editor of SF at Ace Books.
Never highly paid as a group, editors at penny-pinching publishers like Ace
(important as they may have been to SF, often because of editors such as
Wollheim) would have been paid even less. So it was only as the culmination
of a life-time of dedication that Wollheim got New American Library as a
partner in his new publishing enterprise, DAW Books. One can only imagine
what Wollheim's career would have been like if he had been motivated to
work for money.

Or take Cherryh. She has been successful in creating and maintaining an
unlikely career as a freelance writer, and a female writer in a male field—but
it should be noted that a male editor saw no problems with that from her first
submitted novel and told her to quit her teaching job and offered her a
three-book contract in order to make it possible. But Cherryh has had to

write two books a year in order to survive. Would she have liked the luxury of devoting an entire year to a book, or two years, as do some purveyors of best-sellers or popular series? Perhaps. But perhaps, too, this writing habit has demanded constant feeding. She could have adulterated her product (writing shorter sentences is one way she has described a choice she refused), but she never did. Her work has been consistently rigorous. Why?

The answer is love. Science fiction has the capability to inspire it, to create fans. Together fans created fandom—the conventions Carmien describe where writers gather to interact with their readers in a way unprecedented in literary history, the fanzines, the fan publishers, the clubs, the filksongs . . . . Something about science fiction turns readers into fans—people who not only read it but live it. *Fiawol,* as the fans say: fandom is a way of life. I have pondered what makes it happen: Is it because the literature, when it is done properly, requires its readers to collaborate in creating alien worlds? Is it because SF is not simply a fiction but a commitment to a better way of life, to the human species itself, that in giving ourselves over to it we enter a kind of monastic order, what H. G. Wells called "an Open Conspiracy" to work toward human survival and even improvement?

Maybe all of these things. Sometimes this kind of affection is bestowed, as in real life, on unworthy recipients. That is one of the risks fandom takes, and even then the generous act redeems the error. But often it leads to revealing what we all should see and admire. In the case of Caroline Cherryh, a worthy recipient of such affection, that is the obvious outcome. There is much to admire, and much to learn from these acute observers, whose eyes, though starry, are not blinded.

They, too, do it for love, but it is well to remind ourselves that everything is better when it is done for love and not for money. The entire history of science fiction is proof.

I hope you will allow the powerful and effective rhythms of Jane's prose to take you into the legacy Cherryh has provided so far in her career. No one has a better perspective, and no one can tell the tale better than Jane Fancher. Her article is a well-informed and valuable look at C.J. Cherryh's writing and literary career.

After 17 years in the ivory tower it is easy to forget how distant from ordinary discourse the usual academic mode of discussion can be. Working with Jane to arrive at this article required a good deal of cajoling, but once a comfortable mode of expression was found there was no stopping her.

From the very beginning of this project Jane Fancher was a "must have" author for the anthology. A talented novelist with a number of titles under her belt, Jane is also an artist and worked on the sadly incomplete graphic novel version of *Gate of Ivrel*. Working with Cherryh on the graphic novel was enough to bring her to the world of fiction, and she has been steadily publishing ever since.

THE CHERRYH LEGACY
... AN AUTHOR'S PERSPECTIVE

Jane S. Fancher

Legacy. A strange word to use for a writing career that is, at most, only half over, and yet for many of us writing today, that legacy began on a fateful day in 1976 when we picked up a little novel, *Gate of Ivrel*, by an author with the enigmatic name, C.J. Cherryh.

I was a college student at the time, a triple major in Math, Physics, and Astronomy with a persistent interest in Anthropology. I had little spare time and less money for entertainment. Suffice to say, as a consumer, I was a picky reader, but not a particularly critical one. Once I discovered them, I wallowed happily in this C.J. Cherryh's rich worlds and richer characters, the complex, mind-challenging plots and wickedly Machiavellian politics, never thinking twice either about how the books came to be, or to the person behind them, having no idea at the time that I'd one day be writing myself—at the suggestion of this same, phenomenal C.J. Cherryh.

Over the years fate has handed me a unique opportunity to observe the phenomenon in action, a journey that has taken me from simple consumer, to business partner (on the *Gate of Ivrel* graphic novel project), to apprentice (as I took up writing myself), and, ultimately, back to business partner (as we became each other's alpha readers).

Carolyn Cherryh is my idol, my business partner, my mentor, and my best friend. I've heard her personal stories and her writing advice countless times in dozens of contexts, and over the years patterns have begun to emerge as I've endeavored to sort process from talent, to separate that which I could learn from that which I would have to discover within myself. Patterns of causality, not only in her work as it affects consumers and inspires fellow writers, but within the publishing field itself.

Patterns of causality as wonderfully interwoven as one of her plots.

The Foundation

C.J. Cherryh is quite simply one of the finest stylists ever to commit words to paper.

If pressed to pick a "favorite passage" to demonstrate, it would have to be the opening passage from the critically quiet, stand-alone novel, *Faery in Shadow* . . .

> The water flowed first from a spring in Teile, clear as glass, and out of the loch in broad Gleann Teile it emerged rich, peat-dark, its brown-stained bubbles swirling over tumbled basalt. Guagach was the name of this stream, and it plunged through sun-touched bracken and over rock as it began its chute into Gleann Fiain, a noisy fall into a barren chasm, whence it issued whispering and babbling madness. It was born bright and clear and clean on the mountains, it became one thing in the peat of Gleann Teile, and it became something else again in that pool, down among the dark-leaved trees of Gleann Fiain. A single shaft of sunlight pierced the branches and spread itself through the spray in a rainbow that made the woods and rocks seem the blacker about that boiling cauldron . . .

With the skill of the finest movie directors—and the relentless force of gravity—she uses that water and an ill-fated leaf to slip the reader from one world into another—that of the even more ill-fated character.

> A trio of bubbles danced in the whirlpool it left. A brown leaf fell in the treachery of a breeze, as if the evil in the water had caused the limbs above the stream to move and to rattle.
>
> If that was the cause, it was a very vile thing which lived beneath that willow, and travelers would be well-advised to take some other course than that stony, breakneck

path which led down the fell. Such travelers would have been wiser still to seek at once back to the braes of Gleann Teile and their sunlight.

But Caith mac Sliabhin and his companion walked beside the darksome water under that autumn dearth of leaf, and Caith never lifted his head until a breeze sported ashore and touched him with its cold.

Exquisite, lyrical use of the English language, setting the stage perfectly for a Celtic-based fantasy full of darkness and moody magic. We're led to wonder, Does Caith sense that darkness, or is he, like the leaf, caught in the whims of fate?

And just as we begin to wonder, the poetic, descriptive prose slips seamlessly into the background, leaving the story firmly in the hands of the viewpoint character.

Then he wrapped his grey storm-cloak about him, realizing how dark the path had become since they had left the pool behind; while his companion cast a look toward the dark water and that spinning leaf, and walked down to lean over the brink, hands on kilted thighs.

Caith paid him no heed. A great many things distracted Dubhain, half of them nonsensical—a butterfly, the flutter of a leaf, the rising of a bubble in a brook.

In stark contrast are the similarly stage-setting paragraphs of her award-winning *Cyteen:*

It was from the air that the rawness of the land showed most: vast tracts where humanity had as yet made no difference, deserts unclaimed, stark as moons, scrag and woolwood thickets unexplored except by orbiting radar. Ariane Emory gazed down at it from the window.

She kept to the passenger compartment now. Her eyesight, she had had to admit it, was no longer sharp enough, her reflexes no longer fast enough for the jet. She could go up front, bump the pilot out of the chair and take the controls: it was her plane, her pilot, and a wide sky. Sometimes she did. But it was not the same.

Only the land was, still most of the land was. And when she looked out the window, it might have been a century ago, when humankind had been established on Cyteen less than a hundred years, when Union was unthought of, the War only a rumbling discontent, and the land looked exactly like this everywhere.

Hard SF against a backdrop of Carolyn's vast future history, the needs of *Cyteen* are fundamentally different from those of *Faery in Shadow*. *Cyteen* is a story of science, and politics, and generation-spanning projects and near godlike manipulation by this same Ariane Emory. The setup for all those elements is right there in that opening statement, just as magic and the ancient Scottish hillside resides in the opening to *Faery*. The opening to *Cyteen* retains a hint of the poetic rhythms, but quickly shifts to both the physical limitations and political power of the key player in the novel. Unlike Caith, who, like the leaf, must react and survive the elemental forces at work, Ari is the force with which the rest of the universe must contend. It is her plane, her pilot, her choice whether or not to take control, a choice she makes with ruthless self-honesty, a key character trait throughout the rest of the book.

This facility with words is the most nonreplicable aspect of the Cherryh Legacy because it comes from within, a combination of that elusive, indefinable quality known as "talent" and an even more elusive ingredient: serendipity.

Carolyn's development as a writer gives whole new meaning to the phrase "self-taught."

At the tender age of ten, and needing to fill the hole caused by the cancellation of her favorite TV show, *Flash Gordon*, she began writing. That same day, she left the privacy of her bedroom to announce to her mother she was going to be a writer. Her mother said That's nice; get a real job to pay the bills. That made sense, but she reckoned she'd need a job that gave her lots of free time to write. Teachers had all summer free. Perfect! (The fact that teachers didn't get *paid* for those months off didn't register until somewhat later, when the end of summers found her living on tomato soup.)

Her future settled, she began to write. She discovered that extended writing made her hand hurt, so she taught herself to type on a 1930's government surplus Underwood typewriter which, according to rumor, had taken a dive out a second story window early in its career. But it worked; that's all that counted. Day after day, year after year, she tapped away in her bedroom, her only test audience her seven-years-younger brother, an audience she lost when he got to be a teenager and too, well, *teenager* for bedtime stories.

At first (so she says—I've never seen them) these stories reflected the *Flash Gordon* serials, with character genders and names changed, but little else.

Then, she learned the term "plagiarism" and with visions of the Plagiarism Police beating down the door of the house (these *were* the McCarthy years) she began a serious quest to make *her* stories different from anyone else's.

Serendipity. One does wonder, in retrospect, just how large a part paranoia played in what is one of the largest and most varied bodies of work in the history of literature.

Fate took a hand again in her high school years, when she considered (briefly) taking creative writing classes. As luck would have it, Creative Writing conflicted with Band. She was first chair flute; Band won.

Fortunately.

With all due respect to the value of creative writing classes in all their guises for the masses, ultimately, unique "voices" come from within, not from rules. While tools for analysis are useful—and even invaluable—once the creative muse has been nurtured, trying to force "rules" onto the embryonic muse only stifles its growth. Time and again, I've seen C.J., the mentor, having to pry a potential student's fingers off the rule book superimposed on his creativity in some writing class. I personally had a well-meaning high-school English teacher send my creative muse into a twenty-year coma with her insistence on what constituted the "correct" approach to fictional writing: my own little bit of serendipity, since, had I discovered my love of writing at that early stage, I wouldn't have taken art as my creative outlet, wouldn't have come to work with Carolyn on the graphic novel, and wouldn't be in the position to be writing this today.

Serendipity. It affects us all.

But I digress . . . Fortunately, Carolyn avoided the rules-pitfall and continued to practice her craft in the privacy of her bedroom, sending out manuscripts, collecting rejection slips, even as Fate, having taken away on the one hand, provided an alternative on the other: Latin.

Fate, luck, serendipity—call it what you will, her life took a defining turn when she chose first to take, then to major in, and ultimately to teach Latin and Ancient History.

For one of the premier "Hard SF" authors working today, Carolyn's formal education might seem strangely lacking in the so-called "Hard Sciences." Though Carolyn took an early interest in the sciences (indeed, she consumed Astronomy books—of whatever vintage—as gleefully as she consumed Tarzan and Tom Corbett), though her fascination with forensics and serial killers would garner her an immediate psychoanalysis these days, though she kept a scrap book of every science article that appeared in the Lawton, Oklahoma newspapers, when it came to formal education, her resumé shows only the most basic science classes. The reason for this is quite simple: an unfortunate encounter with a mathematics teacher early in her academic career which set mental barriers against certain elements of higher mathematics, which in turn kept her from ever advancing beyond the non-science-major level of science classes.

Serendipity.

Carolyn laments what she perceives as a weakness in her education, and in fact, there are numerous in-house jokes regarding her "Tau Cetian Math," which is far more suited to reconciling the Big Picture than to reconciling bank accounts, but in my opinion, this lack of mathematical affinity was yet another gift of fate, as it pushed her away from the lure of science and its increasingly specialized classes and forced her to find Something Else. That Something Else (Latin) proved a major key to her stunningly brilliant use of language—thanks to a Latin teacher who inspired her to see past the memorization of words and rules of grammar to the substance behind the words and the reasons for the rules (a knowledge base that would ultimately stand her in very good stead against copyeditors' ongoing attempts to standardize her word usage—but more on that later.)

Along with Latin came the translations: Virgil . . . Julius Caesar. Thanks to these great Latin writers, Carolyn's interest in Ancient History blossomed along with her gift for languages. Even as Virgil's poetic turn of phrase set the bar for her writing skills, Julius Caesar sparked her interest in Roman History, and led her, once she began her higher education, to specialize not only in Latin, but in one of the most politically and sociologically dynamic periods in human history: the transition of Rome from Republic to Empire.

The significance of her study in this area of history is as subtle as the effect of the Latin rhythms on her prose, but a study of Rome at this key juncture is quite literally a study of one "first contact" after another. Some methods worked, others didn't. Some leaders were magnificently effective, others . . . less so. The Romans were physical and social engineers: a study of what made them viable world leaders for over two thousand years is a study rich in possibilities—for a student who would one day create dozens of worlds and political situations.

In her freshman year, fate handed her another subtle educational gem: the perfect roommate for a future Hugo Award contender.

The University of Oklahoma was a closed campus. Freshmen lived in dorms. Second semester freshman Linda Holmes was in search of a room-mate, her assigned roomie being incompatible; Carolyn Cherry was in the same situation. Linda was a genetics student; Carolyn was in Classics. They shared a French class. Linda needed help in French. Badly. Carolyn was available. They moved in together, and Carolyn's third Hugo Award for *Cyteen*, though years in the future, was assured.

As undergrads, Carolyn helped Linda with her French and those pesky Latin terms for anatomical parts. In return, she got a vicarious education in genetics at a time when the discipline was in its wildly speculative infancy. She got an unofficial job cleaning planaria (flatworm) trays for the labs—helping Holmes care for the creatures at all hours of the clock. She was taking Latin and Archeology and History, but she was surrounded with cutting-edge science. Actually, the experiments being done on flatworms gave new meaning to the term, since part of the project involved, quite liter-ally, chopping them up and feeding them to each other—but once again, I digress.

As her senior year rolled around, having no money for graduate school, she prepared to wave goodbye to Holmes, who was off to Johns Hopkins the following year to work under one of the country's premier geneticists. However, unbeknownst to Carolyn, her classics advisor had applied for a Woodrow Wilson fellowship for her. All she remembers was being handed a bunch of papers and told to sign: her first lesson in the "read first" rule.

Suddenly, mid-senior year, she got a notification that she was a finalist for the fellowship, triggering her first solo trip from home: a bus trip up to Kansas City. A bus trip that turned out to be an all-nighter milkrun, stopping (as she puts it) at every mailbox en route. A convict in the seat behind her, a juvenile offender being run out of town who insisted on telling his life story to his seatmate, kept her entertained but awake and wary. She arrived in Kansas City just in time for the interview, if somewhat bleary-eyed. She remembers little about the interview itself except exiting with an assumption that she hadn't a chance at the fellowship.

The return trip, lacking the convict, was simply long and numbing.

Naturally, as she prepared for graduation and began to put together her resumé for teaching applications, the fellowship came through—contingent on her acceptance into a graduate program. Only one problem: she hadn't applied anywhere. Quickly, she sent out applications. Stanford wanted a thirty-page medical history. Buffalo, NY required similar masses of paperwork. Johns Hopkins, where roommate Holmes was bound, sent a one note-page "welcome aboard" from the major professor in Classics.

Once again she'd be rooming with her best friend, the geneticist, who was, it so happened, going to be working on one of the first serious studies of genetic links to psychological abnormalities, a project taking head-on the politically hot question of "nature" versus "nurture", a topic at the core of the aforementioned award-winning *Cyteen*.

Serendipity.

By the time she graduated and began teaching, she had all the pieces, but potential is only the first step.

The Creation of a World Class Author

A phenomenon takes more than potential, it takes single-minded, dedicated production.

At twelve, Carolyn Janice Cherry collected her first rejection slip for a poem submitted to the *Saturday Evening Post*. Undaunted, she kept writing, but not submitting, with no professional instruction, waiting for another twenty years before making her first sale to DAW Books, Inc.

Today, with over sixty novels to her credit thus far (and nary a ghost writer in sight), C.J. Cherryh is one of the most prolific writers in modern science fiction. When you compare that number to actual word count . . . novels varying from the 80,000 word *Gate of Ivrel* to the 350,000 word *Cyteen,* averaging some 130,000 per novel, the sheer output of just under thirty years is staggering. (I might also add, she had no "closet novels" to pull out once she began publishing. Only *Hestia, Hunter of Worlds,* and *Brothers of Earth* existed, and those only in rough draft, when she sold *Gate of Ivrel.)*

When you consider that for the first three of those years, she was teaching school full time, and for several years following her official retirement from teaching she attended conventions at a rate of one a month, promoting her career; that she nursed her parents through multiple bouts with cancer and other health problems, and worked extensively with young writers . . . not to mention helping a certain Jane Fancher with a graphic-novel adaptation of that same *Gate of Ivrel* . . . you begin to believe the woman's fingers work the keyboard in her sleep.

I'm not altogether certain they don't.

And then there's the equipment. She wore out the keys on four standard typewriters, sent the subsequent Selectric's ball flying in pieces across the room more than once, and typed her rough drafts on a endless roll of shelf paper to avoid time-wasting paper-changes. She had her first Atari wired with buffers until it looked like some alien monster before finally attaining her first PC and laser printer, those marvelous monsters of technology which have made "writers" out of half the American population, and have given the term "padded prose" a whole new meaning within the publishing industry.

Nothing stopped her active mind from producing, and there's nothing "padded" about *her* prose, before or after the PC.

The Mentor

Quality, quantity . . . next, she needed an echo in the dark: a mentor of her own. Once again, fate took a hand in the person of Donald A. Wollheim, owner/publisher of DAW Books, Inc.

Carolyn sent *Brothers of Earth* to DAW in the mid 1970s. A few months later, she received an actual personal letter (as opposed to the generic rejection forms of the past) from Don Wollheim himself. He expressed his appreciation of the manuscript, but said it was a bit long for the current market. Did she have something of about 80,000 words?

Well, no, but two months later, she did . . . an "I'm working on something" to Don Wollheim, and two months teaching full-time, rising at 4, writing, teaching a full schedule, rushing home, writing, eating one-handed, writing until 1 and 2 a.m. . . . and off it went in the mail. DAW's official acceptance of the 80,000 word *Gate of Ivrel* was Don Wollheim's first contribution to the Cherryh Legacy. Don's acceptance letter said DAW would be publishing Gate . . . first. Despite its market-bucking length, he'd accepted *Brothers* as well.

His second contribution.

With her third submission to DAW, Carolyn inadvertently challenged yet another marketing no-no.

Carolyn is a linguist. Her understanding of languages encompasses not only the words and syntax of the language itself, but the origin of words and the psychology behind the connections to other words. Over the years, her readers have become accustomed to the notion that her created alien mindsets, based on non-human genetic hardwiring, will have concepts not easily handled by the English language. They take it for granted that such non-human concepts will have no human verbal representations, and that an entire book might be centered around making these alien concepts clear to both the human protagonist and the reader.

They take it for granted ... now. In 1976, such a story was a potential marketing disaster.

In *Gate of Ivrel* she brushed against this particular technique, introducing the readers to the words *ilin* and *liyo,* a uniquely Ivrel twist on medieval fealty concepts, a relationship between two individuals that involves penalties both legal and spiritual, oaths both legally and spiritually binding, and mandating even (potentially) ritual suicide. Some have tried to describe it in terms of Japanese fealty practices, but, in fact, there is only one word to describe what Vanye is, and that word is *ilin.*

Hunter of Worlds was her first serious foray into this practice. The plot, the world, the technology, the protagonist's personal growth ... every aspect of the novel revolves around the reader coming to understand, and accept, that certain human values simply have no meaning to the ruling alien species. It's not a technical expansion of the reader's universe, but a psychological one. Part of making that understanding happen was the inclusion of a great number of alien words.

When she submitted the novel, Don's response was, quite literally: "Most publishers would make you take all that out and substitute English ... Nah, let 'em work."

Let 'em work, indeed. And shortly after that, on a three-book contract from Don, specifying neither type nor length nor due date, Carolyn quit teaching and went to full-time writing.

To truly understand Don's commitment to the field in backing Carolyn's endeavors, it's useful to consider the state of publishing at the time.

Shortly after *Gate of Ivrel* hit the stores, *Star Wars* arrived on the scene, proving to corporate America that Science Fiction could make money—lots of money . . . if that Science Fiction followed a certain, easy access, media-like format; a format which is the complete antithesis of an author like C.J. Cherryh. We'll never know what might have happened to the Legacy, had Carolyn been working at this formative stage for one of the corporate controlled publishing companies. It's very possible that in order to sell, she'd have felt compelled to fit herself into some predictable mold, possible that today, instead of this wealth of variety, we'd have three dozen *Gate* adventures. Knowing Carolyn today, I doubt it, I simply can't see her prostituting that great wealth of creativity simply to pay the bills. More likely, she'd have found some way around the orders and written good, possibly even outstanding, stories, but whether the scope we associate with her work today, not to mention the development of her unique stylistic approach, would ever have been realized . . . is highly doubtful.

At worst, her career would have been over, works rejected, conservative editors refusing to accept what she was willing to write. At best, she'd have become a very good, possibly even wildly successful, "comfortable" read author, destined to sell well as long as she produced to demand, but likely to fade away once the trend died.

Fortunately, that scenario was never put to the test. Fortunately, Don Wollheim, an editor in the field during those rich, developmental years of the sixties, and by the seventies owner of his own publishing company, was free to make his own rules, as long as he was willing to take the financial risk.

And risks he did take.

The simplest, most commercial Cherryh books, books like *Gate of Ivrel*, *Pride of Chanur*, and *Merchanter's Luck*, will make the reader work to follow the nuances of plot and motivation.

Sadly, many readers have been scared off by that "hard read" reputation when in fact books like *Gate* and *Pride* are wonderfully accessible. And for those willing to do just a little more work, there are the *Faded Sun* books, and lately the *Foreigner* books.

Don knew the risk in backing books that were more thought provoking and less "feel good," that were, in every way, less commercial, but he loved the genre as it could be, not as the publishing conglomerates would make it. He saw the potential in the young writer and encouraged her to experiment with concept and style at a time when conservatism increasingly ruled the marketplace. The end result is a series of books that Betsy Wollheim, Don's daughter and heir to DAW Books, Inc., refers to as "magic cookie" books, stand-alone novels which stretch the limits of story-telling— highly experimental books like the existentialist's nightmare, *Wave without a Shore*, or the single man's journey into the nature of Self, *Voyager in Night,* or the Camelot in hyperspace, *Port Eternity*. Magic cookie, experimental, call them what you will, Don Wollheim gave Carolyn a unique opportunity to spread her creative wings.

And spread them she did.

But not so far that she ended up flying in the ozone. Don carefully interspersed the magic cookie books with the more commercially viable books, ensuring Carolyn a long and healthy career, completely free of pigeonholes.

And then, there's that on-going matter of length.

Sometime around 1980, Carolyn had an idea for a nice little 80,000 word, highly commercial space-opera style story eventually called *Merchanter's Luck*. As she got into this nice little book she realized it was part of a much larger universe, a universe she had yet to invent. So . . . in order to write this nice little book, she needed first to write a somewhat larger book called *Downbelow Station*. *DS* was far more complex than anything she'd yet written. Previously, her signature tight viewpointing had been limited to two, sometimes three, viewpoints per book. *DS* required at least twice that just to follow the intersecting plot threads.

I don't know the actual word count on *DS*. . . it was written on the afore-mentioned Atari, and so the file is unavailable for electronic analysis . . . but it was long enough for DAW to create a whole new price category for it—after swallowing hard and admitting it truly did need to be that long.

A whole new category. A huge risk for a small, privately owned publishing company. A company whose distribution (so a number of people within the field pointedly warned her) would prevent her ever winning the cherished Hugo Award for best novel.

But she stuck with Don Wollheim despite other offers and Don Wollheim took the risk with the book, as he had with her conceptual themes, and in 1982 Don's gambles on this prolific if eclectic C.J. Cherryh paid off when she proved the nay-sayers wrong and won the Hugo for *Downbelow Station*.

Determining cause and effect within the publishing industry is a dicey proposal at best, but it's undeniable that in the eighties, in the years following that Hugo award-winning novel, the idiosyncrasies of book publishing made longer books not only viable, but preferable. Carolyn, whose already intricate plots had increasingly pushed that length limit, expanded her stories gleefully in this new freedom to explore elements previously shoved aside for want of word count. She no longer had to choose between idea, world-building, or character motivation, no longer had to limit a complex philosophical question to a one-sided equation, but could at last put all those elements into a single novel.

Her writing had truly come into its own.

Variety: the Cherryh Spice du jour

In the forties and fifties, when Carolyn was busy developing her typing skills, the SF/F field was rich with conceptual possibilities. The gridwork had been set, the surface tests made, but the field far from excavated. Her greatest fears in those years was that all the planets in the solar system would have been explored, their secrets revealed, before she ever got published.

In the sixties and early seventies, the years during which she was quietly developing her own craft, authors were taking the free-wheeling concepts of the Golden Age, the great adventure story-telling of the Sword and Sorcery/Space Opera era, and expanding those concepts to include the human drama, turning the stories increasingly toward an exploration of perception and cosmology, psychology and motivation: intense, personal stories that examine the nature of being human through human relationship to and interaction with that technology. It was a wide-open field, free for the bold and innovative to chart the course for others to follow.

And C.J. Cherryh is nothing if not bold and innovative.

Conservatively-speaking, she has created four distinct future histories: the *Downbelow Station* Alliance/Union, which includes the vast majority of her linked novels (she even figured how to fit the Faded Sun and Morgaine books (very loosely) into that scenario); the Foreigner books; and, from another publisher, the *Fortress* series, now into its fourth book, with all the pageantry and court intrigue of the greatest historicals, and the most subtly beautiful of ecological messages hidden within the World according to Tristen. From other publishers, she has Finisterre (the Nighthorse books), and most recently the Gene Wars books (*Hammerfall*), as well as several anthropologically-based fantasies (the Russian *Rusalka* novels, the Celtic *Faery in Shadow* and from DAW, the *Arafel* books; from Baen, the Far

Eastern *Paladin*) and, again from DAW, a dozen or so independent and conceptually unique novels of both SF and Fantasy.

Her aliens are unsurpassed in their physiological, psychological, and sociological conception, ranging from the near-but-not-quite human mri to the distinctly familiar feline-based prides of the *Chanur* books and, with them, the enigmatic, matrix-languaged knnn. Then there's the biologically-challenging hive mind (and corrugated cardboard internal construction) of the majat in *Serpent's Reach*, the creatively-challenged regul of the *Faded Sun* series, and the charmingly urbane and deadly atevi of *Foreigner*. Each world explores some alternative physical and psychological evolutionary path to technology as elegantly as *Cyteen* explores the nature of human intelligence.

Variety: if you like to read, there's a Cherryh book for you, because she never, ever writes to any formula.

The Legacy

In the fall of 1988, Donning Publishing, the company publishing the *Gate of Ivrel* graphic novel, liquidated their graphic novel line, leaving me jobless. Something in the bridging scenes I'd written for the graphic, in the suggestions I'd made on her manuscripts over the years suggested to Carolyn that I might be a writer at heart. She suggested that, rather than move back up to Seattle, I try writing.

On October 24, 1988, I agreed (somewhat reluctantly: recall my comatose writing muse) to try. But:

"How does story happen?" I asked (such was the depth of my ignorance.)

"Write an outline," she responded, turning again to teaching. "A *very* basic outline, a paragraph or two. No more. A core of an idea. A handful of characters."

I sighed, and went for a walk.

Because I'd become so deeply immersed in her future history by that time, I chose a basic premise that was the antithesis of one of her basic postulates. In her universe, nothing travels faster than the fastest ship, so I gave my future instantaneous communication, and made that technology the core of my "suspension of disbelief" factor. My ComNet was unique in my experience, (at the time, I'd never heard of email, let alone the internet) and so, since my background and education is fundamentally different from any other writer (or person, for that matter), the questions that would arise out of the concept and the answers I'd find would be inherently unique. Having assured myself of sufficient defense against the plagiarism police, I got myself a planet, a starship, a spacer who distrusted planets, the first discovery of non-human intelligence, and an exploding starship climax. That's pretty much it. Nothing special. I just wanted to figure out how to write. I returned to herself with this "masterpiece." Barely glancing at my morning's labor, she said, "OK. Take two of the characters, throw them in a room together, and see what happens."

I sighed . . . and went for a walk . . .

. . . and by the time I returned home (at a run), my question (on my way to my computer) was: "How do you *stop* story from happening?"

The answer? Keep writing and you'll find the end . . . right along with the characters.

A year and three months later, I had a three-book contract based on the rough draft of the book I started that day. For me, Carolyn's very simple suggestion had resonated perfectly, jolting that comatose muse back into action, with all the pent up energy of twenty years' sleep. For me, the process began to be alive, to contain a certain thrill of discovery, like Columbus heading out and running into a very large, unexpected bit of real estate.

Of course, I had to learn to analyze the needs of the book and to edit that initial hodgepodge of scenes and raw prose into something readable. Grammar, punctuation, pacing . . . those are the mechanics, the nuts and bolts, the rationally controllable features.

Carolyn's advice on that topic? "Write it as you hear it; I'll teach you to punctuate it."

But that's the craft of writing. The initial rough draft is where the magic lies, and for me that magic rested and rests squarely in the hands of the characters. Everything else, story, world, even the details of those characters' lives and psychologies arise simultaneously and out of the interactive responses of the characters, to each other and the environment.

I need, in short, the very factor the well-meaning English teacher had derided and effectively shattered twenty years earlier: serendipity.

Carolyn's most recent metaphor for writing is golf: you play the ball where it lies. If the seed of an idea lies in an insect as the basis for an intelligent species (only one of her concepts rife with scientific sand-traps), you don't run away from the course, you don't, godlike, pick up the ball and drop it in the hole—you find the right clubs, use the wind to your advantage, maybe you even build a sandcastle or two, but you find an internal logic, based on real world science, to explore the ramifications of the idea and follow through.

Myself, I think of it more as bungee-jumping, a leap of faith with just enough physics to keep you alive.

To successfully write in this bungee-jumping fashion, an author needs options. Lots of options, based on knowledge. Most authors, particularly those in the science fiction and fantasy fields, tend toward highly eclectic info-junkies. It's practically a job requirement, because a story is only as good (and unique) as the options and resources the writer has to handle the questions that arise in the course of its creation. The more eclectic the knowledge base, the more varied the options for both world-building and character motivation and so the more varied (and unique) the potential story line . . . without spending years in research.

The essential research tool is an ever-expanding junqueyard database

Hard core SF writers tend to collect technical data. Hard core Fantasy writers tend to collect historical information. Most writers fall somewhere in between, then generally find one area within their subcategory just a bit more fascinating than the others and dive more deeply into that data stream, frequently resulting in a body of work that *tends* toward a certain "comfort zone" both for the author and the author's loyal readers. This is by no means a negative statement on such writers. This "homing in" is the means by which the author becomes an "individual" to his or her readers. It's part of the delicate and infinitely precious "partnership" that grows between an author and the reader.

Carolyn is a self-proclaimed media junkie. Early on, her sources of inspiration were TV and radio (Space Patrol, Tom Corbett, Flash Gordon . . .) As she grew older (and with that fear of the plagiarism police in the forefront of her mind) she began collecting raw data of every kind, specializing in the aforementioned ancient history, astronomy, and forensics. But specifics are not the source of free-wheeling ideas. New ideas come from lateral processing, from the intersections of seemingly disparate concepts. Those scattered concepts come from a lifetime of data accumulation, from every available source. Her reading time is rarely spent within the SF/F field. For fiction, she tends to prefer historicals such as Patrick O'Brien's Aubrey/Maturin series, books with good characters, books that provide a sense of living at a given time in a given place. For nonfiction, she tends towards an interest in causality, whether based on people and events such as Asbury's *Gangs of New York* (*Gangs of Chicago, Gangs of New Orleans)* or the world in general, such as the Roadside Geology series, or natural adventure, like *Over the Edge: Death in the Grand Canyon.*

In this day of cable TV, her set is rarely turned off, even when she's writing. News channels, TLC, Animal Planet, Discovery . . . everything from homeowner how-to's to dinosaurs. And if it's about a natural disaster, an earthquake, a dam break, she's seen it—likely a dozen times. Tornadoes? She was brought up an Oklahoman—learned when to take cover before she learned to drive. Not that she really *watches* most of the time; she seems to absorb the useful bits of information through her pores, slowly and through multiple viewings.

All of this input provides an endless source of inspiration for plot-driving what-ifs, alien cultures, world-building and even for human behavior. Inspiration, yes, but as the old saying goes: Ideas are a dime a dozen, it's execution that counts, and execution takes knowing what questions to ask.

Too much knowledge can micromanage a plot; too little, and the story becomes mere self-indulgence

Eclectic data base: that's a given for SF writers, but the real trick is the implementation of that data. There are a variety of techniques for performing that operation. At one extreme, the story is a logical extrapolation of current technology based on an in-depth understanding of the topic; at the other, it's a wide-eyed what-if free-for-all, rife with sparkling lights, but little substance.

Obviously, most SF falls somewhere in between these two extremes. One of Carolyn's greatest strengths is the balance she achieves between details and causality. Despite all this information packed into her head, her wide-eyed "what if?" faculty remains remarkably uninhibited. Instead, she uses that vast, deliberately shallow sea of information to anticipate and address, in her own mind as well as (where appropriate) within the pages of the book, the questions the hard science critics inevitably raise.

"Deliberately shallow." There is such a thing as too much information, at least for the fiction writer: there's a point at which the reader can't absorb more detail. And there is a point, different for every creative individual, at which the knowledge base within the writer becomes too interdependent, too detailed—too stuffed with data and detail. At that point, the *conceivable* answers to the what-if question become too narrow, and the result becomes predictable. That precious creative muse is effectively hamstrung.

On the other hand, the author needs to know enough about the chosen what-if topic not only to find believable answers to technical questions necessarily raised by the plot—but also needs to avoid deeper speculations on technical topics where data is lacking—speculations apt to mislead the reader as to what is known for certain: never good; and equally apt to expose the writer's lack of deeper expertise to the knowledgeable. In other words, it may be speculation, but its feet rest on solid logical ground.

My favorite experiences along these lines centers on my sister, a teacher of college Biology and Genetics, and a very hard sell under the best of circumstances, let alone in subjects on her own scientific turf. She came down to visit us in Oklahoma City the year after *Cyteen* came out. I met her at the airport gate while Carolyn "circled the car" and my sister's first words, once she determined I was alone, were: "How much genetics does Carolyn really know? I can't tell . . . and I can *always* tell."

That pretty much sums up the ideal reaction to the "suspension of disbelief" factor in SF plot devices. You need to know enough to ask the questions that spark the speculative story, and you need to have some idea where to go for the answers to gather the bits of detail that will lend your expert character's voice the necessary verisimilitude. You must have a solid understanding of the current state of the art, and when, precisely, you meet the edge of real knowledge.

Carolyn calls it "murfling," a term she got from a fellow science fiction writer, Gordon R. Dickson.

The question of how much detail is enough also applies to that most peculiar aspect of SF/F writing: worldbuilding. Each to his own, and there are those who enjoy spending a lifetime creating an extensive history, languages, species and team sports for their created world. More power to them. The problem is, that's one world, one idea, and the creator spends an entire lifetime devoted to notebooks full of everything but *story*. With over sixty novels to her credit, I think it's fair to say that C.J. Cherryh has developed more alien species, more worlds, and as rich a future history as anyone who has ever set words to page, but to my knowledge the only notebook she's ever kept amounts to a timeline of her future history in which she jots down ideas for stories . . . ideas which amount to a paragraph or two, no more, ideas which might, someday, become full-fledged additions to that rich future history.

At some point, she says, you've got to quit taking notes and start writing a story. *The key to useful research is learning to recognize what's really important and what is mere side-tracked curiosity.*

Carolyn's books run the full gamut of research styles. Perhaps the hardest type story for her to prepare is what I think of as her anthropological fantasy (books like the Celtic-based *Faery in Shadow,* or the Russian *Rusalka* series). These aren't books based on real history, they're books based on the magical interface between human reality and human belief. Politics isn't important. Economics isn't. These aren't books about Czars and kings but the country folk and their gods. Carolyn prepares for these books not by gathering notecards on how to skin a rabbit with an obsidian knife, but rather by scanning a book of fairy tales, an encyclopedia of the gods and myths of a given region, a Russian children's book on the flora and fauna of a given region, and absorbing all the detailed archaeological material she can conveniently lay hands on. She agonizes over that interface between myth and ancient reality. And at that point, with a vision of the mud-and-bricks world, her understanding of Ancient History and Indo-European cultures takes over, and she's finally off and running—but the story has been in progress at the same time. And she already knew how to skin the rabbit.

Of all her hard SF, the techie, solar-system-based *Heavy Time* required the most work. There were technical manuals lying all over the house. Solar sails, space shuttle diagrams (from the *Columbia's* original press packet: she was at the launch), articles on the medical effects of long-term weightlessness, gravitational effects within the asteroid belt . . . it was a fun time around the office.

For Carolyn world-building is an interactive process. She begins with a handful of postulates based on biological, psychological and economical necessity and as the story grows, she fills in the details of evolution of the species concerned—detail which will almost never be in the book, because, she says, once you know it, you don't need it. She maintains a broad enough generalized database in science to recognize a possible point of questionable science and knows where to go to find the details necessary to flesh out a particular situation in a particular book. That, she says, is the essence of education in a constantly-changing world.

For worlds and universes, a *basic* understanding of the physical sciences (geology, physics, meteorology, astronomy, ecology) is vital for culture-building, anthropology, sociology, history, economics—essential. For non-human species, biology, genetics; for all characters of any species, psychology and just plain life.

But in all these studies, far more important than the details of past civilizations or the equation of the uncertainty principle and how to apply it, are the underlying structures, the concepts, the building blocks. To build worlds and cultures, you've got to understand the synergistic relationship between religion and agriculture and city development (centralized government). You've got to understand why you need trade in order to have silk, cotton, wheat, and barley all available to a small, mountain-dwelling community.

In short, a writer who would create worlds needs to know the processes which affect that world and those people more than he needs to know what they have for breakfast. The details of breakfast are an outgrowth of those causalities; if you understand the causalities, you can figure the details when and if the story demands you have your character eating breakfast. If s/he doesn't eat breakfast onstage, what does it ever matter? Conversely, if you desperately *want* your mountain-village character wearing silk as she sips a good whiskey and peels an orange, you can find a justification for all those factors in her life—as long as you know processes.

This sounds haphazard, but when it comes to bungee-jump writing, the fewer "givens" at the start, the more options you retain as the story progresses. The better you understand the processes that affect culture in general, the better equipped you are to supply the causality for whatever the story demands.

This is not to say that the more formal approach, complete with outlines and character sketches is, by any means, "wrong." There is no "right" answer for how to write a novel, there are simply options and methods. Unfortunately in her experience and mine, those options seem to be rarely, if ever, acknowledged in formal, academic writing classes. I suspect this has to do with outlines and character sketches being far easier to standardize, to explain to people who *demand* notes, and, on the junior level, to judge and grade—a necessary by-product of our current educational system.

And for the organized, structured, rule-based mind, I suppose the assumption is that *everyone* can learn by that method. Unfortunately, for someone with the bungee-style muse, writing an outline and character sketches can be excruciating, silly, or even creatively debilitating.

Fortunately for us bungee-jumpers, there's C.J. Cherryh to validate our approach to the art.

For us bungee-jumpers, it boils down to a pretty simple equation: there's only so much time to write. We can spend that time writing manuals for our worlds or we can spend that time writing stories about the people living in those worlds, and keep the data floating free and useful inside our heads.

The ultimate legacy: TPI[2]

Carolyn's stories are about characters. Period. Beyond character-driven motion, there *is* no story, no plot beyond a general direction of events, until the characters declare their intentions to her at each given juncture. This "making it up as you go along" is another typical aspect of the bungee-jumper approach. With each decision made, the character's options become more limited, both as a character and within the confines of the simultaneously developing world and plot—rather like real life. The character becomes defined by his or her internal analysis of options and ultimate choices and those choices drive the plot forward. Multiple characters. Multiple decisions. Interweaving causalities which ultimately find resolution.

Living on the creative edge? Absolutely.

Rewarding? Unimaginably.

But in order to pull off this style effectively, Carolyn had to develop the perfect writing tool. She began consciously considering the question of viewpoint when she was a freshman in college. Back in that dark age of manual typewriters, CJ decided that how she wanted to write wasn't really covered by what she was reading. First person had the intimacy, but inherent limitations of scope. Multiple viewpoints allowed stories to develop along disparate lines that ultimately intersected, which pleased her complex, lateral processing, but didn't create the necessary intimacy for motivational currency within the novel.

So she began working out her own guidelines for a style of viewpointing she calls "Third Person Intense Internal."

I'd never presume to suppose she is the first or only writer to write in this fashion—indeed, I've read other authors whose work I would tend to classify similarly, and my own one-shot, abortive high school attempt at writing would indicate it is, for some, the "native" story-telling voice. But since becoming aware of the concept I've never encountered the term or philosophy in any writing text or in any writerly discussion outside Carolyn's writings on the topic of writing. I certainly think it's safe to say Carolyn, with that vast array of novels, has explored the ramifications of it as no author has before her.

Conceptually, TPI [2] is very simple. Reaching beyond camera angle, beyond the five senses, the reader/writer dives into the head, heart, and soul of the viewpoint character(s) and never strays, focusing the story less on events and more on the causality of those events.

Operationally, it's a bit more interesting.

Viewpoint is the ultimate reader/writer contract. It absolutely controls how deeply the writer involves the reader with the character. Traditionally, viewpoint falls into a handful of basic categories: omniscient (he/she/it), second person (you), third person (he/she/it), first person (I).

Second person is used within fictional prose only for the occasional effect, and so . . . ignore it.

Omniscient viewpoint is the ultimate safety-zone. At its simplest, it's simply a god-view describing the events:

> *John Smith sat on a bench in the corner of the waiting room of The Golden Goose restaurant, watching the guests come and go through the carved and gilded doorway.*
>
> *Outside the Barbary Hotel, Daisy May Grubecker got out of a Yellow cab, nodded to the doorman as she walked past, turned down the hall to her left headed for the Golden Goose. As she passed the maitre d' and entered the restaurant, John stood up, holding out his hand to welcome her.*
>
> *Suddenly he stumbled.*

Yawn. Oh . . . sorry. Omniscient doesn't need to be *that* boring, but in order for it to live up to its "most reliable narrator" billing, it must remain purely observational, reporting events and dialogue, but never entering the heads of the characters. Not the best for reader involvement with the characters.

Once you pass that barrier, you enter the realm of third person wandering viewpoint narrative:

> *John sat on the edge of the restaurant's waiting room bench, watching the customers come and go, shadowy silhouettes against the bright lights of the exterior corridor. He ran his sweaty hands across the worn red velvet upholstery, wondering which of those shadows could be Daisy May Grubecker, his blind date.*
>
> *Daisy May, DMG to her online friends, tugged at her too-short skirt, and glared at the cabby as she slid her legs out the door. Her spike heels wobbled ominously. She swallowed hard, found her balance, and walked grandly into the Barbary, nodded to the doorman, and following her nose, headed down the hall to the Golden Goose.*
>
> *A man rose as she passed through the gilt doorway, took a step forward, and the next instant, he was in her arms.*

Third person, still a bit remote in this example, but beginning to achieve some identification with the characters. The big problem is, it's a floating ·viewpoint. You get potentially a lot of information, but never actually settle into, or center your loyalty on, a single character.

Many people would claim the ultimate reader identification viewpoint is first person:

> *I sat in the corner of the waiting room, feet flat on the floor, terrified I'd wrinkle my rented suit, and rubbed my hands across the worn red velvet of the couch, trying unsuccessfully to dry the sweaty palms.*
>
> *I stared at the doorway, half-blinded by the exterior corridor lights, wondering which of those shadowy silhouettes was . . . her. DMG. Daisy May Grubecker.*
>
> *My blind date.*
>
> *Email, God's own gift to nerds, had brought us together and I'd just begun to wonder whether I should leave it that way, when suddenly, one of those shadows paused. Slim. Elegant in a sleek black dress and sexy, impossibly high, spiked heels. Could it be . . . ?*
>
> *I swallowed hard and rose to my feet, took a final swipe at my slacks to dry my hand, and stepped toward her, hand outstretched.*

My foot caught on the thick carpet. I was falling, clumsy fool that I am, right into her waiting arms.

And indeed, with first person, you finally begin to get some sense of causality, emotion and intimacy. However, for me this style is a bit voyeuristic. There's less direct identification with good old John Smith than there is a sense of sitting beside him as he tells you all about this disastrous date. If emotions run too high, if the world (read plot elements) turns against him, there's a serious danger that John will begin to whine as he attempts to make me understand the depth and pathos of his travail.

Besides . . . the one thing you know going into a first person book is that John Smith survives his date: he must, because he's sitting there telling me (or at least his diary) all about it.

The beauty of third person intense is that is gives you all the intimacy of first person, plus the flexibility of multiple viewpoints.

Feet planted flat on the floor, terrified lest he wrinkle his rented suit, John cowered in the corner of the Golden Goose waiting room, keeping the potted palm between him and the overbright entrance. Shadowy silhouettes came and went through that gilt and carved doorway, and with each new arrival, he sank a bit deeper into the worn velvet cushions.

He should forget this nonsense, leave well enough alone. Email was God's own gift to nerds like —

A shadow paused in the doorway. Sleek. Dark-haired. Impossibly high heels—

Could it be . . . ?

Daisy May Grubecker—DMG, thank you very much—paused in the doorway, waiting for her eyes to adjust to the restaurant's dim lighting.

Made a gal suspicious, that did. Made her wonder just what they were trying to hide in their mystery meat.

And speaking of meat . . .

She resisted, not for the first time since escaping the cabby's rude gaze, tugging at the much too short dress she'd "borrowed" from her roommate, fought the tendency of her left foot to topple off center, and searched the shadowy foyer for one John Smith.

Like she believed that. As much a handle as DMG, she'd bet.

Beyond an over-watered palm, a slim figure slowly rose to its feet. Not bad. Not the whale she'd feared, not the Adonis of her fondest dreams. Light glinted in the head area. Glasses? She could live with that. Besides, if he had nice eyes, there were always contacts.

He was bright enough, she knew that from the emails. Now . . . to see if he was housebroken.

Oops. Sorry. Got a bit carried away. Want to know what happens? Well, he falls. She catches him. The stilettos break and they go down. He hits his head on the potted palm, and she at least thinks he's dead. Beyond that? Well, gee, I dunno. They haven't told me yet. If I'm lucky, I'll never think about it again. Unfortunately, thanks to that last bit from DMG's viewpoint . . . I might wake up in the middle of the night with her story in my head: such is the insidious nature of this style of storytelling.

Insidious, indeed. If C.J. Cherryh's a "hard read," her TPI [2] is an even harder "write."

But wait! (You cry, in frustration and distrust.) Didn't you just say it was *easy?*

It is. Very. At least when a character wants to talk. It's not the writing that's hard, just as it isn't necessarily simply following the story that makes her a hard read; it's that same character identification. Sometimes viewpoint characters are nice folk, whose minds are like comfortable slippers and a warm fire. Sometimes, again, they aren't very nice at all. Sometimes it's necessary to slip on the cloak of the antagonist, and sometimes the protagonist is less than well-wrapped, a victim of child abuse, or a leader who must wield great power ruthlessly.

A reader lives with this identification for at most a few days, and only experiences those elements of character history and psychology necessary to the book. Then, they move on to other books, other characters, likely to more comfortably remote viewpoints. A writer lives with the characters for months, experiencing *all* the details that made them what they are, sometimes receiving the news from a recalcitrant character in the middle of an otherwise quiet night's sleep. No good villain is simply evil incarnate: something created them, drove them to the depths of depravity. No individual of courage, character and options got to that state without physical and mental tempering. TPI [2], by its very nature, forces the author to face those details, to walk in a character's moccasins in ways no other viewpoint requires.

Never having written a novel any other way, I can't say whether those who write remote third or omniscient or first experience similar identification; I can say it's certainly theoretically *possible* to write remotely without it. It's not possible to write TPI^2 without total commitment to the viewpoint characters. Sometimes, that means waking up in the middle of the night, drenched in sweat from dreams not your own, sometimes it means examining your very thoughts with suspicion, wondering if they're yours or the current character's . . .

Which brings up another cool-Cherryh story. Back in her university days, she had two tests to prepare for: one on the Civil War, another on Machiavelli's *The Prince*. The night before, she studied her notes for American History, then put the notes for *The Prince* on audio tape, which she then played on continuous loop as she slept. (Yes, Virginia, the original *Cyteen* "sleep tapes.") The following morning, barely awake, she got her Civil War essay question: It's the day before the attack on Fort Sumter. You're President Lincoln. What are you going to do to stop the war?

Carolyn's somewhat sleep-deprived answer? A carefully selected series of arrests and assassinations, all well-supported with logic, of course. She says she doesn't recall taking the test, but her horror when she began the test on *The Prince* and realized what she'd done to her American History final in the previous period is quite clear.

She needn't have worried. She (and Nicolo M.) received an A.

The inescapable truth of writing is that all characters ultimately come from within the writer. The truth of TPI^2 is that sometimes, they rule. When Carolyn's writing Signy Mallory, you don't walk up behind her and say *Boo!* Unless, of course, you *want* a fat lip or broken rib. When she's writing Caith, you don't let her drive because cars flowing through an intersection might just become a flock of sheep. (They did, to the horror of all of us in the car.)

Suffice to say, in a household full of TPI^2 writers (and at one time we had three living together) the term "designated driver" takes on a whole new meaning.

Are there TPI^2-specific mechanisms? The dreaded "rules"? Well, yes, in a way there are, and such as they can be codified, Carolyn has done herself, free to all at her website (http://www.cherryh.com), where she has posted an entire section on writing tips that is fun and fascinating reading, even for the non-writer, and one of those articles is specifically on viewpointing.

In the above example (remember John and DMG?) I . . . stretched one of the guidelines. In general, a scene is "dedicated" to a single viewpoint. This creates an instinctive trust between reader and author, a trust that allows the reader to settle firmly into that character for the duration of the scene. Establishing the various viewpoints early in the book creates . . . pockets of resonance, if you will, within the reader's gut that automatically kick in every time the story slips into a character's voice. Once that trust exists, a single hint at the beginning of the scene triggers the inward resonance, and the viewpoint is set.

In the above example, in order to illustrate the dual viewpoints and to reflect the previous examples, I shifted viewpoint as DMG enters the room. This is something of a "pseudo scene break," but is seriously stretching the definition. Also, the beginning of John's viewpoint reads like the establishing opening of a scene where the viewpoint is being set. The subsequent handful of paragraphs doesn't allow time to settle into him.

Alternatively, were this well into the book, his viewpoint could be set so firmly that it *is* sufficient trigger for the reader.

Never, as Carolyn stresses, follow a guideline over a cliff. They are suggestions for achieving an end, no more, no less. They are neither comprehensive nor universally applicable. They are the means to an end, not an end in themselves, and that end is character identification on a gut level, not an intellectual one.

Never follow rules over a cliff. And that includes the so-called "rules" of grammar.

TPI [2] subset: copyediting

Language, like technology and society, is constantly evolving. Grammar and punctuation, creatively combined, have the ability to create a virtual reality as potent as any computer. Strict application of a single codification, of any particular era, stagnates evolution and creates uniformity of presentation. Predictability. Reduction of literary storytelling to a set of frozen concepts, not the engulfing virtual experience it can be.

TPI [2], being internal-logic-thought based, strains the rules of strict, by-the-book copyediting more than any other viewpointing style. Convolute thinking creates convolute sentence structure; varying education shifts grammar; impressions better filled by the reader are deliberately left hanging.

The question is, or should be: is the "rule-breaking" consistent and to a purpose? All too often these days, in copyediting, the question of author intent is never even asked before the rule book is applied like a hammer. Worse, the rule book most often employed by copy-editors is one of the most stifling pieces of grammatical codification ever perpetrated on a creative species: the *Chicago Book of Style*. (For a true rant on this subject, I again refer you to Carolyn's website. She expresses the objections to that project far more eloquently than I could hope to achieve in this limited space.) Over the years, Carolyn's dogged protection of her stylistic approach against this over-simplified standard (dumbed-down English is the mildest of her expressions) has given her a Reputation within the copyediting world.

As long as Don Wollheim was personally editing her books, this was never an issue. As with other elements, he left her free to experiment, his input not focused on grammar and punctuation, but rather on clarity of impression. However, all that changed with the hard cover edition of *Angel with a Sword,* a novel whose page proofs came through at a time when she was too busy to check them. Besides, to that point, page proofs had been a matter of looking for typographical errors, editorial changes having been mutually agreed upon by her and Don before setting. How could she have anticipated that a copyeditor would (among other egregiously arrogant shifts in the prose) change all the gutter-rat protagonist's viewpointed prose to textbook English? Most notoriously he shifted Jones' "ain'ts" to "isn'ts," even within the dialogue, which rather well undermined one of the ongoing bits of business: Mondragon's ongoing battles to improve Jones' grammar and to get her to cease using the "a" word.

Go figure.

You can imagine the horror when she finally read her first hardcover book and realized what had happened. Fortunately, DAW had the entire book reset, restoring the original text for the paperback.

This same copyeditor had edited *Cyteen,* where he had proceeded to work a similar hatchet job on Ari II's prose. Carolyn discovered it, his copyedits were simply thrown out, and the book went to press directly from Carolyn's computer file.

(This copyediting nightmare, while common, is also not a universal experience. I personally had great copyeditors on my first series. They not only understood when to set the rule book aside, but cheerfully included explanations for their suggested changes. And when I chose, for *specific* dramatic purposes *which I was able to express,* to keep my original prose, my decision was final.)

Understandably, Carolyn's gotten just a bit testy on the topic, and she protects that viewpoint with a solid understanding of exactly how TPI [2] works, combined with her extensive knowledge of grammar and its *raison d'etre.* Please note: I'm by no means advocating ignoring all rules of grammar and punctuation. One of the things I've learned from Carolyn is how useful those rules can be, both in smoothing out prose and defending your decisions against copyeditors. *It just sounds right to me,* is *not* a viable reason. Knowing the rules—but more importantly, knowing why those rules exist—so you know how and why you're breaking them—is a key to success-fully preserving your character's voice.

Because of the aforementioned Rep, when she handed *The Paladin* in to Baen Books, Jim Baen himself opted to perform the copyedit. By his own admission, when he'd finished he discovered the first half of the book looked rather like a Persian carpet, there was such a fringe of Post-its marking so-called grammatical errors. But at a certain point late in the book, the Post-its disappeared altogether. He realized that at a certain point he'd quit reading as an editor and begun reading as a reader. He then went back, reex-amined all the instances, and ended up pulling all but two, both of which Carolyn freely conceded needed to be changed.

Bottom line: as a reader, it's far better to simply read and experience a Cherryh book. As a writer, if you take those conceptual guidelines as presented on her website and try to deconstruct her prose accordingly in order to apply what she does in a given instance directly to your own work, you're in for unnecessary frustration. TPI [2] originates within the writer, not within the rules.

As is the case with most creative endeavors, the secret lies in learning to look critically at one's own work and learning what questions to ask. For TPI [2], those questions become pretty simple, questions such as (but certainly not limited to): Is the viewpoint character in a position to know/notice this information? *would* he notice? (i.e. a character who saw only black and white would never comment on the color of an object), and is the comment structured in his particular voice? And stance. If he's an alien—can he put his hands behind his back? Not if he's a kif. If he's amaut, his hands will join behind his knees. And so on. In his viewpoint, that's only natural. Pyanfar sheds when stressed, as a human might sweat.

TPI [2] forms the core of C.J. Cherryh's story-telling. It's the underlying secret to her incredibly believable aliens and her loveable but nuttier-than-a-fruitcake protagonists, as well as to the creation of a cast of lead characters (and their associated prose) as varied as Ariane Emory (I and II) and *Fortress'* Tristen:

> Winter was a Word, howling white and bitter cold. Straw was a little one, yellow and dusty and hot. Dewdrops he knew from spider-webs on the shutters, and the old keep had many spiders.
>
> But where did candles come from, that they were at once so scarce, and yet vanished every handful of days, for new ones to fill their holders?

(Gratuitous inclusion of yet another beautiful passage.)

Ideally, TPI [2] creates an environment into which the author's own voice *never* intrudes, and where the book itself becomes as much an examination of the viewpoint character(s) cosmology as a portrayal of a series events. As a result of that immersion for a time into a different viewpoint, the reader is forever and subtly changed. You know you've been "had" by a Hani when you find yourself reaching with a "claw" to push a button rather than using the human fingertip pad; you know you've been "infected" by Tristen's viewpoint when you find yourself stopping to enjoy a butterfly or a pile of leaves—not because they've been described in endless, breathtaking detail, but because you've shared Tristen's fascination and joy of discovery. You're infected with the emotion and the sensation, but it's a good kind of infection.

The wide scope of Carolyn's body of work—as well as her everlasting gift to the SF world—is based on the inherent flexibility of this core approach. Combined with her incredible control of language, her vast imagination, her warped and subtle sense of humor, her sheer talent, her incredible productivity, and last but most definitely not least, a publisher ready and eager to take a chance, you have the phenomenon known as C.J. Cherryh.

Curiously, the very aspect that makes her work most valuable to the field limits her distribution. Her very scope makes her work impossible to describe in the modern sound-bite approach to advertising.

Possibly because of this failure on the part of modern advertising, her work has never gotten the huge numbers of a New York Times bestselling author, but that is a commentary on modern commercialism, and a sad loss to any reader who has never encountered the "right" C.J. Cherryh book to get him hooked. When I worked in a bookstore, I *never* had someone come back disappointed, once I got them connected to the "right" Cherryh book.

Fortunately again for us, Carolyn has always held that self-challenge of greater value to her than her income.

The result of this interface of individual talent and publishing support is a body of work that establishes new territory in the art of storytelling, not just for the SF/F field, but all of literature. And she's not through yet. At a time when the tide of conservatism and commercialism threatens to consume the SF genre, C.J. Cherryh's body of work reminds us all, writers, readers, publishers and editors, that SF is not just a genre of entertainment, but a genre of experimentation, of individuality, and of challenge, to ourselves and to the world.

Another non-academic who was uncertain of the value of any contribution she could make to *The Cherryh Odyssey* is Betsy Wollheim, President and Publisher of DAW Books, Inc. Luckily, she agreed to contribute. I would argue there is no one in the publishing business with a longer association with Cherryh's work, as she joined (at the urging and invitation of Donald A. Wollheim, her father) DAW close to the publication of *Gate of Ivrel*.

While not all of Cherryh's publications have been DAW projects, many have, and by many measures Cherryh is one of DAW's most significant authors. Betsy's perspective is therefore unique. I hope you will enjoy this view of Cherryh's contribution to the field of science fiction and fantasy.

A PIONEER OF THE MIND

Betsy Wollheim

I suppose every serious science fiction writer could be called a pioneer of the mind. After all, it's the job of science fiction writers to take readers to places in their fiction to which mankind has not ventured, nor often even imagined. But somehow, I've always felt that the work of C.J. Cherryh has a more genuine pioneer spirit than any other writer I've read. When I read Cherryh's work I feel things that I rarely experience with other science fiction writers. Something about her work is just so real—so believable, and there are reasons.

I first read *Gate of Ivrel* before I started working at DAW. It was 1975, and I had just returned to New York after a six-year absence, during which time I had completed my college education and afterward worked with magazine printing houses.

Although he never said so at the time, I guess my dad, Donald A. Wollheim, wanted me to come and work with him. There was no doubt that he hoped *Gate of Ivrel* would be the lure to draw me to DAW. Obviously, it worked. That I could theoretically "discover" new talent, by finding novels like *Gate of Ivrel* in the slush pile was too seductive an offer to pass up. Of course now, with thirty years of editorial experience under my belt, I know that finding just a single author of Carolyn's stature once in one's career is a huge accomplishment. I also now realize that the Morgaine books are truly unique—and were especially so in the mid-seventies—for they meld a heroic fantasy protagonist, and a woman at that, with a science fiction setting.

Don, an editorial veteran, knew immediately that this new writer, Carolyn Janice Cherry, was something special. She certainly wasn't a "one-shot wonder" (she had submitted two manuscripts simultaneously). But there was no possible way for us to realize just how important she would come to be. Not yet. In the beginning, Don just had to figure out which manuscript to publish first. Years later, I remember Carolyn telling me that the way she knew that she had sold both books (the other was *Brothers of Earth*) was that my dad's letter said: "I think we'll publish *Gate of Ivrel* first." So Carolyn, who had been writing for years (as most professional writers do), made her first sale with two books at once. In retrospect that seems prophetic.

Carolyn set about promoting her career with a real vengeance—traveling from convention to convention, meeting fans and other pros. Her efforts were especially impressive under the circumstances: for in the early days Carolyn was extremely shy—almost painfully so. Introspective and quiet, except with family and her closest friends, I've always thought it must have been terribly difficult for her to go from convention to convention, sometimes several in a given month. But this is just my point of view—I know Carolyn would beg to differ, for Carolyn has reserves of personal strength that many of us lack. She may have been shy, but she was never timid: in fact, I've always thought of her as very strong, even ferocious when appropriate.

In the mid to late seventies Carolyn also traveled to New York often, staying in our family home in Queens, coming into the office with Don and Elsie on the subway, even reading manuscripts from hopeful new writers and critiquing them. She seemed to enjoy the daily workings of our little publishing company, and I know that Don and Elsie enjoyed having her here. Looking back on that time, I see how very magical it all was. My father was a difficult and very private man. He didn't like to socialize. Yet there was something about Carolyn and Don that just *meshed*. They would sit at the kitchen table talking late into the night about books, space, history, politics, philosophy—anything and everything. My parents had close relationships with a number of authors during their lifetimes, but no author was ever taken into the Wollheim family as completely as Carolyn was. The bond between Don and Carolyn was truly remarkable, and though as Carolyn became more established, more famous, and busier, she didn't come to New

York as often, I know that everyone involved looked back on that time as something special. Carolyn is, and always will be, part of our family.

In the sixties and seventies the world of science fiction publishing was very different than it is now. It was smaller, less competitive, and authors were freer to write whatever they liked—they were under less pressure to publish strictly commercial books. It was a truly golden time for science fiction and fantasy writers. Readers of the genre were hungry to consume any books they could find, and unusual, experimental, and outré works were as welcome as blockbusters. And Carolyn savored the moment. It was during these years that she wrote her "magic cookie" books—books that stretched the boundaries of imagination, and took readers on unusual paths. These novels, *Port Eternity*, *Voyager in Night*, and *Wave Without A Shore*, (now available in an omnibus called *Alternate Realities*) remain to this day some of my personal favorites. It makes me sad that these lyrical, philosophical, fascinating and in some ways whimsical books might be hard pressed to find publication in today's world. In the seventies, Carolyn had carte blanche to write whatever she wanted, and when a package arrived from her in our office, Don and I never knew what we were getting—it was very exciting.

I feel privileged to have known Carolyn in the early days. Having known the younger unproven Carolyn has given me a more personal insight into the person she is today than I would have if I had met her years later, with three Hugo Awards and five dozen novels under her belt. Maybe it's a deeper, or perhaps, more accurately, a longer insight as well, for when I think of Carolyn, her heritage always resounds clearly in my mind.

Carolyn's forebears crossed the Great Plains in a Conestoga wagon, and the echoes of these determined, brave, stoical people still reverberate in the Cherry family. It's an impressive heritage, one which I feel has deeply influenced Carolyn's writing on many levels. From where people from a nearly-extinct race travel from star system to star system searching for others of their kind, to the Chanur series where a lone human inadvertently makes first contact with several alien races, so much of C.J.'s work addresses the needs of the individual to adapt to the demands of an alien situation or circumstance; to do things and go places which have not been attempted before. The cultural influence of Carolyn's pioneer heritage, in all its various aspects, echoes throughout her impressive backlist. Her most recent DAW series, *Foreigner*, is literally about a lost ship, and a human colony struggling to survive on a world populated by intelligent, but not necessarily compatible, aliens.

But nowhere does this heritage resound so loudly as in her most famous work. The complex, elaborate, and long history of Earth's space pioneers—those people who expanded our society to the stars, creating a civilization which evolved and broke from its parent human society on Earth—is an actual pioneer story, perhaps the ultimate pioneer story. Many writers have addressed this theme, which may be the most common theme in all of science fiction literature, but in Carolyn's Alliance-Union novels, especially in her most important works, *Downbelow Station* and *Cyteen*, I believe she transcends the norm in ways never before achieved.

I don't remember when I became aware of Carolyn's cohesive universe-view, but certainly by the time she wrote *Downbelow Station*, it was clear to me that something bigger was happening in that novel. The book was originally called *The Company War*, a title I now wish we had kept. In 1980 when we saw the first draft of *The Company War*, Don felt that no one would be the least bit interested in a company—any company. That may seem hard to believe now, for *The Company War* is an extremely commercial title for today's market, but Don was probably right. It was a different age and Carolyn's title was way ahead of its time.

Carolyn went through hell with that book. It was an extremely long work for its day, so long, in fact, that Carolyn cut descriptive passages out of the first draft thinking that it was too long to publish. (The average science fiction novel of the time was 80,000 words.) So, the draft we first saw was too bare—too stark. Don asked Carolyn to add physical description, connections. So Carolyn had to reintegrate the very bits she had taken out.

When we got the second draft in the mail, it was made up almost as much of scotch-taped segments as original paper. Don passed the book to me. As I read it, I found that each time there was a chapter change, I spent several pages trying to work out two of the five w's: where and when. So I asked Carolyn to please provide headings that answered these questions for the reader.

It seemed to me to be a simple solution to a problem, but providing this solution proved extremely difficult for Carolyn. Time and space have a complex mathematical relationship, and Carolyn was writing in the BC era: Before Computers. I remember Carolyn telling me that in the figuring of time she discovered that there needed to be additional connecting bits—bits she hadn't before realized she needed.

Carolyn worked harder on this novel, which was re-titled *Downbelow Station*, than on any novel she had thus far written. And she got a huge reward: she won the Hugo Award for Best Novel of 1981, defying all sorts of odds, including the widespread belief among fans that a DAW book (our company still had a pulp reputation at the time) could never win a Hugo.

There is no question that the pioneer heritage of the Cherry family influenced Carolyn, and is woven into the fabric of who she is, but the Alliance-Union novels are true pioneer works in an even more literal way. In writing *Downbelow Station*, Carolyn mapped a trail for these books that humans on Earth could one day follow to the stars—she actually studied the heavens and worked out the route—a pioneer's road. Though the story is fiction, the world of *Downbelow Station* is based on our real universe. Pell is Tau Ceti, Viking is Epsilon Eridani, and the route to these stars is worked out in Carolyn's mind. As she says in the introduction to the twentieth anniversary edition of the novel: "I selected a set of insignificant stars that lie near enough to each other to serve as a highway of way stops on the route to another truly interesting star: Tau Ceti . . . I worked out my distances and adopted a reasonable territory for a young interstellar civilization. And in doing that, I created trade routes and more history."

In fact most of C.J.'s novels take place in actual star locations—have been worked out on an astral map. The action of the Chanur series occurs close to the Orion stars, the territory of the Faded Sun lies more toward Castor and Pollux. Even her recent Foreigner series, which is going into its seventh volume, though technically the story of a lost branch of humanity in an unknown sector of space, is a branch lost from the Alliance-Union worlds.

When so much science fiction takes place so far both in time and in space from the world we live in that this sort of interstellar planning is not strictly necessary, one has to wonder why Carolyn was motivated to do this. To me, the answer is simple: she wanted a greater feeling of reality.

Why did she crave a greater grounding in the real universe?

Theoretically all science fiction is grounded in the real universe, and is based on the human reality of whatever era the writer lives in. But for Carolyn, I think there is more to it.

She really wants to go out there.

Carolyn once described her literary voice to me as "intense internal." I think that's enormously perceptive, because I have always seen Carolyn as someone who genuinely wants to go into space, to live in space. As an allergy sufferer, she once told me she thought she was "better suited to life in space." By writing in an intense internal voice, it must almost be like being there.

I don't think all science fiction writers want to live in space. And I'm sure there are worlds and situations that Carolyn has created in which she would not like to live. But if given the chance, I truly believe that she would live somewhere in the Alliance-Union universe. Sincerity is a very powerful force in fiction. The reader can always recognize a cynical writer. When a writer truly wants to be in the places she or he creates, how can a reader not want to go there, too?

Carolyn's sincerity has always shone through. Even her aliens are more believable—more thoroughly worked out in every way. I think if they weren't, she herself couldn't believe in them, and that simply wouldn't work for her. She takes this very seriously.

If it were five hundred years in the past, Carolyn would want to be on a sailing ship seeking strange new shores. If it were the far future, she would want to be on a different kind of ship seeking even stranger new horizons. Carolyn is a true inheritor of the Cherry family genetic code. At this point in time, our technology is not capable of allowing this would-be pioneer woman to seek the frontiers that she would wish for. For now she must continue to be what she has been: a pioneer of the mind. Thankfully, on that kind of trip, she can take us along.

Brad Sinor's contribution represents a series of firsts. This is not his first publication—he is a novelist and freelance writer with years of experience. However, Brad was the very first to respond to the call for papers for this project with a contribution. And while not the very first, Brad is one of the very first writers Cherryh influenced back in Oklahoma. Brad's article was the first accepted for *The Cherryh Odyssey,* and it represents just the sort of non-academic yet vitally important content this book is intended to convey to readers.

His narrative represents the kind of influence Cherryh has wielded for decades. How Brad benefited you can see for yourself. He is in one sense emblematic of the legacy Cherryh has provided so far during her career.

Ready yourself for a journey in the wayback machine . . .

OKLAHOMA LAUNCH

Bradley H. Sinor

There are some friends whom you have known for so long that you really can't remember where or exactly when you first met them. Well, in the case of Carolyn Cherryh and myself, that isn't true.

It was in April 1976 that I encountered her for the first time. It was all because of another science fiction writer, Philip José Farmer.

I happened to stop at a local Oklahoma City bookstore one afternoon before returning to the University of Oklahoma where I was a student. I was in search of a new Farmer novel, *Ironcastle*, that was due to be released that month from DAW books. Founded four years previously, by sf pioneering writer and editor, Donald A. Wollheim, the company had already become a major force in the field.

In those days the very distinctive yellow spines marked all of DAW's books, a shrewd marketing decision by Wollheim, so I spotted them right off and had no trouble finding the book I had come after. With my prize in hand I scanned the display of the other DAW releases for that month. One that caught my eye was a novel called *Gate of Ivrel* by C. J. Cherryh. Looking at the by-line, I casually wondered what the initials might stand for—Carl Joseph, maybe, or Charles James.

The cover featured a woman wearing very little, a sword held over her head, with her cape flapping in the wind, standing on a mountain top. Next to her was a man on one knee. A fairly new artist in the sf field, Michael Whelan, had done the painting. The artwork, along with the back cover copy, were enough to pique my interest and get me to take a chance on what appeared to be a first novel.

With a career as both editor and writer that reached back to the 1930's, Don Wollheim had developed an eye for talent. Beginning as member of the legendary fan group, The Futurians, which produced many of the significant names in the sf field, such as Frederik Pohl, Damon Knight and Isaac Asimov, Wollheim helped to forge the history of the sf field, from pulp magazines to paperback originals and hardback bestsellers.

Gate of Ivrel also featured a glowing introduction by one of the most notable names in the sf field, Andre Norton. Carolyn got to return the favor, some years later, by writing an introduction to Andre's collection, *Lore Of The Witch World*, published by DAW books in 1980.

A few days after acquiring the book I was sitting at my typewriter in the newsroom of the *Oklahoma Daily*, the student newspaper at the University of Oklahoma, working on a feature story about the Stovall Museum. One of my friends, an Oklahoma City native, was talking about how a History and Latin teacher from his old school, John Marshall High, named Carolyn Cherry had just published her first novel. When he mentioned the title I stopped typing and reached into my briefcase, pulling out my copy of *Gate of Ivrel*. I handed the book to my friend and asked, "Is this the one you're talking about?"

A week or two after that the University of Oklahoma Science Fiction Association, of which I was a founding member, extended an invitation to Carolyn to come and speak at the Norman campus, about a forty-five minute drive from her home in north Oklahoma City. Besides R.A. Lafferty, who lived in Tulsa, she was the only publishing sf writer living in Oklahoma at the time, so we were all quite interested in meeting her. At the time I was surprised that she accepted the invitation. But as I got to know her I realized that Carolyn enjoyed spending time with others who had an interest in the sf field.

To break the ice, some of us arranged to meet Carolyn at a local Chinese restaurant for dinner, before the meeting. I had intended to be there on time, since that particular restaurant had been chosen at my suggestion, but as it happened I ended up being the last to arrive. Carolyn, on the other hand, had gotten there fifteen minutes before any of us and had been worried that she might not be at the right place.

Afterwards we escorted her to a room in the basement of the OU Student Union, where there were a dozen other people waiting for us. One thing I recall about that room was that someone had jokingly scribbled a Lovecraftian basketball score on the blackboard: Miskatonic University 34, R'lyeh Tech 29. Instead of giving a set talk, Carolyn preferred to answer questions about herself and her novel. She mentioned that she had already sold a second book, *Brothers of Earth*, due out in October, and had a third that would appear the next year, called *Hunter of Worlds*.

One of the first questions had to do with the spelling of her last name. Her name was actually Cherry, but she had added the second "h" at the request of her publisher, to make it a bit more exotic. "But even so, there is only one way to pronounce it, and that's Cherry," she was quick to point out.

As for her background, Carolyn explained that she had started writing when she was ten years old, after a Flash Gordon serial had finished running on television. Most of her early stories were written on a battered old manual typewriter that "looked like it had been dropped off the roof of the Security Bank building in Lawton, Oklahoma."

Lawton!? I was from Lawton!

After the meeting I went up and confirmed that I had heard her correctly. It turned out that we had lived there at the same time; in fact, we had gone to the same junior high school and high school. She had even gone to the drive-in theater that my dad had managed for more than 30 years.

The idea that someone who wrote science fiction had grown up in Lawton just blew me away. Growing up in a town in southwestern Oklahoma and reading SF, let alone wanting to write it, was unusual, to say the least. If you mentioned it to anyone, the usual reaction was "That's nice, but what do you want to really do with your life?"

I got used to that attitude; so did Carolyn.

A few years later I learned that Lawton had also been the home for other major genre writers. At the 1980 World Science Fiction Convention I met hard sf writer Gregory Benford, and learned that he had also lived in Lawton when his father had been stationed at nearby Ft. Sill. A few years later in Piers Anthony's autobiography, *Bio of An Ogre* (Ace 1988), he mentioned that he had also been stationed at Ft. Sill and got his American citizenship at the Comanche County courthouse in Lawton.

That talk she gave was just the first of a number of events that the OU science fiction group would sponsor that would involve Carolyn over the next several years. She came to an OUSFA-sponsored speech given by fantasist and screenwriter, Harlan Ellison, who, impressed by one of her books, was especially keen to meet her. Carolyn returned to Norman to introduce the talk given by sf writer and computer guru Jerry Pournelle, also sponsored by OUSFA. When her publisher, Don Wollheim, was in town, she drove him and his wife to a dinner and party that the group held in their honor.

Most writers don't make enough money to write full time. Carolyn continued teaching for three years, before she became a full time freelance writer. I don't know if I would have had the confidence to go without the reassurance of a regular paycheck.

In the late 1970's and through the 1980's, one of the big trends in the fantasy and science fiction field was shared-world anthologies, projects where contributors use a single, consistent background for their stories, often intermingling each other's characters and plot lines. The first one, *Thieves' World*, created by Lynn Abbey and Robert Asprin, spawned a dozen volumes and half that many spin-off novels. For a time, it seemed as if every publisher wanted to have his or her own shared world series.

Carolyn was invited to contribute to several of them: *Thieves' World*, *Magic In Ithkar* and *Heroes In Hell*. In 1986 she opened her own shared world franchise, *Merovingen Nights*. This one was based on her novel, *Angel With A Sword*, published the year before.

For contributors to the Merovingen series Carolyn assembled a list of veteran writers, including Janet and Chris Morris, Lynn Abbey, and Robert Asprin, whom she had worked with on previous projects such as *Heroes In Hell* and *Thieves' World*. She also held the door open for newer writers like Mercedes Lackey, Nancy Asire, Leslie Fish and Roberta Rogow.

From the beginning, I really wanted to be a part of the Merovingen Nights project. When I approached her about it, Carolyn was willing to look at a submission from me. There were no promises made about an acceptance, and none expected, just an agreement to look at the story.

For me the problem was that my first few attempts were not, in my opinion, of good enough quality to submit. It wasn't until she was reading for number five in the series, *Divine Right* (1989), that I actually produced a story, "Foggy Night," I judged ready to send to Carolyn.

She didn't take it. However, she did give me a detailed critique of what was wrong with the story and an agreement to look at a revised version. That was on a Friday afternoon. On Monday morning version 1.5 went off to her office. Not too long after I got word that she was taking "Foggy Night." While I had sold stories and articles to a few magazines, I've always considered that sale to be the real start of my writing career.

Of course, that wasn't the first story of mine she had read. At a science fiction convention not too long after I first met her, Carolyn asked if I would be interested in being part of an SF writers' critique group that she was trying to organize. I agreed at once. She gathered a list of names and mailed a form letter to a lot of people who seemed interested, playing host to the first meeting of the Oklahoma Science Fiction Writers organization. Amazingly enough, the group still exists more than a quarter of a century after she founded it, and a number of its members continue to sell short stories and novels. I think I may be one of the last few original members in the organization.

A number of the people who came that first night went on to make professional sales: Mike McQuay, Ron Wolfe, A. E. Silas and myself to name a few. Others, such as David Thayer, have become active in the SF fan community. Under the pseudonym Teddy Harvia, Thayer has been a nominee and winner of the best fan artist Hugo several times.

Over the years, Carolyn read many of my short stories, both through the writers' group and one-on-one. She would critique them with an expert eye on what I was doing right and doing wrong. But always there was the admonition to keep on writing, because only by continuing to write would I improve my skills, an admonition I have passed on to others over the years.

On one occasion I sent her a story that I wanted to submit to a particular anthology series I had heard many good things about. Since I was planning to be in the Oklahoma City area the next week, we arranged to get together for pizza.

I called her to confirm the time, and the day, and casually asked how she liked the story. Her reply was that she wanted to wait until lunch to talk about it. I didn't think this boded very well at all, but I told her that was fine.

After we ordered lunch I asked the dreaded question, "So what did you think of the story?"

"That wasn't a short story," she said. I had a sinking feeling in the pit of my stomach. "That was chapter eight of a novel." Carolyn then handed me a very lengthy critique of the story with suggestions on ways I should consider expanding it to novel length.

I never did get around to submitting a story to that particular anthology, but I sweated blood over the novel, learning things with every page I wrote. The manuscript still exists in my files, and will never see the light of day. I know now that it wasn't very good, but the encouragement that Carolyn gave me helped me to finish it and become a better writer.

It was sometime after that when it dawned on me that Carolyn had never really given up being a teacher. The only thing she had done was to move to a different sort of classroom. I'm not the only student to have sat in her classroom. The list of other alumni of "Cherryh University" includes novelists Mercedes Lackey, Robin Bailey, Nancy Asire, Leslie Fish, William Mark Simmons, Beverly Hale and Jane Fancher. Some years later, when I did sell my first novel, a trip to Oklahoma City to tell Carolyn, in person, was definitely called for. The look on her face made the hour-and-a- half drive worth it.

Carolyn's readers have shown their appreciation of her work, not just by reading her books, but also by writing songs about characters from Morgaine to the Hani of the Chanur novels, and the Merovingen Series. Dubbed filk singing because of a misprint in a convention program book, sf- and fantasy-based folks songs have been a staple of fandom over the years.

SF conventions happen, somewhere in the United States, almost every weekend. They attract anywhere from a few hundred to a few thousand, who come to enjoy the company of people, both fans and professionals in the field, who share their interests. After the panels, the movies and the parties many can be found gathered in bardic circles singing until dawn. Every now and then Carolyn herself can be found, guitar in hand, ready to take her turn singing.

Besides singing, she has penned a number of songs herself. They've ranged from ballads like "Sam Jones", set against her own Union-Alliance universe, to one inspired by a *Scientific American* article that she had read, "Molecular Clouds." The latter deals with the discovery of a distant space cloud filled with the exact same combination of molecules that go into the making of ethyl alcohol—in other words, vodka.

There have even been two complete collections of songs inspired by Carolyn's work: *Finity's End* (based on the Union-Alliance stories) and *Fever Season* (based on the Merovingen Nights series) released through Firebird Arts and Music.

In 1979, after leaving OU and moving back to Lawton, I got a phone call. It was from a friend named Mike, who was one of the managers of the local TG&Y, a regional variety store chain. For some reason, that store always got new books, especially the newest science fiction, before any other store in Lawton, so I was a frequent visitor.

Mike had heard me mention Carolyn on several occasions, although he had never read any of her books. After the book jobber left, Mike noticed *Fires of Azeroth*, the third book in the Morgaine series, among the new titles and picked it up. That was when he let me know I should come take a look.

Okay, I was curious. While she was writing it Carolyn had talked a little about it to me and, of course, I was quite anxious to read it. While I like the book the best part was the words on the copyright page. "To Audrey, who is Kurshin at heart and to Brad who asked the right question." As I stood there looking at it Mike asked, with a grin, "That is you, right?"

I was on the phone that evening with Carolyn, thanking her. I also had to ask just what the question had been. Since, allowing for the lag time that publishing a novel involves, I had to have asked it more than eighteen months before, I now had no idea what it was.

Even over the phone I could "hear" her smiling that enigmatic smile of hers and telling me that I was just going to have to remember it on my own. She was definitely having fun with that. It took awhile, but after reading *Azeroth*, I realized that the question had been something to the effect of, "What about Morgaine's family?"

In 1981 Carolyn made a trip down to Florida where, staying with Joe Haldeman and his wife, Gay, she witnessed the launch of the space shuttle. Within the next few weeks the shuttle was being returned to Florida from its landing site at Edwards Air Force Base in California. One of the stops was to be at Tinker Air Force Base in Midwest City, a suburb of Oklahoma City.

When it was announced that the shuttle would remain there for a day and the public would be allowed in to see it up close, I definitely planned to go.

Big surprise: Carolyn wanted to go. I picked her up early and we headed out. The traffic was light until we were about a mile and a half from the base. There, traffic had slowed to a standstill, and to say it was moving at a snail's pace would have been saying we were moving twice as fast as we were. Normally we could have traveled that length of road in perhaps five minutes; this time around it took nearly three hours.

It was worth it.

Once we had parked the car, we walked the half-mile around the hanger to where the 747 with its piggyback passenger was parked. It was one of the most fantastic sights I had ever seen, the kind of thing I had been dreaming about since those long gone days in grade school when I read every science fiction novel in the library of Lincoln Elementary school and the Carnegie Library in Lawton.

Back then, pre-Columbia, pre-Challenger, pre 9-11, we were allowed to get within five hundred feet of the shuttle. This was closer than the five miles distance everyone had been allowed at the launch Carolyn had attended. One of us, I'm not sure which, observed that the only thing better than what we were looking at would have been to see a whole line of them poised to return to Florida for new missions. The other one agreed, but added "Or maybe hearing a speaker announcing . . . next flight for Luna City leaving in fifteen minutes."

I took a photo of Carolyn with the shuttle just over her shoulder. She then took the same shot of me. That picture still hangs on my wall. Not too long ago I got the chance to say thank you to Carolyn for her belief in me. I dedicated my first short story collection, *Dark And Stormy Nights*, to Carolyn. I am sure that there are others to whom Carolyn has reached out her helping hand that feel the same way I did. Not only has she made her mark on the field with her tales but with her friendship and willingness to help others find their way along the same path that she treads.

Because of Carolyn, my life was changed in a major way unrelated to writing, and the funny thing is, she didn't actually do anything. Sound strange? Good.

In 1988, on the weekend before Thanksgiving, I had gone to the annual Soonercon SF convention in Oklahoma City. Since it was local, Carolyn was there, along with her housemate, artist Jane Fancher. That evening Jane organized a group of what turned out to be about twenty people to go out to eat at a BBQ place across the street from the hotel.

The restaurant didn't have enough seating to allow everyone to sit at the same table, so we had to break into smaller groups. One of the people I wound up sitting with was a very pretty blonde woman from Tulsa named Sue Truelove. She had actually gone along with the group because she had enjoyed Carolyn's work and wanted to visit with her.

I spent most of the evening and much of the rest of the convention with her. Over the next year or so, I saw her a number of times and eventually moved to Tulsa to be with her. On my birthday in 1990 I asked Sue to marry me, and she accepted. Other than our respective families, the first people we wanted to tell were Carolyn and Jane.

We had visited them at their house on several occasions, so it was no surprise when we called Carolyn, said we were in town and suggested getting together for dinner. I suggested that same BBQ place. After ordering the ribs, just as we had that first night, we told Carolyn and Jane our news.

Several months later, on April 13, 1991, Carolyn and Jane made the trip to her old hometown, Lawton, to attend our wedding.

Gratis tibi ago, amicae meae
(Thank you, my friend and my teacher.)

Of all the authors I've worked with on this project, Burton Raffel is the most—something—of them all. I invite readers to execute an Internet search using Burton's name. Be prepared for a large number and variety of results. A translator with astonishing output, Burton is also a fiction writer, poet, and . . . well, I suggest you find out for yourself.

This piece first appeared in *The Literary Review* (vol. 44, No. 3) during the spring of 2001, and it is perfectly suited for *The Cherryh Odyssey*. As we move beyond the personal observations of Cherryh's work and influence on the field, Burton's piece is an excellent introduction to a slightly more detailed and critical (in the sense of academic perspective) kind of writing.

C.J. CHERRYH'S FICTION

Burton Raffel

Consider, first, a novel about a thirty-seven-year-old ship's crew-woman, thrown up on the beach by an economic squeeze, unemployed and unemployable because she's unwilling to change a way of life that simply does not exist on shore. She has been left in a dying port, where ships seldom dock and those that do cannot offer her employment. Without alternatives or resources, she contemplates starvation (or even suicide). She is becoming physically shrunken; her clothing is worn, almost tattered. "She smelled strongly of soap, of restroom disinfectant soap, a scent [one] had to think awhile to place."

A local resident, struck by her persistence and pride, gives her what work he can, illegally; a sex-driven barkeep gives her a place to sleep (with him, of course) and a bit of food. The barkeep turns sadistic; trained in violence as well as ship-board mechanics, she kills him. Unexpectedly, a disguised quasi-military ship arrives, and she talks her way into a rock-bottom berth. But before she can leave, the dead man is found, she is arrested—and then freed when the ship uses its military status and authority to claim her. Safely on board, still half dazed, "she avoided looking at people, especially looking them in the eye or starting up a conversation, just stared blankly at the main-deck [which she has been ordered to clean] and all those possible foot-prints people were making walking back and forth—footprints had occupied her mind all day, still occupied it, in her condition—and she mentally numbed out, tasting the food and the tea down to its molecules, it was so good, and finding her hands so sore [that] holding a fork hurt."

Written throughout in consistently clear, probing prose, perfectly suited to both characters and subject matter, C. J. Cherryh's *Rimrunners* (1989) is obviously a tale of adventure. Less obviously, it is also a close, intense psychological study and a keen exposition, in strongly presented, deeply imagined detail, of complex inter-relationships between and among individual and social forces, in a time and place not our own. In pure stylistic terms, some of B.J. Traven's work comes to mind; so too does other determinedly non-Literary literary fiction. Cherryh writes: ". . . they were a little gone, having a damn good time, but gone, and NG [short for 'no good'] was gone too, out-there, deep-spaced and having trouble breathing." Plainly, her prose has strong rhythms of its own—but how different is this, qualitatively, from, say: "Helene was not a teetotaler by any means. In fact Ed encouraged her to drink. She was more fun when she drank. But she was liable to get drunk tonight, because it was Christmas, and Ed didn't want her to become reckless with the spirit of giving." That comes from John O'Hara's *Appointment in Samarra* (1934), which Alfred Kazin called "the best of the 'hard-boiled' novels . . . [and] a very serious book indeed." (*On Native Grounds*, 388) Nor would there be any difficulty setting out stylistically related passages from other American writers, notably the original hard-boiler himself, Ernest Hemingway.

The "beach" in *Rimrunners* is literally a space station; the "ships" are space-going. The fiction is *science* fiction. But genre labels become irrelevant, at such fully realized and masterful levels. *The Lord of the Rings* is high-quality fiction, period. It is not simply or primarily fairy-tale or fantasy fiction. *Alice in Wonderland* is high-quality fiction, not a children's book. Both are unassailably (and enduringly) literature. And so too are the adventure tales (though we tend for obvious reasons not to think of them as adventure tales) of Joseph Conrad, Albert Camus, Franz Kafka and Joseph Roth, Robert Louis Stevenson and Herman Melville—and those of C. J. Cherryh.

Like most genuinely literary (not Literary) writers, Cherryh is not limited, either stylistically or in subject matter or approach. She employs "hard-boiled" prose when the particular book or approach seems to her to require it; from time to time, unpredictably and driven only by authorial impulses, she chooses to write of proletarian, feminine, or epic, or heroic, or genetically alien characters and themes, for, as she quite typically says, different subjects and approaches "stretch different muscles" (Amazon.com interview):

> It was from the air that the rawness of the land showed most: vast tracts where humanity had as yet made no difference, deserts unclaimed, stark as moons, scrag and woolwood thickets unexplored except by orbiting radar. Ariana Emory gazed down at it from the window. She kept to the passenger compartment now. Her eyesight, she had to admit it, was no longer sharp enough, her reflexes no longer fast enough for the jet. She could go up front, bump the pilot out of the chair and take the controls: it was her plane, her pilot, and a wide sky. Sometimes she did. But it was not the same.
>
> Only the land was, still most of the land was. And when she looked out the window, it might have been a century ago . . .

Thus begins the first chapter of *Cyteen* (1988), a massive, intricate, wise, and compelling novel (first published as a trilogy) to which I will return. I want to do no more, at this point, than simply note *Cyteen*'s substantive as well as its quite apparent stylistic expansiveness. Indeed, *Cyteen* has been called Cherryh's masterpiece, and though that seems to me a valid judgment, the book's brilliance, its intensity, its depth are, I think, very closely matched many times over in her work.

Port Eternity (1982), for example, is an absorbingly passionate study in isolation and dream-worlds—not "fantasy" fiction, which Cherryh also writes (and which I will not here discuss), but plainly "science" fiction. The novel's narrator is Elaine, an android servant on the private spaceship of lady Dela, a rich and spoiled aristocrat, who amuses herself by naming all those who serve her after the Arthurian characters in Tennyson's *Idylls of the King* (freely quoted throughout) and having them constantly act out those roles. Dela's current voyage becomes, unwittingly, her last, when her ship and all its occupants are seized—they do not know how or why, if there is in fact a "why"—by a silent, unbreakable, unknowable power. Dela's response is to stage an elaborate banquet:

We came topside, into that huge formal dining room with the weapons and the real wooden beams and the flickering lights like live flame. All of them who had sat down at table got up again to help serve, excepting Griffin [the last of the lady's paramours] and Dela of course, who sat together at the head of the table. It was a scandalous profusion of food, when we were only then setting up the lab that was, at best, never going to give us delicacies such as this: but Dela was never one to scant herself while the commodity held out—be it lovers or wines or the food we had to live on. Maybe it pleased her vanity to feed her servants so extravagantly; she had brought us to appreciate such things—even Mordred was not immune to such pleasures. Perhaps it was humor. Or perhaps it was something more complicated . . .

I trust that, by this point, something of Cherryh's literary range begins to become apparent. We can also see very clearly one of her most distinctively literary traits, namely, her reluctance to deal in straightforward, black and white terms. Except in a very few of her earliest and somewhat raw books, Cherryh's work is in many ways an elaborately detailed, wondrously extended commentary on the universe's irresolute subtlety and deeply determined indeterminedness. *Port Eternity* is a vividly drawn, eerily compelling narrative, for despite the unusual range of her fiction, its analytical depth and imaginative variety, Cherryh remains first and foremost what all of fiction's major figures must be, a storyteller.

The Faded Sun (1978-79), like *Cyteen*, is a trilogy of novels: *Kesrith*, *Shon'jir*, and *Kutath*. Cherryh—something of a pseudonym, her birth-name being Carolyn Janice Cherry—is a trained classicist and archaeologist as well as a joyously creative linguist, formulating beautifully conceived languages for her invented cultures as fluently and realistically as she builds the cultures themselves and their intricately evoked settings. Extraordinarily different from *Cyteen* in subject and style, filled with bleak but glowing desert landscapes and dark, shrouded characters with burning motivation and the purest of unchanging principles, *The Faded Sun* may well be in strictly narrative terms more far-reaching, though nothing could be more fully realized. Cherryh's creations are sometimes worlds having no contact with or awareness of humans; more often, as in *The Faded Sun*, alien and human are obliged, by differing blind circumstances, to closely and vitally interact. In this case, though not invariably in Cherryh's work, the interaction is not only exceedingly violent but involves humans and aliens, each in their own ways, in powerful, dangerous, often fatal attractions to one side or the other. Fascinatingly, these are not necessarily the sides into which they were born.

> There was a division in the world, marked by a causeway of white rock. On the one side, and at the lower end, lay the regul of Kesrith—city-folk, slow-moving, long-remembering. The lowland city was entirely theirs: flat, sprawling buildings, a port, commerce with the stars, mining that scarred the earth, a plant that extracted water from the Alkaline Sea. The land had been called the Dus plain before there were regul on [the planet] Kesrith: the mri remembered. For this reason the mri had avoided the plain, in respect of the dusei [beasts of great bulk, sensitivity, and intelligence, bound to the warrior mri]; but the regul had insisted on setting their city there, and the dusei left it.

The second chapter of *Kesrith* opens with this intricately woven paragraph. So clear and always urgently to the point is Cherryh's writing that (1) every unfamiliar word and concept in this passage has already been more than satisfactorily explained, in the few pages of the short first chapter, and (2) in addition, time- and value-dimensions of great weight and power have been attached to each and every such term. The trilogy has large and pressingly important ecological dimensions—totally and very powerfully integrated into the plot. In Cherryh's work, one intellectual or analytical dimension tends to be no more insisted upon than any other. She has no need to proclaim, to thunder, to hammer at her readers with her ideas. In short, her literary confidence is as high as her literary energy level (she has said that, in full spate, she writes eighteen hours at a stretch); it enables her to operate in taut synch with her material:

> He was tall, even of his kind. His high cheekbones bore the seta'al, the triple scars of his caste, blue-stained and indelible; this meant that he was a full-fledged member of the Kel . . . Being of the Kel, he went robed from collar to boot-tops in unrelieved black; and black veil and tasseled headcloth, mez and zaidhe, concealed all but his brow and his eyes from the gaze of outsiders when he chose to meet them; and the zaidhe further had a dark transparent visor that could meet the veil when dust blew or red Arain reached its unpleasant zenith. He was a man: his face, like his thoughts, was considered a private identity, one indecent to reveal to strangers. The veils enveloped him as did the robes, a distinguishing mark of the only caste of the [mri] that might deal with outsiders.

The sheer *authority* of this seems to me all-compelling. And the weight of the conflicts and questions revolved in front of us, always in measured but only slowly apprehended and even more slowly appreciated fashion, is still further enhanced by heavy narrative reliance on dialogue. Cherryh's characters do not "converse," or merely talk: as all fictive masters know, novelistic dialogue at its best and most effective is a kind of embedded plot. Constantly thus revealed, and then still further revealed in action (as well as in active introspection: Cherryh handles internal rumination as fluently and judiciously as she does that which is actually spoken), the carefully colored personages moving through these densely woven novels are opened to us as significantly, created as fully and as coherently spun into their and our orbits, as the characters who inhabit any fiction I know. "[The mri] were a beautiful people," thinks a human at the beginning of *Shon'jir* , looking down at an unconscious, barely living mri warrior, "tall and slim and golden beneath their black robes: golden manes streaked with bronze, delicate, humanoid features, long, slender hands; their ears had a little tuft of pale down at the tips, and their eyes were brilliant amber, with a nictitating membrane that protected them from dust and glare. The mri were at once humanlike and disturbingly alien. Such also were their minds, that could grasp outsiders' ways and yet steadfastly refused to compromise with them." Another human, at the end of *Kutath*, and at a moment of decisive and intensely dramatic choice affecting both peoples, thinks to herself:

> . . . Fear had killed the worlds between.
>
> To use the mri, one had to play the Game, to cast them from the hand and let them go.
>
> The belief that it would be different . . . this, she cherished, as she believed in humankind.
>
> She played the Game.

Accordingly, these are novels that, inevitably, like *Anna Karenina* and *Middlemarch*, like *A la recherche du temps perdu* and *Don Quijote*, like *The Magic Mountain* and *David Copperfield* and *The Brothers Karamazov*, have no real ending, at least in sense of narrow, two-dimensional, cartographic finality.

Cherryh is fiercely prolific. It would be foolish to expect that each and every novel she writes will maintain absolute, soaring levels. ("Even Homer nods," as Horace observed two thousand years ago.) Still, only *Hestia*, published in 1979 but probably written well before, and *Wave Without a Shore* (1981—but, again, probably written earlier), offer anything less than the subtle, passionate writing she has been giving us for more than two decades. *Brothers of Earth* (1976), which deftly and convincingly explores the effects of new and long-separated environments on groups of human beings, is more than sufficiently memorable. *Hunter of Worlds* (1977) impressively explores not only multiple-levels of species relationship, but species differences of an extraordinary nature. Cherryh's driven imaginative urgency pushes her, in this novel, into a realm she does not usually deal with, namely, a race which is unquestionably, unalterably, almost unthinkably superior. *Serpent's Reach* (1980) focuses powerfully on humans and a fascinatingly imagined ant-like species. Many of the scenes Cherryh here conjures up are profoundly unforgettable. *Voyager in Night* (1984), perhaps more intellectually than emotionally intense, once again deals with humans and a "species" far beyond human capacities. But *Cuckoo's Egg* (1985), which seems to me almost a study for the writing of *Cyteen*, is as fine and stirring as anything Cherryh has ever done. It is in a way a brilliant tour de force, looking at humans entirely from an alien perspective—beautifully suggested in the book's very first paragraph, describing *the* alien at issue, as he waits for an infant human to be brought to him for rearing, in a cause no less than the ultimate survival of this aristocratic tutor's race:

> He sat in a room, the sand of which was synthetic, and shining with opal tints, fine and light beneath his bare feet. The windows held no cityview, but a continuously rotating panorama of the Khogghut plain: a lie. Traffic noise came through.

This is prose of perfect suppleness, delicately aligned on word-choices of impeccable selection. The character may seem familiar, at the very first: he is sitting, which is completely within our human ken, and he is in a "room." But then the floor is revealed to be "sand," and not natural sand but "synthetic," and not merely synthetic but "shining with opal tints." Clearly, this is *not* a humanly familiar setting—and though the person being described (whatever his nature) is a house-dweller, he sits with "bare feet." What the windows display is a "continuously rotating panorama." This is pretty readily imaginable, if not precisely common in our world—but "the

Khoggut plain"? And just who is adding the sarcastic aside, labeling the rotating panorama "a lie"? There is "traffic" in the streets; this is obviously a city. But traffic and a city of exactly what sort? The concepts may be familiar, but by this point the reader is aware that the realities, the living, animate details, the sights and smells, the shapes and colors, cannot be ones with which we are acquainted. Cherryh presents us with all of this, and indeed more, in just three sentences, none of which is overlong, and the last of which is exceedingly short. It would be hard for prose to do more, or better, in so compressed a space.

And the five volumes of the *Chanur* series (1981-92: Cherryh intended only four, but apparently, as well as understandably, found herself unable to abandon so glowing a creation), like the seven volumes (ten, if *Cyteen* is added) that begin with *Downbelow Station* (1981) and have progressed to *Tripoint* (1994) and *Finity's End* (1997), draw with loving care and great skill two distinctly variant worlds. Cherryh *works* her materials, in the very highest Henry Jamesian sense. "Humanity is immense, and reality has a myriad forms... Experience is never limited, and it is never complete; it is an immense sensibility, a kind of huge spider-web of the finest silk threads suspended in the chamber of consciousness, and catching every air-borne particle in its tissue. It is the very atmosphere of the mind; and when the mind is imaginative—much more when it happens to be that of a man of genius—it takes to itself the faintest hints of life. It converts the very pulses of the air into revelations." ("The Art of Fiction," 1884).

Which artistic conversion is exactly what Cherryh gives us, in *The Pride of Chanur,* the first novel in that series:

> ... [C]aptain Pyanfar Chanur ... [was] setting out down her own rampway for the docks. She was hani, this captain, splendidly maned and bearded in red-gold, which reached in silken curls to the middle of her bare, sleek-pelted chest, and she was dressed as befitted a hani of captain's rank, blousing scarlet breeches tucked up at her waist with a broad gold belt, with silk cords of every shade of red and orange wrapping that about, each knotted cord with a pendant jewel on its dangling end. Gold finished the breeches at her knees. Gold filigree was her armlet. And a row of fine gold rings and a large pendant pearl decorated the tufted sweep of her left ear. She strode down her own rampway in the security of ownership, still high-blooded from a quarrel with her niece—and yelled and bared claws as the intruder came bearing down on her.

This is the book's second, not its first paragraph. The first establishes the existence of some furtive, unknown, unkempt "bipedal, brachiate" creature, skulking in the background as the captain disembarks. Cherryh conjures the grand, hirsute captain in all her lush finery and love of display, then deftly re-introduces the skulker, combining his/her appearance with the captain's no longer merely showy leonine characteristics. (There is so little question of patriarchal suppression, and so little need for militant feminism, in any of these novels, that the subject seems entirely moot.) Cherryh has subtly prepared us for this revelation of lion-ness, not simply by describing the captain's "mane" but, delicately, by seeming to focus our attention on the *fact* that the captain sports a beard while, as if merely in passing, informing us that said beard is red-gold. Indeed, "gold" suffuses much of the paragraph, along with "every shade of red and orange." This is plainly no zoo lion, nor do we meet the captain on an African veldt. When the skulker, wounded, dashes past the captain and onto the ship, Cherryh again lets us see, even hear and feel, the functionally leonine aspects of this splendid, commanding personage as, turning to chase after the intruder, her "claws [are] scrabbling for traction."

Both leonine qualities and showy love of pomp and dazzle are in fact integral, basic and important aspects of Pyanfar's colorful, idiosyncratic character. It is she, as captain, who creates, complicates, endangers and ultimately redeems *The Pride* [a resplendent pun] *of Chanur*. This too is thoroughly in Cherryh's style: every small event is discovered to be linked to larger and larger causes and effects, to perhaps endlessly radiating circles of involvement. Cultures, worlds, and—in the Chanur universe—*our* human world come to have connections of a profoundly apposite sort. Cherryh is far too dedicated an explorer of other worlds and ways to allow readers merely passive engagement.

Humans, then, are by no means always set either at the center of Cherryh's vision, or off to the side. On the one hand, human beings are unsurprisingly quite like some of the sentient species she has created. Yet they are distinctly unlike others, much as the methane breathers Cherryh has imagined are inevitably unlike any of the oxygen breathers. It is in that context, I think, that it is most helpful to look at *Cyteen*, a book which cannot be diminished by being considered apart from the nine other novels (to date) which set out what Cherryh envisages as the events and consequences of human space exploration.

The circle-upon-circle of endlessly out-reaching civilizations does not press so visibly or so immediately, in *Cyteen*. But even in its own farflung universe, Cyteen (the planet, not the book) is no more the center than, once upon a time, the Earth itself was thought to be. Cyteen is indeed a world, but it is an expropriated world, intrinsically hostile, and only in part terraformed and human-inhabited. Occupation and the partial transformation of a deeply alien environment have occurred relatively recently. And this planet, which in a very real sense can only be conquered step by step and keeps fighting back every moment of every day, is also the setting for a singularly powerful vector in Cherryh's picture of humanity's post-space-explorations, namely, a great functioning laboratory and factory, called Reseune, where ideas are turned into realities, and inanimate matter is turned into fully functioning, indistinguishably human creatures known as azi. (Indistinguishably human—but *differently* human.) More: *Cyteen* the book is built around this ability of Reseune to create human beings, almost without quantitative limits, in whatever mould is wanted, including industrial or military drones as well as men and women of enhanced ability. Most especially—for the purposes of this novel—Reseune's capabilities have, after years of working toward that goal, achieved the more or less exact re-creation of human beings, in the form of perfect genetic, though of course not psycho-social, clones.

One such cloning, though for policy reasons disguised, is Justin Warrick, officially the "son" of Jordan Warrick, who is a Special—humans of so high a caliber that, by statute, they have vast privileges and protections. There are only twelve of them, in all; the most powerful, as well as the most visible and without question the imaginative center of *Cyteen*, all throughout its three parts, is Ariane Emory—already introduced in the book's first paragraph, which I have quoted earlier. Ari (as she is called) is herself genetically the child of two human parents, rather than a planned gene-set. Her genetic mother and father were both geneticists and, in fact, the founders of Reseune. More than a hundred years old when Ari was "conceived" (in and by the apparatus of Reseune, which provided a sustaining womb and thus became her physical birth place), the parents are long dead. The rejuvenation techniques that so long preserved them, techniques that have been still further perfected, have brought Ari herself to the age of a hundred and twenty,** which starts to approach rejuv's outer limits.

Much feared, for good reason, and much hated, also for good reason, Ari is suddenly mysteriously murdered, midway in the trilogy's first volume. The murderer's identity is and remains unknown, though Jordan Warrick is maneuvered into a confession. Falsely? We never know, though he seems likely to have been guilty. But Reseune cannot manage without Ari, and the decision is made to immediately produce a clone, a possibility which Ari had anticipated and for which she has elaborately planned: her instructions, tapes, videos, and the like, are designed to carry the re-creation to full maturity. The birth, rearing, and coming to adulthood of the clone are then stunningly traced across the often breathtaking pages of volumes two and three. Similarities, and differences, between Ari I and Ari II are developed no less profoundly or achingly affecting than the evolving similarities and differences of Don Quijote and Sancho Panza, over which readers and critics through the centuries have wondered and exulted.

This is however only the basic, more or less skeletal structure of *Cyteen.* I will leave for discussion by others such quietly dropped clues as that the expansionist drive of the interstellar Union, shaped and still dominated by Cyteen, was directly and unquestionably a continuation of that "fervor which had led to the establishment of *the original thirteen star stations,*" or that "Cyteen was founded by people seeking independence from colonial policies of the Earth Company" (315). We even hear of "the framers of the [Union] Constitution." (The very word "union" has of course its own reverberations in these contexts; the names of humanity's other two branches, in Cherryh's grand scheme, are "Sol" and "Alliance," which have no such political echoes.) The heart and soul of the book is the flawlessly interwoven stream of meaningful story and high-powered insight, of fascinating character and palpitating event, all of it embedded in and sometimes set against a detailed matrix that can and regularly does flash with the beautifully melded incandescence of intelligence and sensitized experience.

- "Remember," says the senior Ari's pre-recorded message to the younger Ari, "what you do is your own choice. What I did was mine." (363)
- "We tunnel between realities," says Justin Warrick, explaining born-men's mental processes to an azi. (333)

- "You didn't get anywhere by telling people to be nice," thinks eight-year-old Ari junior at her birthday party. "You just got their attention and shook them up until they fixed on you instead of what they had fixed on, and then you could do things with them." (261)

- "It's real hard to understand humanity," says the old, experienced man to the younger, relatively inexperienced but very very smart Justin Warrick, "when you keep attributing to everyone around you the complexity of your own thinking." (444)

- "It's not a Game, Catlin had said sternly when [her new partner in CIA-type training] had called it that. A game is what you do on the computers in Rec. This is real, and they cheat." (250)

- "Gloria [a child about to leave her planetary home for a far distant space station] had no idea in the world what she was going to. No idea in the world what ship discipline meant, or the closed steel world of a working station." (226)

- "Hormones were still crazy," thinks the adolescent younger Ari, beginning to deal with the struggle between sex and analytical thought. "But the brain was starting to fight back. // The brain has to win out, Ari senior had said. But the little gland at the base of the brain is the seat of a lot of the trouble. It's no accident they're so close together: God has a sense of humor." (441)

- "A vase set on a table stayed a moment and [then] sought its old position, not violently, just persistently," an azi undergoing hostile psych-probe assures himself. "That was not the way it was, of course. It was only the image he had . . . But he was still largely *not-there*. He was exhausted, and the rooms kept coming disarranged, the furniture flying about at random, requiring him to order it again . . . He was coming apart inside and . . . he was not sure things would go back where they belonged." (115-16)

- Two azis are addressed by their Supervisor, and react exactly as they have been bred—literally—to do: "Two perfectly attentive faces turned to her, open as flowers to light." (440)

- Ari senior to Ari junior, posthumously: "Human technology as an adaptive response of our species has passed beyond manipulation of the environment; beyond the manipulation of our material selves; beyond the manipulation of mind and thought. . . We must compress experience in the same way human history compresses itself. . . Ultimately only the wisdom is important, not the event which produced it. But . . . experience is a brutal and an imprecise teacher at best." (472)

- "As women six times his age went, she was still worth looking at. . ." (65)

- "Reseune operates in the place of time and natural selection," declares an "educational publication" prepared and released by Reseune. "Like nature, it loses individuals, but its choices are more rapid and guided by intelligence." (94)

Were all of these complex matters handled, fictively, as mere concepts, abstractions, the novel would be a boring tract—intelligent, well-informed, but lifeless. Take, for example, the last snippet I have quoted, which taken out of context might allow the reader to think that those who set up and those who now control Reseune seriously confuse themselves with Charles Darwin, at the very least, and at the worst, with God Himself. That is a real issue; it is frequently and realistically—as well as highly dramatically—discussed and debated, in these pages. (The level of intellectual talk in *Cyteen* is astonishingly high, just as it is incredibly fascinating.) But this issue, and many more, are both enacted and, as I have said, completely embedded in the novel's fabric. Here in its entirety is section iii of chapter 3, pages 102-03 of *Cyteen*, bringing to life the original Ari as she works in her laboratory—and as we very soon thereafter find out, these are almost the very last moments of her life. Her murderer enters at the end of this brief section:

The new separator was working. The rest of the equipment was scheduled for checkout. Ari made notes by hand, but mostly because she worked on a system and the Scriber got in her way: in some things only state of the art would do, but when it came to her notes, she still wrote them with a light-pen on the TranSlate, in a short-hand her [computerized] Base in the House system continually dumped into her archives because it knew her handwriting: old-fashioned program, but it equally well served as a privacy barrier. The Base then went on to translate, transcribe and archive under her passwords and handprint, because she had given it the password at the top of the input.

Nothing today of a real security nature. Lab-work. Student-work. Any of the azi techs could be down here checking things, but she enjoyed this return to the old days. She had helped wear smooth the wooden seats in Lab One, hours and hours over the equipment, doing just this sort of thing, on equipment that made the rejected separator look like a technologist's dream.

That part of it she had no desire to re-create. But quite plainly, she wanted to say *I* in her write-up of this project. She wanted her stamp on it and her hand on the fine details right from the conception upward. *was most careful, in the initiation of this project —*

I prepared the tank —

There were very few nowadays who *were* trained in all the steps. Everyone specialized. She belonged to the colonial period, to the beginnings of the science. Nowadays there were colleges turning out educated apes, so-named scientists who punched buttons and read tapes without understanding how the biology worked. She fought that push-the-button tendency, put an especially high priority on producing methodology tapes even while Reseune kept its essential secrets.

Some of those secrets would come out in her book. She had intended it that way. It would be a classic work of science—the entire evolution of Reseune's procedures, with the Rubin project [cloning Specials] hindmost in its proper perspective, as the test of theories developed over the decades of her research. *IN PRINCIPIO* was the title she had tentatively adopted. She was still searching for a better one.

The machine came up with the answer on a known sequence. The comp blinked red on an area of discrepancy.

Damn it to bloody hell. Was it contamination or was it a glitch-up in the machine? She made the note, mercilessly honest. And wondered whether to lose the time to replace the damn thing again and try with a completely different test sample, or whether to try to ferret out the cause and document it for the sake of the record. Doing the former, was a dirty solution. Being reduced to the latter and, God help her, failing to find solid evidence, which was a good bet in a mechanical glitch-up, made her look like a damn fool or forced her to have recourse to the techs more current with the equipment.

Dump the machine *and* consign it to the techs, run the suspect sample in a clean machine, and install a third machine for the project, *with* a new sample-run.

Every real-life project is bound to have its glitch-ups, or the researcher is lying...

The outer lab-door opened. There were distant voices. Florian and Catlin. And another one she knew. Damn.

"Jordan?" she yelled, loud enough to carry. "What's your problem?"

She heard the footsteps. She heard Florian's and Catlin's. She had confused the azi, and they trailed Jordan as far as the cold-lab door.

"I need to talk to you."

"Jordie, I've got a problem here. Can we do it in about an hour? My Office?"

"Here is just fine. Now. In private."

She drew a long breath. Let it go again. *Grant*, she thought. *Or Merild and Corain.* "All right. Damn, we're going to have Jane and her clutch traipsing through the lab out there in about thirty minutes.—Florian, go over to B and tell them their damn machine won't work." She turned and ejected the sample. "I want another one. We'll go through every damn machine they've got if that's what it takes. I want the thing cleaner than it's providing. God, what kind of tolerances are they accepting these days? And you bring it over yourself. I don't trust those aides. Catlin, get up there and tell Jane she can take her damn students somewhere else. I'm shutting down this lab until I get this thing running." She drew a second long breath and used the waldo to send the offending sample back through cryogenics, then ejected the sample-chamber to a safe-cell and sent it the same route. When she turned around the azi were gone and Jordan was still standing there.

This is as close to a clear picture of the "crime," if indeed it was a crime and not a complex accident, as Cherryh ever give us. The irresolution is typical. But so too is the patient build-up of detail, of which every smallest item is totally consistent with everything else we are told, anywhere in the novel. No one in *Cyteen* is any more black-and-white than are any of the book's inanimate furnishings, whether small or large or in-between. Ari is "mercilessly honest" about an experimental error, and fantastically careful about the necessary follow-up. She is also casually arrogant and profane, simultaneously an egomaniac and a person of great and patient consideration. Which matters more, the positive or the negative? For Cherryh, obviously, the answer is regularly: neither.

And Ari senior prevails. In *Cyteen*'s penultimate chapter, Justin Warrick suddenly looks up at Grant, an azi of Alpha status specially and purposefully designed by Ari, and sees him "as a stranger would, in an objective way he had never looked at Grant, the unlikely perfection—Ari's handiwork too, from his genesets to his psychset. // Everything was, everything. No good, any longer, in fighting [her] design. Even Grant was part of it. He was snared, he had always been.// *She wanted Jordan. Jordan failed her. She saw to my creation. Designed Grant.// Fixed me on her. . .* // Everything's connected to everything— " (604) Cherryh is completely conscious of that

87

universal connection. "Everything is related to everything," she says in the Amazon.com interview already cited from—and then she adds, "especially in my writing."

How many writers have both that degree of awareness *and* the literary power needed to make their thought brilliantly real, passionately true, and beautiful?

** Just as Cervantes has Don Quijote making absurd mistakes in arithmetic, so too Cherryh has the original Ari's "parliamentary" opponent, Mikhail Corain, reflecting that she had died at age "one hundred forty-odd." Don Quijote's and Corain's mistakes are totally in character, and characterologically revealing. So too the re-created Ari, in a state of psychological turmoil after claiming vast new freedoms for herself, at age twelve, uncharacteristically but revealingly fumbles and bumbles over the first Ari's age at death, calculating "a hundred fifty" and, a moment later, "a hundred-twenty-something." Cherryh, like Cervantes and indeed all masters of literature, constantly "works" stories and readers, to the enrichment of everyone and everything concerned. That sort of almost endlessly complex self-enrichment is perhaps the clearest mark of great as opposed to merely good literary art.

Novelist and critic, author of 15 books, the most recent of which, *Scores: Reviews 1993-2003* is the source for part of his contribution here, John Clute is a name impossible to escape in the world of fantastic literature. First published in 1959, he is best known for his work on the great encyclopedias of the field, one each for fantasy and science fiction.

If Cherryh were a critically monotone author, it would be possible for readers to love and appreciate each of her books equally, provided that boredom is not a question. Thankfully, Cherryh is a flexible and ever-evolving writer, which leads us to John's not-entirely positive review of *Hammerfall*, the opening book in Cherryh's new series. There is nevertheless much praise here: Clute's keen eye sees Cherryh's skill and professionalism and his perspective on her literary career is of course without match in the field.

Do not fail to peek beneath the surface of John's words here, for there is depth to plumb in this seemingly simple review.

A GREAT DEAL IN SAND: HAMMERFALL BY C. J. CHERRYH

John Clute

In the end, it was impossible to think of *Hammerfall* (New York: Eos, 2001) as entirely doofus. Every now and then over the week it took to get through this big first volume of a sequence whose ultimate dimensions remained at time of reading beyond mortal ken, a wee negative thought or two might have welled up through the teardrops of exhaustion. But I fought on. After all, C. J. Cherryh, who has written at least 50 novels in an intensely active career, is no fool. If she wanted to ride *Hammerfall* all the way to the last page, a reviewer should trust her enough to follow, and to follow, and to follow, and I did. Call me Ishmael.

There certainly is a problem here. The real weariness one feels after closing the last page of *Hammerfall* cannot have been an affect Cherryh failed to mean to engineer, for she is one of the most professional of all sf writers, and she *must* have known she was asking a great deal of those of her readers who stuck with her to the end. If she applied the pared-down, unrelentingly forward-march idiom she has mastered to a book like *Hammerfall*, a book with an Idiot-Plot storyline that bites itself in the ass three or four times before subsiding deep in sand, a storyline which only exists because (inexplicably in the high-tech world of *Hammerfall*) telephones do *not*, then she must have known that readers would suspect she was using all that hard-earned skill, which they had learned to trust, to take them for a ride. Cherryh's narrative voice developed, at least in part, in order to control the baroque high-wire multi-layered space-opera plotlines that govern the best novels in the Union-Alliance mega-sequence which has occupied most of her time for decades. What was that voice doing here? Why was competent, trusted, trustworthy, tough C. J. Cherryh insisting that we pay sedulous heed to a vicious circle?

The action of *Hammerfall* takes place in a desert called the Lakht, on a planet seemingly colonized centuries earlier by humans whose genes are monitored and occasionally tweaked by nanoceles controlled at first by the tyrant who brought them here, and subsequently by his sort-of-immortal She daughter, known as the Ila. She (or Her Indoors) has long ruled the roost from the city of Oburan in the center of the Lakht, which is dominated by wandering tribes, whose males very much resemble Bedouin males on Earth: phallocentric adolescents fixated by territory, procreation, patriarchy, honor, superba, spite. They ride camel-like creatures called beshti. Closer to the edge of the Lakht are villages, whose inhabitants are comparatively cowardly (or adult), and treat their women better.

For 30 years now, a madness has been infecting humans. They hear voices calling them eastwards, they have visions of a hall of stars and a tower, and the planet seems to tilt under their feet at dawn and dusk. And they feel an irresistible compulsion to follow their visions into the east. It is a bit like *Close Encounters of the Third Kind on Dune*. Strangely, each society in the Lakht (there are a lot of them) treats the victims of this compulsive madness in *exactly* the same fashion: by driving them from their homes. Not one Lakhtian society thinks of these voice-hearers as worthy of care, or as seers, or as holy. As the novel begins, Her Indoors has finally begun to show some interest in the growing plague, and has her guards gather victims from all corners of the land, and bring them, by force if necessary, to the central city.

Our hero, Marak, has been disguising his madness for decades, but is finally found out by his patriarchal pa, who gives him over to the Ila's guards. As the story opens, he is being driven *west* across the desert towards Oburan, along with others of the afflicted. It is a hard trip, especially as the dreams of the afflicted attempt to draw them eastwards. En route, we are told about the great stretches of sand that stretch in every direction, about the water that is scarce, about the sun that is very hot. The afflicted prisoners reach Oburan at last. Her Indoors interviews Marak. She boasts a translucent beauty (Her Indoors doesn't get out much). She commands Marak to lead a small expedition back to the *east*, in order to find out what's going on. He sets off, retracing his steps. En route, we are told about the great stretches of sand that stretch in every direction, about the water that is scarce, about the sun that is very hot, about the beshti who have certain habits. It is a long trek.

But Marak, nothing daunted, manages to lead his expedition to the tower which the voices have told him is his goal, and which is also the goal of the two women who have become his wives. Here he finds Ian and Luz, two advanced humans from off-planet. It is their voices he has been hearing, their voices which the afflicted have been hearing for decades. They have come down to Lakht in order to attempt to save its inhabitants from an alien race which fears that Her Indoors's experiments in geneshaping mark a resumption of a long-ago war in which they (the aliens) suffered deeply; in retribution, the aliens plan to devastate the planet by (I think) tossing big asteroids at it. In fact, lo!, some asteroids are already en route (hence the dreams of Hammerfall the afflicted have been afflicted with by Ian and Luz).

There is no time to waste (decades have already passed)!

Marak must therefore return *west* all the way back to Oburan and tell Her Indoors the score. (It is at this point that the reader begins to wonder why Ian and Luz don't simply telephone Ila and tell her the jig is up. No satisfactory reason is given for their inability to use the technologies they must possess, in order to communicate with an individual whose experiments in geneshaping mark her as equally likely to own a cellphone.) Marak sets off bravely. En route, we are told about the great stretches of sand that stretch in every direction, about the water that is scarce, about the sun that is very hot, about the beshti who have certain habits, about the danger of the shale which trips the unwary. He reaches Oburan, where all the tribes have foregathered, because they now believe the sky is about to fall. He persuades Her Indoors that she must allow her peoples to travel eastward through the desert to the tower, where they will be safe from Hammerfall. Wise readers will note that the route they will have to tread we have already trod thrice.

And all the folk begin to travel *east* (and we are there with them, every trod). En route, we are told about the great stretches of sand that stretch in every direction, about the water that is scarce, about the sun that is very hot, about the beshti who have certain habits, about the danger of the shale which trips the unwary, about the genes which heal, about the sex that is good between a man and his wives in turn, about the storms which sting, about the sand which blinds and muddies the water which is bitter, about the beshti who piss in the water which is bitter, which is only one of the habits of the beshti, and about the predators who have learned by now to lie in wait along the deeply worn paths that the west-east-west-east hegira-haunted humans adorn like so much smorgasbord. Lots of humans are eaten. The asteroid falls become more frequent.

There is no time to waste!

Marak, who has become a very great leader of the folk, gets most of them to safety, just as a great asteroid half-splits the planet in two. But just in the nick the aliens are persuaded to lay off because Ian and Luz's "makers"—their own new brand of nanoceles—have neutralized Her Indoors's treaty-violating gene shapers, making it impossible for her old-brand nanoceles to start the war again. In a short final chapter, we learn that Marak and his wives have become immortal, in readiness for volume two.

It is a most extraordinary text. It walks in its own bitter water. The book is told with all the intensity of an epic, with prose rhythms that evoke the Bible, with a strange wild-eyed earnestness—a faux-naif bardic yawp that Cherryh seems almost to be uttering out of a conviction that she is telling us the truth, that the bone-wearying back forth back forth back forth of *Hammerfall's* storyline is justified because it's *true*. The reviewer shuts up, abashed. He awaits the sequel. He has not solved *Hammerfall*, but he has finished it before it finished him. But the New Testament better be something else.

Editor's Note: The following are some last-minute thoughts about the sequel to *Hammerfall* John Clute was able to provide as this book was going to press.

Three years later, just too late to submit itself to sustained scrutiny here, a sequel has indeed arrived. *Forge of Heaven* (New York: Eos, 2004) is not quite yet the New Testament we might have thought imminent, though it is—indeed, and necessarily—very different from its predecessor. Geological epochs have passed, hammerfall's scars have diminished, much else remains the same as hitherto. Ian and Luz, immortalized observers from the previous volume, continue to keep tabs on the Ila, similarly deathless; Marak and one wife (a skim read failed to uncover any reference to the second) still survive, also immortalized and kept in extremely good health (Cherryh tells us they still have good youthful sex after aeons of it) by nanocele nannies in the blood, continue to do what they did before. As in the previous tale (but only once this time), Marak goes somewhere and comes back again; but he is not the main character in this volume, which comprises a pretty-well organized squabble of Apocryphae in preparation, we must guess, for the New Testatment—where one suspects he may well assume the garb of Paul Atreides (but this is to find out) . In any case, his trip downhill into the ands of the about-to-be-flooded-desert, in search of some stray earth-quake-spooked beshti whose habits we do not wish to discuss at length, and then his trip back again uphill with beshti in tow, seems mainly intended to keep him busy spinning his wheels until the next instalment.

Most of the action of *Forge of Heaven* takes place in Concord Station, where various complicated interstellar factions, which represent various facets of a typically complex Cherryh galaxy, quarrel and jostle and make pact together over a crisis which affects all of them, and maybe (we are warned) the whole universe. The aeons'-long task of maintaining watch over Marak's World, mainly in order to prevent the escape of any gene-engi-neered modifications to the human genome (to which Earth adheres with fundamentalist passion), has been put at threat by an assault, and a plethora of spies, and a virus-like invasion, and a certain amount of guff.

This is all sort of sorted hereabouts. At novel's end, decks cleared, we stand at the brink of another novel, where the positional shuffling will (I think) cease, and some intensely interesting action could begin.

Here, there is relatively liltle of interest to learn about anything to do with genetic change, or about a civilization which cannot tolerate change (Earth's, in constant conflict with the genetically modified Outsiders who are also main players in the game, along with the ONDAT, the alien civiliza-tion which inflicted hammerfall in the first volume). The payoff is not yet. The texture of the book is all prelude and talk. It is, as a text, queerly and fascinatingly *Asimovian* , not only as regards the conflict between change and stability which also governs much of the argument of both the FOUN- DATION and the ROBOT series, or the concept that whole civilizations can revolve around a refusal to cohabit with the unknown (genetic change here; robots in Asimov himself); but also as regards the structure of the book itself. Its narrative pacing—its 400 pages constitute a slow crescendo from abstract precis to pellmell action—may be more sustained than anything Asimov himself ever mustered; but the fact that so much of *Forge of Heaven* is conducted through interviews and conversations between princi- pals—separated by short spasms of action that require, and get, *lots* of debriefing afterwards—hearkens straight back to the Talking Head mara- thons that so intrigued the readers of Asounding Science Fiction in 1940s, back when the road to the future was an Open Conspiracy. (Just as Isaac Asimov stirs beneath C J Cherryh's feet, so H G Wells agitates under Asimov.)

Independent business consultant and interaction designer Heather Stark is not a critic in formal terms, yet she, as an extremely well-educated fan of Cherryh's work, brings forth an interesting perspective about what she perceives as a difference between Cherryh's work as a science fiction writer and as a fantasy writer. While many might doubt there is a difference between the two roles, Heather's view is not uncommon among Cherryh fans—some read the science fiction, others the fantasy, and some read both.

That Cherryh is a literarily flexible author is a given. Her long attention to the craft of writing is manifest in her many years of providing help to new and developing writers as well as her writing on the subject.

Is there a difference, literarily, between the two bodies of Cherryh's work? Is one inherently better than the other? As you read this article (please note as editor I have allowed it to remain in its British English form) I hope you will enjoy the metaphor of Two Cherryhs.

C.J. CHERRYH—IS THERE REALLY ONLY ONE OF HER?

Heather Stark

For over a quarter century, more often than not, C.J. Cherryh has published several books each year (*Bibliography*). Can one person really publish so much, so quickly? Or could there be some other explanation?

Her productivity is astounding. Excluding co-authored, edited, and re-issued works, the odd translation here and there, and miscellaneous dollops of generous advice to writers, in the 27 years since 1976 she has published around 60 novels. Using a back of an envelope estimate of 100k words per novel, what this means is that she has written at least 6 million words in 27 years—probably more.[1] This works out at about 1,100 published words per writing day.[2] Cherryh herself says that on a good day she gets down 2,000 words a day—and on a bad day, none (*Panel room*). So, if over the past 27 years she has had more good days than bad days, which I do hope is the case, it is possible—just—that there is only one of her.

But I have my reasons for thinking there might be two C.J. Cherryh's, not just one very hard-working one. For over twenty years, I've been reading just about every C.J. Cherryh I can get my hands on. I have come to learn that there are two different types of C.J. Cherryh books:

- The ones I admire and enjoy. Written by of the greatest writers of all time.
- The other ones.

I'm talking about Cherryh's science fiction and her fantasy. I'm really not sure they are written by the same person. (In fact, I kind of hope they aren't.)

It's not just me (. . . is it?)

I'm not the only person to have noticed that Cherryh produces different types of work. On her web site, Cherryh herself handily divides her oeuvre into science fiction, fantasy and miscellaneous (*Universes*).

Life would be simpler, and this chapter would be a lot shorter, if I could accept that Cherryh's output is more versatile than my taste for it. But I can't. I've tried, and I've failed. And I keep failing. Those Cherryh books with floaty hair all over the cover, the ones that look like an art rock album (or a shampoo bottle) from the 1970s. I buy them. Inevitably, they disappoint me. Time and time again, I tell myself that this time it will be different. This time it will be OK. This time it will be good. Or even better. And so I buy them. Again. And again, I'm disappointed. I feel like Charlie Brown after Lucy has pulled the football away. Again.

Even worse than the fact they disappoint me, these books puzzle me. I keep thinking there must be something here that I'm just not getting, and if I just tried one more time, or thought about it harder, or differently, I'd understand them and love them. At the very least, I'd understand why I didn't like them, and learn to leave them well enough alone.

Survival of the fantasist?

It's a known fact that Cherryh's work is very varied. However, it has also been suggested that this variation is actually the result of an evolution:

> Ursula Le Guin and C. J. Cherryh are examples of writers whose work has taken major turns from their earlier fiction. Some critics hail the ability of these authors to transcend the concerns and direction of their early work to be a sign of genius, while some of their fans get grumpy and miss the more familiar styles. (Wiscon Panel 139, 1997).

What kind of evolution seems to be at work here? If, in 1997, when this theory was put forward, you had looked at Cherryh's output to date, it certainly would have seemed that she was phasing out science fiction and switching over to fantasy.

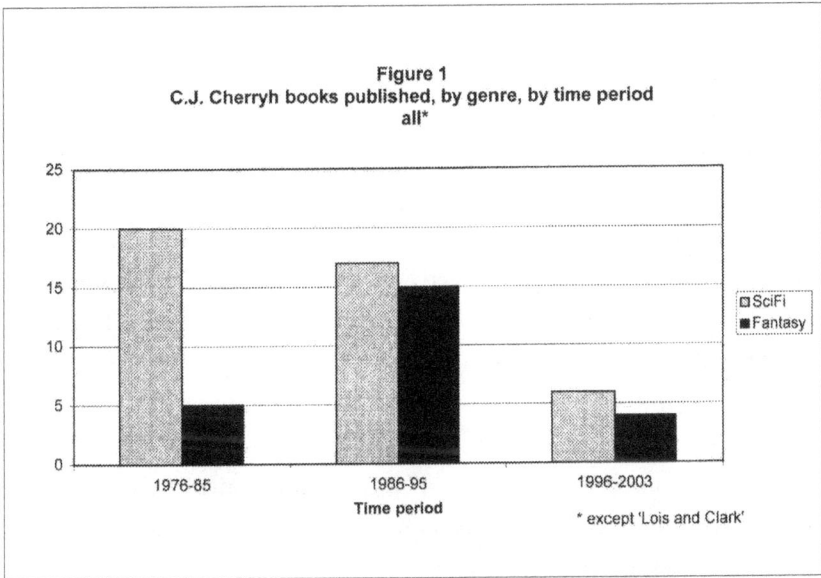

Figure 1
C.J. Cherryh books published, by genre, by time period
all*

Figure 1 tallies up all Cherryh's books including co-authored and edited volumes according to the genre classification on Cherryh's web site. If you look at the difference between 1976-85, and 1986-95, what's going on appears to be pretty clear: science fiction output is shrinking and fantasy is on the up—so much so that it appears to be on the verge of edging out science fiction. The 'evolutionary process' at work seems to be that fantasy is competing with science fiction—and winning.

However, if you look at what has happened post-1995, you might, if you were an optimist, think there was cause for optimism. Fantasy output has not edged out science fiction, and has shrunk, pro-rata, compared to the previous period. Science fiction still outweighs fantasy. A pessimistic interpretation of the very same graph is that science fiction output is going inexorably south, and it is only a matter of time before it disappears entirely.

One Cherryh or two?

Even the most starry-eyed optimist must accept that C.J. Cherryh appears to be creating less and less science fiction as years go by. But to better understand what is really going on here, we need to take a closer look at the differences between the fantasy and the science fiction work involved. Are they, perhaps, so different that they could only be the work of two different authors? Or, conversely, do they show unmistakable signs of being the work of a single controlling intelligence?

The rivet test: entirely accurate, but otherwise entirely useless

One industry-standard way of telling the difference between fantasy and science fiction is the Orson Scott Card 'rivet test': if it has rivets, it's science fiction. The rivet test works perfectly, for the classifications the *soi-disant* C.J. Cherryh provides for her work: what she calls science fiction has rivets, and what she calls fantasy doesn't.

Like the MBA who tells you that you are floating in a hot air balloon when you ask where you are, this is perfectly accurate, but perfectly unhelpful. It is not because I'm a rivet fancier that I admire Cherryh's science fiction. The rivet test does not explain what it is about the difference that makes one riveting, and the other not.

A lesson from the rank and file

Even Cherryh's more 'rank and file' science fiction works have special qualities which set them apart. Take *Hellburner*, for example. It's set on space-ships and on space stations, so there are lots of rivets.

Also on the plus side, there is a lot of dark humour. The protagonist of the first chapters, Ben Pollard, is a young man in a hurry, fast-tracked for greatness because of his skill at computing and his talent for political ladder-climbing—no small part of which lies in identifying which side is butter side up in sticky political situations. Because of a seeming snafu that threatens to whisk him off-base, and entirely off-message, he ends up at risk of missing an opportunity to interview for a key post that is critical for his advancement. His first thoughts on the situation have to do with the pros and cons of asking for help from his mentor, Weiter:

> If he risked a phone call to Weiter to request a rescue, it was a 90 percent certainty that Weiter couldn't do a damn thing. . . and he'd be screwed with Weiter for putting him in a Position. (11).

This is just a simple, small moment. But it reveals a characteristic Cherryh precision and economy in detailing thorny dilemmas where choices must be made with partial information, high stakes, and uncertainty about the possibility of a good outcome.

Very soon, our Ben quickly becomes entangled in inter-service rivalries, hopeless double-binds, and military double-speak of the highest order that may—or may not—originate from big bad gorillas at the very top of the tree. Cherryh is very good at allusive, knowing, and chilling evocation of power games based on partial knowledge and shifting mistrust between people and between factions. But this never tempts her into neglecting the rich opportunities for satire that are provided by military-industrial bureaucracy: our pro-tem hero soon finds that, because of the snafu that dragged him off message, he no longer has the requisite authorisation to have lunch. Not only that, but his luggage has gone missing. It's nobody's job to care —and so, of course, nobody does.

Shortly afterwards Cherryh gives a forensically accurate—and darkly hilarious—account of the nasty twists and turns and inner dynamics of a decision made by a committee hearing. It's the kind of thing you might get if you crossed Jane Austen with Machiavelli.

In the book, these personal vignettes have their equivalent, at a larger scale, in a much larger set of conflicts occurring across a broad sweep of (alternative future) history. In much of her science fiction, Cherryh explores variations on the shenanigans that the Roman Empire did so well. She puts themes of conquest, culture, conflict, and power in a new context, by setting them in the new material culture, practicalities, and constraints of life in space, and on planets that are linked by space travel. However, Cherryh's science fiction is not just 'Caesar in Space.'

Speculative anthropology with rivets

Cherryh's science fiction has a recognizably 20th Century sensibility. In a small but perfectly formed squib giving advice to would-be world-builders, which she has generously put on her web site, Cherryh recommends that the world-builder consider, amongst other things: biological and environmental constraints, the nature of the built environment, cooking and eating practices, cultural transmission of knowledge, burial practices, afterlife beliefs, beliefs in the nature of self, and the natural divisions of consciousness (*Panel room*). The 'modern equipment' which Cherryh brings to her science fiction is not the space ship—or even the rivet —it is the critical and analytical weaponry of social and cultural anthropology.

Cherryh's science fiction worlds unfold to us via complex and multi-layered interactions of political, social, economic, and material culture. Their richness is not a matter of the amount of detail, but the type of detail their descriptions contain.

However, a rich way of structuring an answer is not very useful without a good question to exercise it on. Space is just more of the same, except elsewhere, if you don't look at it in a new way, with new questions in mind. One of the things I really admire about what Cherryh does in her science fiction is the way she poses what-ifs, and plays out the answers in terms of cultural, economic, political, and social consequences, as well as personal ones.

Some of the what-ifs she explores have to do with variations on historical patterns of economic development: for example, how might the patterns of colonial expansion differ, under the different constraints on communication and trade that are imposed by space travel? Some what-ifs are not specifically tied to outer space, but are easier to set there: what if assassination was an enshrined element of the legal system? What if human clones produced and trained according to a strict caste system, designed for highly specific roles, found themselves in a radically different physical and social environment from that for which they were designed?

In playing out possible answers, Cherryh gives her questions the full-service treatment, creating answers which encompass military strategy, political economy, and cultural anthropology, and using these answers to explore the possibilities of what might happen as space is colonized, and alien conditions and intelligences change what we know of as reality. She works with a very broad sweep of (alterative future) history. But she can pull focus when it suits, too.

Consciousness: the final frontier

The boundaries and nature of individual consciousness is another concern of Cherryh's science fiction. Pilots in *Hellburner*, and in other novels, work in drug-altered states of consciousness that enable them to transcend the limitations of corporeal space-time. Cloned non-citizens in the Merchanter-Union universe, the subject of 20 of her books, listen to subliminal 'tape' that provides accelerated instruction in the skills that their particular class of clone is specially designed to learn. With tape-teaching, consciousness itself becomes a designed product where choice of action is narrowed to the point where it may no longer even be an illusion. In the dark alien encounters of *Voyager in Night*, one of the human captives is given relief from the prison of his solitary and unreliable consciousness through being administered a sensation of maternal love. It is an illusion, which is just being used by the alien captors as a drug which will strengthen the human victim enough for another round of torture.

The archetypal Cherryh science fiction character lives in a bad world in which an individual consciousness is fundamentally alone. The solitude of the individual is not solely a result of the difficulty of communication across cultures and species. This solitude also reflects an attitude of fundamental —and all too often justified—mistrust. In Cherryh's worlds, the impulse to affiliate is an important weakness that can be used by counter-parties in games of power whose outcomes determine each world's course of events, and each individual's chances of survival. In the culture of the dominant species of *Foreigner*, 'Fourteen words, the language had for betrayal, and one of them doubled for "taking the obvious course"' (358). As a vision of what existence is like, it isn't exactly pretty—but it's gripping.

Can it be . . . love?

Most of Cherryh's science fiction characters don't have a great deal of fun: they are too busy struggling. Their sex lives usually aren't so hot either, mostly because they have more important things to be getting on with—like survival. Epic geopolitical conflicts do not leave a great deal of time for recreational activity.

But even in the harshest *mise en scène*, love—or something like it—usually seems to make its way through to the surface, at least for a while, like a weed pushing through the cracks in the pavement. It may be unlooked-for, it may be unwelcome, and it may not be obviously useful, but it is capable of flowering in the most unlikely circumstances.

Cherryh is not by any means a conventional romantic novelist. But, in amongst the riches of her science fiction list, there is a genuine adventure/romance: *Angel with the Sword*. It is one of the regrets of my reading life it hadn't yet been written when I was 12 or 13. (I know how much I would have enjoyed it then. But, that said, I still enjoy it now.)

Our heroine, Altair Jones, is an orphan of 16 or 17 who makes a precarious but independent living by running a pole-boat for hire on the river Det, in a strange watery city with hints of mediaeval Venice to it. She is a bit of an artful dodger, and bit of an entrepreneur. She needs to be.

One day, a beautiful naked blond man is thrown into the canal right next to her boat. After considering the pros and cons of interfering with what might be a gang matter, she hauls him out, and while she is giving him resuscitation, her boat twists and turns, crashing against the pilings on the pier:

> Push and shove when he choked, till he heaved it up and got another half-liquid suck of air down his throat.
>
> *Bang, broadside onto the timbers of the pier with a shock that popped her teeth together. Old Det was lively when the tide was turning. Push and let be. Push and let be, until the gasps got smaller and equaled her own.*
>
> *Thump*, against another piling, in a dizzy spin into moonlight towards the dreaming clutter of night-tied boats at Hanging Bridge. (18-19)

The rhythms of the kiss of life weave into the rhythms of the boat banging into the pier, out of control. The pace is measured, but the situation is urgent. It's a lovely passage that shows Cherryh's mastery of the moment, and her strong feeling for meter.

Altair fishes the beautiful naked blond man out of the river, and saves his life again by keeping him warm by chafing him with her own body. With virginal enthusiasm, she makes up her mind to offer herself to him, as soon as he wakes up. He, however, is still concussed, which might possibly be why he doesn't think much of the idea. (But it might also have something to do with the fact she has never in her life had the luxury of a hot bath.)

Needless to say, she eventually gets her wicked way with him, and although in some ways he turns out to be an excellent lover, he also turns out to be a spy, a former assassin, and a rogue, dependant on a shifting series of alliances with the various factions vying for power in the city. She needs to chase him around town a fair amount, pursued by villains, before he accepts her affection, and she accepts his protection. Many adventures are had by all. Perhaps it's a romance more suitable for Tank Girl than Barbara Cartland—but it's a romance none-the-less.

There are even rivets, although they are kept offstage and offplanet, because the aliens who, unseen, control the world Altair lives on have embargoed contact between the humans trapped on the planet, and the rest of the human space-faring diaspora.

What happens when there are no rivets?

Before I undertook to write this chapter, my attempts to understand what was going on with Cherryh's fantasy works were hampered by the fact that although I kept buying them, I couldn't actually force myself to get all the way through any of them. However, in the interest of research, I have now read *The Tree of Swords and Jewels* from cover to cover.

What did I look for? I looked for what I love about Cherryh's work. Dark humour. Scope. An intriguing what-if, with a multi-layered answer. A lesson or two in political economy or military strategy. A bracing dose of Machiavellian viperishness. Something strange and insightful about the material culture of a foreign, possibly alien, civilization, and the difficulty of cross-cultural understanding. Something gloomy and compelling about the futility and isolation of individual consciousness. Lovely prose. Maybe, if I'm lucky, a bit of love on the side to keep me warm.

What did I find? A mediaeval setting. A tenuous and treacherous telepathic link between the iron age conquerors, and the fleeing fairy folk. Overlapping realities. A nameless horror or two. Plucky children. A Hero. A Quest. All the accoutrements of a full-on Celtic twilight.

A passage from the prologue gives a flavour:

> Now young Evald had known only cruelty of his own father and only kindness of Niall—so he worshipped Niall Cearbhallain, growing into young manhood under the close guidance of Niall and Caoimhin and Scaga. But in the end this devotion of his doomed Niall to die, for Faery would have taken Niall back to its heart if Evald had not driven its emissary away from Niall's deathbed in what he thought was his foster-father's defense. (12)

Cherryh can't help but write with good rhythm. This enlivens the first sentence for just long enough to keep me awake all the way through it. But by the second sentence it's all getting just that little bit too complicated. The reader is trapped in a myth-laden syntax that barely seems worth the bother of parsing it. This sensation is Nothing Less Than a Harbinger of the Doom that Awaits the Reader in Subsequent Pages.

By the end of the book, endless mythic fog swirls even more thickly over her style, obscuring all in its wake:

> The earth quaked. The drow shrieked one awful cry. "No," one shouted, who lifted a venomed sword. "Fall back—O cousin, you do not defeat us! You only draw new battlelines. And she is there, our cousin, when you release the Worm—A world divided, Liosliath! That is what you win—but Aoibheil is ours!"
>
> They retreated; the lesser evils flowed after them, less swift, leaving mortal allies in confusion and panic on Aesebourne's wooded shores.
>
> "Lord!" Beorc cried. "O gods, my lord—"
>
> A second time he set the horn to his lips and pealed out a note wilder and louder than the first. (231)

By that point, I was well past the point of caring what might or might not be going on. I had the sense that I'd probably seen it before somewhere.

It's this been-there-done-that feel of this work that gets me down. It's like being trapped in someone else's Tolkien story. You feel that you know the landscape, the costumes, and the local customs. If you could just remember who you were, and find your carven oaken shield . . . you would probably also remember the plot you were trapped in, and thus finally escape from the seemingly endless cycle of fictional rebirth.

Such a place might well be a nice enough place to wallow around in wearing your fluffiest pair of slippers and clutching your snuggliest fleeciest most beloved hot-water bottle. But it's not the place to hang about if you are looking to be surprised—or, indeed, interested—by anything that goes on.

Of course, not all of Cherryh's fantasy is set in an alternative Celtic twilight. But, personally, I find that it all has a faint, unmistakable tinge of re-circulated air. When there are no rivets, it all falls apart.

Let me be clear. It's not because I have something against fantasy that I don't like *Cherryh's* fantasy. I don't like Cherryh's fantasy because, in it, everything that I think is truly excellent about her work is missing and what's there doesn't make up for what isn't.

Will the real C.J. Cherryh please stand up and get back to work?

The fantasy works and the science fiction works published under Cherryh's name are so different that it's hard to see how anyone (except C.J. Cherryh) could have written them both. But since it *is* Cherryh we're talking about, it's difficult to say with any confidence what's going on. Within her science fiction *oeuvre*, Cherryh did, after all, write both the sweet, sexy adventure-romance, *Angel with the Sword*, and *Voyager in Night*, in which the aliens have angle bracketed names straight out of a formal semantics textbook, and the plot is just as difficult to warm up to.

So, really, anything is possible. Given the versatility she displays within a genre, it is, sadly, all too possible that she could have written the fantasy as well as the science fiction. And sometimes, in the fantasy works, if you listen carefully, Cherryh's naturally strong sentence rhythms can be heard trying to escape into the light and fresh air.

However, it would not be fair to condemn her on such flimsy evidence as this. The fairest conclusion that can be drawn, based on the facts, is that equivocating and faintly annoying Scots verdict of 'not proven.' Not guilty enough to be found 'guilty,' but not innocent enough to be found 'not guilty,' either.

I really do hope there are two Cherryh's. Because if there is only one, then the more fantasy gets written, the less science fiction there's going to be. I'm not just being selfish. I think this would be a loss to the world.

Cherryh's science fiction can be bleak. Her worlds are not nice places to be. They are strange. They are premised on conflict. They show new and subtle ways in which hell can be other people. Her characters don't often have nice days. But she's a genius of an explorer. She brings with her all the cultural richness of earth, and humanity, uses it to push the boundaries of what it is to be human, and to understand others.

My personal appeal to C.J. Cherryh is this: please don't get too cosy in faerie. Go out again, into the future, into the dark, the unknown, and the cold. And come back safely, and tell us what you find.

WORKS CITED

Cherryh, C. J. *Angel with the Sword*. London: Victor Gollancz Ltd., 1987.

—. *Blog*. Personal web site. March 24, 2004. http://www.cherryh.com/www/blog.htm .

—. *Bibliography*. Personal web site. March 24, 2004. http://www.cherryh.com/www/foreignbiblio.htm .

—. *Foreigner*. New York: Daw Books Inc, 1994.

—. *Hellburner*. London: New English Library, Hodder and Stoughton, 1993.

—. *Panel room*. Personal web site. March 24, 2004. http://www.cherryh.com/www/panel_room.htm

—. *The Tree of Swords and Jewels*. London: Victor Gollancz Ltd., 1988.

—. *Universes*. Personal web site. March 24 2004. http://www.cherryh.com/www/univer.htm .

—. *Voyager in Night*. London: Methuen, 1985.

Wiscon Panel session 139, "Authors whose work changes dramatically: signs of genius?" WISCON 21, May 1997. March 24, 2004. http://www.sf3.org/wiscon/21/program.faq.html .

END NOTES

[1] This back of an envelope estimate uses an estimate of 100k words per novel. This estimate is conservative —it is probably too low. In early 2004, Cherryh's weblog said she had recently completed a novel in the Foreigner series which weighed in around 120k (*Blog*), and a few of her novels (most notably Cyteen) are truly huge. But it doesn't matter to the conclusions that can be drawn whether the estimate is precise or not. If you work the numbers using an estimate that is 50% bigger —say, 150k words/novel —an estimate which is probably too high, bearing in mind the number of DAW type books (preferred length 80k) that go into the total —the overall conclusion doesn't change. It would still be possible for there to be only one C.J. Cherryh. But she would have had to have had many more good days than bad days, over the past 27 years.

[2] Again, this is based on an underlying back of an envelope estimate of 200 writing days per year. Given that writers have administrative overhead, and undertake PR activities, not every working day is necessarily a writing day. Again, it doesn't matter if this assumption isn't exactly correct: the conclusion about whether it is possible for C.J. Cherryh to have written everything with her name on it would be the same, for assumptions that are within shouting distance of this one.

[3] If you exclude co-authored volumes and edited volumes from the analysis,

there is less of a fantasy bump in the middle, but most of the same growth patterns hold: science fiction declines monotonically, and fantasy crests in the middle time period.

Janice Bogstad's contribution is at the far end of a long process of acceptances that began with Bradley Sinor's. Last in this case is far from least. This academic view of Cherryh's "Russian" trilogy is valuable and revealing to non-academic readers (as well as to those of us in the ivory tower) as it examines in detail an important pattern of meaning in these now-out-of-print books. Perhaps renewed attention to them will summon them forth to the shelves of booksellers once again.

Note the setting aside of the word "Russian," above. Historical events have overcome old terminology, and Janice's article is probably the very first to use a post-Soviet understanding of the cultural geography as regards these Cherryh novels. It also contributes an interesting element to the discussion of the perceived, in some quarters, split between the purely fantasy and science fiction aspects of Cherryh's output.

I hope you will find Janice's examination of these now hard-to-find Cherryh novels of interest. Note in particular the extensive bibliography that is part of this article. A fact of life that often confuses undergraduates is that MLA format is a guideline, not an absolute rule. In this case Janice provides far more than merely the sources she cites, leading curious researchers beyond what one might expect in an article devoted to a science fiction and fantasy author. Interested readers have access to much more than the article itself, and I suggest the curious seek out further reading.

SHIFTING GROUND:
SUBJECTIVITIES IN CHERRYH'S
SLAVIC FANTASY TRILOGY

Janice M. Bogstad

C.J. Cherryh's work and popular reception

C.J. Cherryh is both "fiercely prolific" (Raffle 581) and a versatile writer of popular fictions. As Thomas P. Dunn points out in his article in *St. James Guide to Science Fiction Writers,* her work was undervalued and dismissed as space opera or popular heroic fantasy for many years until the vast, saga patterns of her various series began to be discernable in such bodies of work as the Morgaine series, the Alliance-Union Universe series, and, more recently the Foreigner series. He later notes: "It became clear that Cherryh was not writing mere space-and-critter yarns or attenuating series of sequels for the sake of product, but was using established SF clichés to outline an entire galactic future history" (182).

While most of her works are either a combination of fantasy and sf tropes, such as the Arthurian legends in the Morgaine sf series, in-depth humanistic explorations of technologies over vast stretches of time such as the Alliance-Union Universe books or explorations of human/alien interactions such as the Chanur series, she has also created several groups of works that employ high-fantasy tropes, explorations of good and evil played out in fantastic landscapes and stories derived from her studies in languages, history, folklore, ethnography and magic. Such was her lyrical Dreaming Tree series and such is her Slavic Folklore trilogy, *Rusalka* (1989), *Chernevog* (1990) and *Yvegenie* (1991). Yet this unusual fantasy trilogy was initially received very well and then virtually disappeared from the critical and popular attention, at a time when her other works, and especially her science fiction, was become extremely popular. The reviews of the first, *Rusalka*, were both hopeful and favorable. By the third novel, reviewers were criticizing the pace, characterization and plot of the story. To speculate on the reasons for the neglect and progressive criticism of these works as a trilogy, and to establish their difference from other modern mass-market fantasy, it will be necessary to look at the subjective position that her characters take up in relation to magic, and the differing typologies of magic that figure in this humanization of the wizard's life.

C.J. Cherryh's fantasy and series fictions

Much popular fantastic fiction falls into the mold of heroic "sword and sorcery" fantasy after the pattern of the Conan series: prehistoric heroes slashing their way across a brutal landscape or chivalric tales where nebulously medieval knights fighting for castles, or the virtue of their ladies, slash their way across the landscape for noble ends. More specifically, the Arthurian legends, compiled in various versions with the most popular being the *Morte D'Arthur* of Sir Thomas Mallory or the fairies and other folk of Celtic mythology, also form a backdrop for some of Cherryh's works. Even Tolkien's massive invention of Middle Earth can be traced to Nordic and Anglo-Saxon myth and legend. While Cherryh has dabbled in these traditions, her Slavic series attempts to explore a totally different one. It deserves attention because, for some reason, she has chosen to step out of those tried-and-true story patterns while still exploring the world of magic and its menace, and the old battle between good and evil, that characterizes the plots of most fantasy.

This investigation of her Slavic folklore series focuses on the critical properties of such a choice in relation to the Western reader whose background does not prepare them for the tropes and characters of the southern Slavic territories (currently Ukraine). Her trilogy is set along the Dnieper River in the forests north of Kiev, current capital of the Ukraine. In addition the expectations of heroic or high fantasy do not allow for the careful detailing of social and psychological implications of personal magic, both for those who practice it and for those upon whom it is practiced. At the same time, the same psychological explorations that Cherryh incorporated in the Dreaming Tree trilogy had perhaps less success because they were set within a familiar, Celtic tradition. When the legendary tradition is so familiar, readers are not very tolerant of alterations in the formula.

Writers choose to set their fantastic works in known bodies of folkloric tradition for a reason. Investing a work with plot, characters and setting that are all unfamiliar ground for a reader is a daunting task. Therefore, if one can call up the world of the Arthurian romance tradition, or Celtic or Norse legend, less detail of setting and character are necessary and one can focus on the plot. Better yet, as in the many retellings of the Arthurian legend, one can then embroider alternative understandings of human nature onto a well-known plot such as the heroic, wronged king and the love triangle. Cherryh, on the other hand, after more than fifteen years of popularity as an accomplished writer in a range of fictional genres, chose to introduce a lesser-known mythology, that of Slavic folk tradition, into a story of seeming mischance that quickly becomes an exploration of magic *as* chance. In her trilogy, Cherryh introduces a number of folkloric characters in addition to the Rusalka who is a central figure. These range from the simple homestead and local spirits, the field-things, yard things (bannik) and forest things (leshy or leshi) to the inimical, water-demon shapeshifters such as a vodyanoi called Hwiuur (*Rusalka* 70). And she also explores the concept of layers of magic, of natural and unnatural magic, of chance, choice and determination.

The Slavic Trilogy and the hierarchy of magics

One can easily determine the source of her legend, the gypsy tale of the rusalka (Ivanits 120), a drowned person whose spirit tries to regain life from the land, trees and hapless travelers in the forests along the Dnieper. Ivanits, among others, identifies the major fantastic players in Slavic legend that Cherryh borrows for her drama of the young wizard Sasha and his feckless friend Pyetr. These two unassuming young men are pursued into the dangerous forest lands between Vojvoda, their home town and Kiev, their goal. The homely spirits—Babi, who guards his masters yard and friends; banniks who reside in outbuildings of farms and give sometimes uninterpretable predictions; leshy or long-lived, wise, tree-like beings in the dark forests of the north—all crop up repeatedly in Slavic legend, especially those of the roving gypsy tribes. Ivanits describes the leshi as "master of the forest and guardian of the beasts within"(65). She then goes on to postulate the real-life origins in demobilized soldiers and robbers hiding in the forests and preying upon travelers, identifying them with medieval Russia and detailing a heavily embroidered tradition for creatures that can both menace and aid those humans who encounter them. She later describes the vodyanoi or vodianoi that is responsible for creating the eponymous rusalka of Cherryh's trilogy: "Regarding the nature of the Vodianoi there is no such controversy. Since the spirit's purpose was to drown people, almost everywhere the peasants viewed him as evil and dangerous and they often referred to him as the 'water devil' (Vodianoi chert)" (Ivanits 70).

But this trilogy is not the simple retelling of the Slavic folklore of agricultural peasants collected and studied by Slavic folklorists through the 20th century. Although it is pleasant to detail and recognized the completeness of Cherryh's borrowings, the folkloric world of the Slavic peasant which she is able to both recall and formulate into a worldview within her novel, falls into a long tradition of folklore that has been variously analyzed as a "science" by Propp and a manifestation of the unconscious by Todorov. It should be clear from the complexity of Cherryh's approach to magic that this is not simply an attempt to tell the story of an unfortunate young girl turned into a water spirit, a rusalka, and then rescued. While that could potentially be an absorbing story for the Western reader unfamiliar with this body of legend, she rather uses the story as a device to humanize the experience of magic. In other words, she creates, through the unfamiliar folkloric tradition, a critique of simplistic assumptions many writers make about the human subject when confronted with the vast unknowns that surround us. Her satires of conventional science fiction and fantasy tropes are characteristic in Cherryh's works. Whether in space, between worlds, or in medieval southern Slavic territories, Cherryh's fiction engages her readership through details of character and because her characterization questions the usual portrayal of easy human adjustment to shifting frames of knowledge—like deep space, like chaos theory, like entropy, like extended life, like magic that operates according to laws that are beyond human comprehension and the distress that generates in the subjective, affective universe of the individual.

The Slavic trilogy focuses on familial relationships that have been deformed by various kinds of magic, the simple magic of the forest and the complex magic of the powerful wizard in consort with unnatural demons. Each of these deformations of the human relationships with one another and with nature, set in a tradition unfamiliar to the majority of Cherryh's readers, resists our tendencies to classify the struggles of the characters according to known story patterns. The wizardry and magics of this series are revealed to the reader as the characters learn them. The works cross generations, focusing on three generations of interconnected families but centered on the lifetime of two young men, Sasha and Pyetr, who are really outsiders. The trilogy both begins and ends with Sasha, as first a boy of fifteen who doesn't know for sure that he's a wizard (*Rusalka*) and then a man in his thirties who has gradually learned what it means to be a wizard as well as a man (*Yvgenie*), for it is both friendship and family relations that motivate the majority of his and other humans' actions in this set of stories.

This close-knit group of individuals united by ties of friendship, love and family are pitted against several kinds of magic with increasing magnitudes of power that are potentially or actually inimical to their survival. Three generations of wizards are involved in the struggle and another, preceding generation is often mentioned, so that events are given a prehistory as well as a recent past. Thus the reality of each crisis, and there are many, large and small, is played out on a constantly shifting ground of subjective comprehension and analysis. The reasoning of wizard and non-wizard, experienced and inexperienced wizard, younger and older wizard are detailed in contrasts that slowly come to define an array of magic that interacts but is not of the same magnitude, with no authoritative interpreter of the phenomena. No one can be trusted to have a complete picture of any crisis, nor can anyone trust their own perceptions, a state of affairs which Cherryh achieves by interrogating the disruption of cause-effect relationships in the presence of magic. These speculations about the meanings of phenomena on the part of different characters, each with different levels of access to the breadth of the phenomena, are what transform this story into a kind of science of magics. Sasha especially investigates documents and interprets each of them. His is the most fully represented consciousness, the one which

Todorov, in his *The Fantastic*, would probably identify as "the collapse of the limit between matter and mind" (114) that characterizes much fantastic fiction. And what emerges is Sasha's science of magic.

As the three novels trace Sasha's gradually expanding command of several magical realms, they also paint both a psychological effect and a science of magic. He begins with a simple understanding that people can be affected by creatures of the earth familiar in many folklores. By the end of the third novel, he has identified at least three magnitudes and their patterns of interaction. *Rusalka*, the first novel, chronicles the ensnaring of these two young men in the rescue of a rusalka from her half-life in the forests along the Dnieper north of Kiev. The majority of the story takes place within the confines of a large forest and the players in this drama have very little contact with people from the outside, save occasional short trips to market for one or two of them.

Sasha begins as a teenage orphan living and working in his aunt and uncle's inn and at their sufferance, and Pyetr is a slightly older family-less man in his twenties who has had some success living on the coattails of the lesser sons of rich men in the small Slavic village of Vojvoda. The rusalka's father, Uulamets, traps them into helping him to rescue his young daughter, who has been drowned or committed suicide in the river. His own less than pure motives are slowly revealed when he protests his daughter Eveshka's preferences in a mate. Released from her existence as a half-ghost preying on the life-force of trees in the forest and the occasional hapless traveler, his daughter falls in love with Pyetr, a non-wizard rather than Sasha, the young wizard Uulamets had intended to sacrifice. Her rescue is complicated by the intervention of the vodyanoi, Hwiuur, who had drowned her and the wizard Kavi Chernevog who led her to her death. Yet Sasha is there to protect Pyetr and to respond to another fantastic invention, the Leshy. They request that he replant and re-grow the forests that the rusalka has killed in exchange for their help. These same powerful creatures render Chernevog comatose in a far corner of the woods where he's to be guarded: "Weave him tight, so he can't do harm. Make his sleep deep. This is Leshys' work," (368) say these ancient ones, with names like Misighi and Wiun.

The second novel describes the life of the three young people together in the forest. It is entitled *Chernevog* after this same Kavi Chernevog who bears some responsibility for Eveshka's earlier transformation from human girl to rusalka. Chernevog returns, seemingly to recapture Eveshka, but his motives are much more complex and, in fact, it is Uulamet's wife (Eveshka's own mother) who is really trying to control the girl. Where Kavi Chernevog seems like evil incarnate in the first book and acts so at times in both the second and third, he becomes much more sympathetic as the history of the wizard family, and especially Eveshka's mother and father, are further explored. Eveshka ends up ensorcelled within her mother's forest dwelling, only to be rescued by the combined efforts of Pyetr, Sasha, Uulamets and Chernevog, whose motives are still not clear. Her rescue costs the life of Uulamets.

Eveshka's pregnancy is the bridge to the third book of the trilogy, *Yvgenie*, which moves the story fifteen years into the future and focuses on the daughter she has created with Pyetr, and various attempts to ensnare the young Ilyana in the power games of other wizards. For Eveshka herself was the carefully created daughter of two wizards, Uulamets and Draga, her mother, each of whom had intentions for her. And, while Ilyana has a human father, she is still a very powerful wizard, powerful enough even as a young child that she inadvertently calls the spirit of Chernevog from his half-sleep and he grows up with her as her secret friend. When they both reach the age of fifteen, he makes his move. He enters the body of another young man, Yvgenie, who's escaped into the forest from vindictive families in Kiev and Vojvoda, and cohabits it with the hapless young man, running off with Ilyana into the forest and casting further doubt on the depth of his evil.

Be careful what you wish for:
the interaction of folkloric, wizard and power magics

Underlying the story of family relationships cemented and deformed by different magnitudes of magic is the subjective story of humans, wizards and non-wizards, trying to cope with a magical realm which they cannot control. And there is a first magnitude of magic, that of the homestead, forest, and water creatures who must be appeased but are generally more indifferent than inimical to humans. The Slavic peasant magic of the bannik, domovoi and leshy, and even the more inimical brodyachi, rusalka, and vodyanoi form only the backdrop for this investigation of how magic might invade one's consciousness. As described above, Cherryh has borrowed this authentic folkloric framework from Slavic mythology and it is thus the kind of everyday magic which many accept as either superstition or a known, and therefore manipulable, quantity. Thus Sasha can tell his friend how to avoid the ill-nature of a bannik by providing it with certain kinds of food and giving it space just as most children can tell you a little about the Irish "little people." Each plays tricks on humans, tricks that can either be interpreted as mischance to the non-believer (as Pyetr points out, the Cockerel's barn-thing is a cat (*Rusalka* 31)) or guarded against in tried and true fashion (by leaving out milk and grain for the barn-thing). What Sasha perceives is the second magnitude of magic, the wish which responds to reason and craft, a craft that must be learned and carefully practiced but which is accessible only to a wizard born. As yet, he doesn't even suspect the third, the power magic of Eveshka's mother and father. And thus, like "normal" life, this magic gives only the appearance of being controlled and conferring power on its users and over all others. It also has its own logic.

This story begins with simple questions about this second magnitude of magic as Sasha, in the first book, cannot determine whether his ill-wishes actually caused the death of his parents when he was a young boy. Because he has grown up under the mistreatment of his aunt and uncle and the fearful jibes of villagers that he is unlucky, Sasha tries to live his young life carefully, wishing for nothing and acting in as innocuous a manner as possible. He is the Jack of all work at his uncle's inn and overworked, underfed and subject to physical and emotional abuse by all around him, but most especially his family. When Pyetr, another orphan who has achieved some success at gambling, stumbles, injured, into the stables of the inn, Sasha is also ready for a friend. He tries to help Pyetr, even at the expense of his elder, pampered cousin. It seems only natural that Sasha should immediately bond with his needy companion who has been tricked into taking responsibility for the death of a troublesome old man, the husband of his lover, and must flee Vojvoda even though he is ill from a sword-wound. And Sasha's simple characterization as an orphan-servant undercuts the significance of his references to the power of wishing, and the many liminal creatures of village, homestead and field of whom he is fearful. The field-thing, the barn-thing and the forest-thing that he mentions to Pyetr as they set off on their journey, affect both that young man and the reader as superstitions of a simple boy and are only gradually revealed for their part in both past and future of these boys and those around them.

But Sasha fears other kinds of magic. First, he knows of wizards and has even been introduced to them by his uncle. Long ago, Sasha was tested and was assuredly not a wizard. And again we can dismiss these encounters as formulaic as we know of the antics of witches and alchemists in our own past cultures, as well as shamans in the non-European countries, among Oriental and Native American traditions. But there is this troublesome issue of Sasha's wishes. He tells Pyetr that he might have wished his parents dead in a fire and this image comes back in both the second and third novels. He fears that his dislike for his cousin Mischa and wish that the cousin's clothes might be spoiled had actually landed him in a puddle. And this wish has disastrous consequences for Sasha and the ailing Pyetr. He fears that his desire to help Pyetr as they journey through forest and wood may have resulted in worse trouble when they find the empty cabin that belongs to Uulamets. In exchange for healing Pyetr, he commits himself to helping Uulamets capture and revive a long-dead daughter who has become a rusalka, haunting the woods, killing trees and plants, sucking the life out of travelers through the forest paths. And all of these subjective fears occur because he cannot determine the power of his wishes. Uulamets confirms this power, tells him about how real wizards have to keep books of their wishes and deeds because one is never sure how the wishes will be enacted, whether a wish today will result in some strange occurrence in the future, how one wizard's wish will interact with another. Uulamets also reveals that wizards are more vulnerable to this magnitude of magic than non-wizards, but that non-wizards are nonetheless affected.

The subjectivity of magics

Throughout the three novels, the subjective effect of this imprecise science haunts Sasha, Eveshka, Pyetr and later Ilyana. They are haunted because they strive not to hurt people. And this is a daunting task because wishing can take one unawares. Sasha muses constantly throughout the second novel, *Chernevog,* as he lives out his life in the forests around the Dnieper. Protective of Pyetr and Eveshka, he worries whether some wish of his has caused an event that will eventually destroy them all. He wants to keep Pyetr happy, so Pyetr's beloved horse appears in the forest homestead one day. Eveshka is afraid she will wish for something catastrophic, so she goes off for long stretches by herself in the woods, leaving Pyetr to fret for her safety. Both worry so much that Pyetr will become too unhappy with no normal human contact in the remote forest that they send him off to Kiev or elsewhere.

Especially when his daughter Ilyana is small, in the third novel, they worry that she will inadvertently hurt him as Sasha believes he did his own parents. In fact, Pyetr himself complains that he hardly knows his own daughter.

> "It's just that every time there's a difficulty with my daughter, I'm packed off to the god knows where. She's fifteen, 'Veshka, she'd never harm a hair of my head and it's not as if she throws tantrums these days." (*Yvgenie* 23)

And when he returns from one trip to Kiev having disgraced himself with several powerful families, both Sasha and Eveshka worry that it might be might be their own doing and indeed in *Yvgenie* discover that he had planted a seed unexpected by any of them, and with wide-reaching consequences.

Were this second magnitude of magic, the magic of wizard-wishes, their only worry, the consequent disruption in their understanding of cause and effect, and their attempts to control it, might make for an interesting trilogy. Todorov names this type of magic "pan-determinism": "In other words, on the most abstract level, pan-determinism signifies that the limit between the physical and the mental, between matter and spirit, between word and thing, ceases to be impervious" (*The Fantastic* 112).

The second and third novels especially represent the physical realization of wishes planted when, say, Eveshka's daughter was young, coming to fruition when she's a teenager. The wishes that engender the next series of crises have passed through channels and families that reach as far away as Vojvoda and Kiev, and as far into the past as the childhood of her father Uulamets, trained by another evil wizard, Malenkova. As the histories of their dilemmas emerge to clarify their possible courses of action, they also caution against too much wishing. For example, one of Pyetr's early misalliances has resulted in his having a second daughter, Nadya, whose entire life has been controlled by her family's fear that her illegitimacy will lose them their inheritance. And her very existence may be the result of wishes made by other wizards that embroiled Pyetr in a longstanding quest for power-magic. These gradual revelations are enough to make a wizard very cautious.

In *Chernevog*, the third magnitude of magic is firmly established. While hinted at by Uulamets, a kind of power-magic, drawn from a parallel realm to haunt this one, is drawn into play with the introduction of both the wizard Chernevog and Uulamets' wife, Draga. And this heralds another set of disruptions that enters the lives of the younger people through a frightful and troublesome history that casts yet another level of doubt on their understanding of the world. Our first introduction is through the history of Uulamet's training of Chernevog, which is placed in the context of his own training in wizardry. Real wizards are given as children to an adult wizard who uses them as he or she wishes, and, says Uulamets: "Worse than any beating, boy . . . You should have lived with old Malenkova. Crazy as a loon and mean as winter" (*Rusalka* 345).

Uulamets met his wife Draga while living with that wizard whom she eventually killed. And neither Eveshka nor the other young people are sure whose idea it was for Draga to *have* Eveshka, for, as Chernevog explains, Draga could not have carried Eveshka if she didn't want to. And Uulamets took on Chernevog as his apprentice, but at the same time Draga took him on as her lover (*Rusalka* 358) and perhaps also was responsible for his coming to Uulamets for training through the agency of a white owl who later became his familiar (held his wizard's heart). And Chernevog cannot be sure of his own motivations in tricking a Hwiuur, a shape-shifting vodyanoi, into killing Eveshka. But all are sure that Draga wants to control Eveshka, and eventually Eveshka's child. Draga is involved in the most destructive of magics, power-magic which requires the lives of others to be fed to it. This third-magnitude magic is the revelation that underlies the plot of capture and rescue in this second novel. Eveshka is drawn by her mother to a magical location where Draga can make use of her daughter's power, where Eveshka can scarcely be reached by Sasha and Pyetr even with the help of Chernevog and where Eveshka learns that a wizard can cast their heart outside of themselves to be less vulnerable. Chernevog is controlled because his owl-familiar has been killed (*Chernevog* 251) but this owl also allowed Draga to exert control over him. Eveshka mistrusts her mother, like the daughters and mothers of many fairy tales and legends, but can't help being seduced by her seeming affection and her wisdom, as Draga instructs:

"Shhh. You raise a rainstorm. Do you know every leaf that falls? The law is that leaves will fall. Which leaf is meaningless to know. What you care about is that the rains come—and stop in due course. The difference is scope, dear." And her reply: "My husband is not a leaf, mama." (*Chernevog* 207)

And much later, Draga's persuasive argument:

"Veshka. Just follow me. One perfect wish. One wish for everything you want. Is that so hard? You husband—your home—your young friend—isn't that really what you'd choose, over everything in the world?" (*Chernevog* 290)

But even Draga cannot be sure of her ground, for when Uulamets comes partially back into the world to free Eveshka, Pyetr and Chernevog from her power, his explanation—that their old teacher is responsible for unleashing an unearthly magic into the world—is apologetic.

He heard Uulamet's voice say, out of nowhere, forgive my wife. She destroyed Malenkova. But Malenkova's beast was too much for her. She was all its purpose . . . ultimately, that's all she was (*Chernevog* 324).

And while Draga is carried off and Chernevog is neutralized by the forest Leshy, their legacy of evil remains for yet another generation, the generation of Ilyana.

Yvgenie, the third book, begins very lyrically. Ilyana, daughter of the female wizard Eveshka and the normal male Pyetr, has a secret. It's one she's had since early childhood. While most of her playmates are minor supernatural creatures, like Babi the yard thing and an occasional Leshy, she also has a ghostly boy-friend who appears first in the spring when she is just old enough to walk in the woods alone. He returns every spring and summer, growing along with her until, at age fifteen, he kisses her for the very first time, both entrancing and frightening her. By this point, Sasha and Eveshka have a sophisticated understanding of magic. They know that Ilyana is destined to be a wizard and already has some powers. They caution her about wishes, about keeping a wizard's book, about staying away from strangers, and so they eventually find out about this friend. They inevitably recognize him as some embodiment of Chernevog who cannot fully escape his stony forest bed. He eventually finds his way into the body of a young man, and the interlacing of long-ago and present wish-, folkloric/earth- and power-magics. The lives of the little family begin again to build into a crisis of shifting families, loyalties and subjectivities. Whose view of the cause-effect trajectory is trustworthy? Which character's actions are motivated by careful reason and which by emotion? Who is in control of others? And, as especially Pyetr and the hapless young Yvegenie ask, who is in control of themselves?

The third novel, with the grounding of magics already set, is the both the most complicated and the fullest exploration of magical subjectivities, following the travels and self-examinations of several groups, and revealing actions motivated by long-ago wishes, if that is their explanation. Thus it explores more fully the subjective chaos of life lived in full knowledge of magic. For example, all three magnitudes of magic are now understood to a certain extent by the wizards (both alive and dead) that form alliances and oppositions. While it seemed clear that Draga was striving for more control over supernatural beings and power magic in the second book, the third explores other potential motivating forces. Where it seemed in the second book like she controlled a pack of hellish wolves: "Kavi remembered Draga's wolves, and dying" (*Yvgenie* 271), they seem to appear of their own agency in the third. Where Chernevog saw himself as the master of the vodyanoi Hwiuur in the first and second novels, this creature takes on his own agency in his hate for Pyetr who stole away his "lovely bones," Eveshka, and has frustrated his other conquests. In fact, the ghostly Chernevog pits his strength against Hwiuur in order to save Ilyana, as he explains: "He wanted your daughter. But I wouldn't let him" (300). And Eveshka's motives become more ambivalent in his eyes, as they struggle to save Ilyana from the vodyanoi, the leshy who want to preserve her and some other inimical force generated by power magic that predates even Draga:

> She wanted the strength he held. She took it, in one dizzy rush, that left him on his knees and wanted him from her sight, now, that was the single grace she gave him because there was a wisp of life left in him and she would not kill—from moment to moment, so long as she could she would not kill. (*Yvgenie* 273)

Both Eveshka and Chernevog understand that they cannot control the passionate impulses generated by their emotional nature and that this is the ultimate struggle, to remove themselves from the occasions when their passion overcomes their logic and control, their wishes overcome their good sense. While they can ultimately rescue Ilyana from the while palace of skulls where she is held, and from the power-invested vodyanoi who then attacks her, it is the homely earth-magic creature, Babi, who finally devours the vodyanoi they have diminished and frees them from its menace, if not from their own. "Babi pounced, and swallowed, and sat up with his small hands folded across his belly.

And licked his lips." (*Yvgenie* 308)

While Eveshka and Chernevog still possess the spiritual flaws of a rusalka, and Sasha and Ilyana are still uncertain their wishes can be controlled, a creature that has seemed minor throughout the three novels reveals greater discernment about evil and destroys, in the most matter-of-fact way, the embodiment of their ultimate enemy.

By the end of this trilogy, Sasha has gained some understanding that magic is really magics. The folkloric magic of bannik and vodyanoi can only be appeased and may never be understood, but it will strike back if threatened by rusalka or by power-magic such as that of Malenkova. Wish-magic is very chancy as it is filtered through other wishes and through earth magic. Power magic unleashes forces that can inhabit and make use of earth magic, which draw power for intentional acts of will and control from it and from humans, both wizards and non-wizards.

Throughout this exploration, it is the potential for harm to humans that preoccupies and controls. Magic, even within the context of a world that validates it, is far too uncertain a basis for human life. And Cherryh has thus critiqued the blithe introduction of superhuman forces into human life that characterizes so much popular fantasy.

BIBLIOGRAPHY

Armitt, Lucie. *Theorizing the Fantastic*. London: Arnold. 1996.

Attebery, Brian. *The Fantasy Tradition in American Literature: From Irving to Le Guin*. Bloomington:Indiana University Press, 1980.

Barr, Marlene. *Alien to Femininity: Speculative Fiction and Feminist Theory*. NY: Greenwood Press, 1987. Contributions to the Study of Science Fiction and Fantasy, number 27.

Beal, Rebecca S. "C. J. Cherryh's Arthurian Humanism," in: Slocum, Sally K. (ed.); *Popular Arthurian Traditions*. Bowling Green, OH: Popular; 1992. pp. 56-67

Bogstad, Janice M "Fantastic Fiction At The Edge and In The Abyss: Genre Definitions and the Contemporary Cross Genre Novel." *Patterns In The Fantastic, II*. Ed. Donald M. Hassler. Mercer Island, WA: Starmont Press, 1985. 81-90.

Brizzi, Mary T. "C. J. Cherryh and Tomorrow's New Sex Roles," In: Staicar, Tom (ed.); *The Feminine Eye: Science Fiction and the Women Who Write It*. New York: Ungar; 1982. pp. 32-47.

Cherryh, C.J. *Faery in Shadow*. Ballantine, 1994.

—. *Goblin Mirror*. Ballantine, 1993.

Selected Series Fiction:

The Chanur series:
—. *The Pride of Chanur*. NY: DAW, 1981.
—. *The Kif Strike Back*. NY: DAW, 1985.
—. *Chanur's Venture*. NY: DAW, 1985.
—. *Chanur's Homecoming*. NY: DAW, 1986.
—. *Chanur's Legacy*. DAW, 1992.

The Dreaming Tree Series:
_—. *Dreamstone*. DAW. 1987.
_—. *Tree of Sword and Jewels*. DAW. 1983.
Also issued as: *The Dreaming Tree*. DAW. 1997.

The Faded Sun Series:
Kesrith. Garden City, NY: Doubleday. 1978.
Kutah. . Garden City, NY: Doubleday. 1978.
Shon'jir. Garden City, NY: Doubleday. 1979.

The Foreigner Universe:
Foreigner. DAW. 1994.
Inheritor. DAW. 1996.
Invader. DAW. 1996.
Precursor. DAW. 1999.
Explorer. DAW. 2002.
Defender. DAW. 2003

Alliance-Union Universe Series.
Angel with a Sword. DAW. 1985
Cuckoo's Egg. DAW. 1985.
Forty Thousand in Gehenna. DAW. 1984.
Hunter of Worlds. DAW. 1987
Merchanter's Luck. DAW. 1982.
Port Eternity. DAW. 1987.

The Morgaine Saga:
Gate of Ivrel, DAW. 1976.
Well of Shiuan, DAW. 1978.
Fires of Azeroth, DAW. 1979.

The Slavic Series:
Rusalka. Ballantine. 1989.
Yvgenie. Ballantine. 1990.
Chernevog. Ballantine. 1991.

Dunn, Thomas. P. "C. J. Cherryh,: in *St. James Guide to Science Fiction Writers.* Ed. Jay P. Pederson. St. James Press/Gale, 1996, p. 18-183.

DuPont, Denise, ed. *Women of Vision. Essays by Women Writing Science Fiction*. NY: St. Martin's, 1988.

Eisenhour, Susan. "A Subversive in Hyperspace: C. J. Cherryh's Feminist Transformation of Space Opera," *New York Review of Science Fiction*. 1996 Oct; 9 (2 (98)): 1, 4-7.

Freud, Sigmund. "The 'Uncanny'(1919)." *Studies in Parapsychology*. Trans. Alix Strachey. Ed. Philip Reif. NY: Collier, 1963. 19-60.

Heidkamp, Bernie. "Responses to the Alien Mother in Post-Maternal Cultures: C. J. Cherryh and Orson Scott Card." *Science-Fiction Studies* (SFS) 1996 Nov; 23 (3 (70)):

Hume, Kathryn. *Fantasy and Mimesis*. NY: Methuen. 1984.

Hyde, Paul Nolan. "Dances with Dusei: A Personal Response to C. J. Cherryh's *The Faded Sun*." *Mythlore: A Journal of J. R. R. Tolkien, C. S. Lewis and Charles Williams*. Spring, 1992. 18 (2 (68)) p. 45-53

Ivanits, Linda. *Russian Folk Belief* .Armok, NY. M.E. Sharpe, 1989.

Jarvis, Sharon (ed.). "Goodbye Star Wars, Hello Alley-Oop, Cherryh, C. J.," *Inside Outer Space: Science Fiction Professionals Look at Their Craft*. New York: Ungar; 1985, p. 17-26.

Johnson, Greg L. "The SF Novel as an Alien Art Form: C. J. Cherryh's Foreigner Series," *New York Review of Science Fiction*.1997 Nov; 10 (3 (111)): 21-22.

Jones, Gwyneth. "Consider Her Ways: The Fiction of C. J. Cherryh," in Jones, Gwyneth. *Deconstructing The Starships*. Liverpool, UK: Liverpool University Press, 1999. p. 130-140.

Khanna, Lee Cullen. "Frontiers of Imagination: Feminist Worlds." *Women's Studies International Forum*. 7.2 (1984). 97-102.

Lefanu, Sarah. *In the Chinks of the World Machine: Feminism and Science Fiction*. London: Women's Press, 1988.

Markowitz, John . "C. J. Cherryh," *Science Fiction Chronicle: The Monthly Science Fiction & Fantasy Newsmagazine*. 1998 July-Aug; 19 (9-10 (198)): 6, 37-39.

McGuire, Patrick. "Water into Wine: The Novels of C.J. Cherryh," *Starship: The Magazine About Science Fiction* (New York, NY) 1979; 16 (2): 47-49.

Propp, Vladimir. *Theory and History of Folklore*. Trans by A. Y. Martin and R. P. Martin. U of Minnesota Press, 1984.

Raffel, BurtonC. J. Cherryh's Fiction *Literary Review: An International Journal of Contemporary Writing* 2001 Spring; 44 (3): 578-91.

Solokov, Y.M. *Slavic Folklore*. Detroit. Trans. By Catherine Ruth Smith. Folklore Associates. 1971.

Shinn, Thelma J. *Worlds Within Women. Myth and Mythmaking in Fantastic Literature by Women*. NY: Greenwood Press, 1986.

Spivak, Charlotte. *Merlin's Daughters. Contemporary Women Writers of Fantasy*. NY: Greenwood Press, 1987. Contributions to the Study of Science Fiction and Fantasy 23.

Todorov, Tzvetan. *The Fantastic: A Structural Approach to a Literary Genre*. NY: Cornell Univ. Press, 1975. trans. By Richard Howard.

Wiloch, Thomas. "Carolyn Janice Cherry," *Contemporary Authors Online*. The Gale Group, 2001.

Zizek, Slavoj. *Looking Awry: An Introduction to Jacques Lacan Through Popular Culture*. Cambridge, Mass. MIT Press, 1991.

J.G. Stinson is a former intelligence analyst for the U.S. Army who comes to her work as a critic from the world of journalism, where she is a freelance writer of reviews, essays, and feature articles. Her work has appeared in notable publications relevant to the field, and this article, in part, first appeared in the online publication *Strange Horizons*. Here, in greatly expanded form, Jan examines Cherryh's use of the "other" in many of her narratives.

Although not strictly speaking an academic piece, it addresses a literary issue (the "other"). Thoughtful and readable, it provokes many questions about how this aspect of Cherryh's approach to storytelling relates to her effect on her readers and the field at large.

[*Portions of this article appeared in the March 18, 2002 edition of the electronic magazine "Strange Horizons" as "Going Native: The Human as Other in Selected Works of C. J. Cherryh."*]

THE HUMAN AS OTHER IN
THE SCIENCE FICTION NOVELS OF
C.J. CHERRYH

J.G. Stinson

"I write about people who See, who See things differently and who find the Systems
stripped away, or exchanged for other Systems, so that they pass from world to world
in some lightning-stroke of an understanding, or the slow erosion and reconstruction
of things they thought they knew."

—C. J. Cherryh[1]

The preceding quotation could as well describe what a shaman does in some human cultures, if one defines a shaman as a person who can move between perceived realities. In many of her science fiction (SF) novels, C. J. Cherryh's shaman is the maverick or outsider, one who comes from elsewhere and whose arrival signals vast change. Outsiders in their native culture can do little more than show how they're marginalized by the "normal" members of that culture. Take an outsider and transport him or her to an alien culture, however, and two cultures/societies can be illuminated, on both a personal and group level.

As a character in literature, the outsider was born from Carl Jung's group of recurring entities of the unconscious called archetypes. The outsider has links (according to Jungian theory) to the archetypes of the Scapegoat and, in some cases, the Sacrifice. In literature, the outsider has been variously embodied as the Flying Dutchman and the Wandering Jew (both doomed to eternal rootlessness for a heinous crime), and even the Bible's Cain.[2]

But the outsider isn't always a criminal, and death is not always this character's destiny. In many of Cherryh's novels, the outsider plays roles as varied as political sacrifice, agent of vengeance, whistleblower and liaison. Each of these roles is embodied by the characters discussed in this essay. They all feel alienated from their birth cultures, and find much that welcomes them in the alien cultures which they illumine for the reader. Each of them is also accused of "going native" by someone in their birth cultures.

The pejorative phrase "going native" connotes regression from a "civilized" mode of thinking and/or behavior to that of a less-sophisticated, less technologically advanced mindset. The characters examined herein show such changes not as regressions, but as lateral shifts to alternate ways of thinking and being, of experiencing one's environment. These characters are all mavericks of various kinds, personifications of the outsider or the Other (not-us). Several of them take conscious steps toward alien cultures; some have no choice.

The idea of the Other in human cultures is ancient. It can be embodied by an actual person or other living being, or an idea or philosophy. Human societies formed partly as a way for humans to gain protection greater than they had as individuals. Over time, being more like the group one lived in became more important than whatever traits made one unique. Religious beliefs sprang up around the concept that homogeneity in a group was preferred by supernatural powers, and deviations from the group's physical characteristics, accepted beliefs or customs was enough for a society to ostracize—or sometimes kill—those who offended them. As human societies gained more contact with each other and made technological advances, their tolerance levels for "difference" increased, and the boundaries between acceptable and unacceptable stretched out a little more. But the boundaries have always been there.

In physical terms, outsiders can bring disease or invaders (or both) with them, as well as beneficial change in the form of new technologies, ideas, or knowledge of tribes or cultures yet unmet. The Other can represent change, the unknown, or danger (among its many facets). Perhaps in early societies, wariness in encountering strangers was seen as a survival trait: stay away from potential disease or other physical harm and live longer. Over time, this led to a generalization about outsiders which is encapsulated in the concept of the Other, which represents that which is not known or is different from the accepted norm of a group.

Once the Other becomes known, however, the major strength of humans as a species usually comes forth—they adapt. Lack of adaptation endangers the potential for survival; human history is littered with the remains of cultures that didn't adapt to change and died out. But there is a constant tension between staying within what is and looking beyond to what might be. The Other often acts as a catalyst for change, whether the society involved perceives it is ready for change or not. Perspective and adaptability can be said to chiefly govern how humans react to encounters with the Other, regardless of its form.

The characters Elizabeth McGee (*Forty Thousand in Gehenna*)[3], Sten Duncan (The Faded Sun series)[4], Thorn (*Cuckoo's Egg*)[5], Raen A Sul hant Meth-maren (*Serpent's Reach*)[6] and Bren Cameron (the Foreigner series)[7] all absorb elements of the thinking, behavior, and worldview of their "adopted" cultures. Each had personal and moral reasons for their choices, and each was automatically suspected by their "parent" cultures of being a traitor at worst, and mentally unbalanced at best.

McGee is a scientist who discovers a nasty underhandedness in her government's treatment of the planet Gehenna's "residents" and tries to change that treatment, even when events catch her unprepared and force her hand. Duncan is a military officer and survivor of several combat missions who, when captured by humanity's foe, the mri, learns that his enemy is more after his own heart than humans, and does all he can to protect them as the last of their kind journey homeward. Thorn, a human baby raised by an alien, must seek answers from his foster father concerning his own origin, his differences, and how he came to be among nonhumans. Raen is a child when her clan is slaughtered, her immediate family and most of her kin murdered in a House vs. House battle in which she is the only survivor. The insectoid majat take in the starving and half-mad Raen, and she comes to rely on and trust them more than she can ever trust any human again; she makes the majat the instrument of her revenge, and in the process of changing the majat she is also changed. Bren Cameron is the ambassador for humans to the atevi, a race both alien and tantalizingly similar to humanity but apparently lacking the concepts of friendship and love; while he learns more about how to survive among the atevi, he strives to protect them from human treachery and petty politics that could spell disaster for both species.

Forty Thousand in Gehenna is one of several novels set within Cherryh's "future history" known as the Alliance-Union universe, where humans have expanded into space from Earth via commerce, and the Earth Company's previous stranglehold on its merchanters and space stations is broken in the Company Wars. There come to exist three economic powers among humans: the Earth Company, weakened but still active; the Alliance, a loose confederation of stationers and spacers; and Union, a planet-based government formed by scientists.

Union's eventual wholesale use of cloning (resulting in the cloned humans called azi) is viewed by the Alliance and the Earth Company as reprehensible, at best. The Alliance and Union also have their conflicts, which result in Union's covert plan to seed potential Alliance space with as many of its own colonies as possible.

The story of the colony of Gehenna is a generational one, beginning with the original "born-man" government personnel and azi who first arrived on that planet. The colonists expect other ships to follow, but these ships never appear. The born-men die, from age and disease and violence, and the azi are forced to begin their procreative programs earlier than they expected.

The native lifeforms aren't as well understood as the colonists were led to believe, and the azi children grow further and further away from their bewildered parents, drawn in fascination to the calibans, the "aliens" of Gehenna.

Although arriving later in the story than most of the other viewpoint characters, Elizabeth McGee is pivotal to the conclusion of the story because she is the first to see (and to be allowed to see) that there is something new evolving on Gehenna. The human-azi society of the Union colony has collapsed, along with most of its culture, and in its place a partnership between azi descendants and the sentient, nonhumanoid calibans is rising. Gehennans and calibans have taught each other about each other, and both groups have gained new perspectives on themselves and their worldviews. The two species construct enclaves called Towers, in which they both live. New ways of thinking pass between humans and calibans, and at the end of the book this intellectual cross-pollenization is brought into use, in order that humanity might make sense of another, even more different culture.

McGee enters the story after several generations of azi have passed, when a Union ship finally returns to see what has happened to the colony on Gehenna. She meets and helps a wounded Cloud Tower child, Elai, and is later allowed into Cloud Tower to observe the struggle between Cloud and Styx Towers for supremacy in Gehenna's settled area.

McGee is a scientist, sent to Gehenna to study and observe the interaction between the azi descendants and the calibans, and to learn what happened to the original colonists. What she discovers is more alien than she expected, yet her mindset is such that she can eventually determine how the Gehennans think, how the calibans communicate with each other and with humans. She isn't locked into a certain way of seeing things, and thus is able to achieve a gestalt-like jump of comprehension. Other scientists assigned with her on her mission aren't as flexible, and end up paying a fatal price for their narrow-minded perceptions.

Elai, who becomes leader of Cloud Tower several years after first meeting McGee, has her own reasons for allowing McGee into her life and her home. McGee goes along with Elai's actions in order to gather information on the culture that has developed between the azi descendants and the calibans. But when Elai rides to battle with those of Cloud Tower against Styx, McGee must decide whether the "new" humans of Gehenna deserve her help and loyalty more than her own government. She decides for the Gehennans, and in doing so promotes further contact between them and the Union government, albeit at a slow pace. This is a pace Elai prefers, caliban-like, and McGee's superiors have the good sense to heed her advice and do likewise.

Thus, McGee has essentially "gone native" in the interest of preserving a unique human culture, and because her moral compass points her in that direction. Without McGee acting as a linchpin between established human culture and Gehennan culture, resolving the differences between them would have been much more difficult, perhaps impossible.

The events chronicled in the Faded Sun books (*Kesrith*, *Shon'jir*, and *Kutath*) are set about 400 years after the Gehenna colony's founding. Three years after Alliance ships first encounter the species known as the regul, a forty-year war between humans and the regul breaks out. The mercantile regul employ another species, the humanoid mri, as their soldiers. Mri warfare—based on an honor code and ritualized combat—is neither recognized nor adhered to by humans, and the mri are forced to learn their opponents' ways.

For their periods of service to the regul, the mri always ask that one world be ceded to them as their homeworld, to be inhabited only by regul and mri, and never to be surrendered to any foe while their contract was in force. But the regul conveniently ignore this central element of their deal with the mri when they begin peace negotiations with the humans. When their property and interests are threatened, the regul begin giving orders which prove deadly to the mri, and thousands of them die needlessly.

Sten Duncan is a veteran pilot of the human-regul war, selected as an aide to George Stavros, the soon-to-be human governor of a new human region of space, whose base is on a world called Kesrith—also the current mri homeworld. Human presence on that world would void the regul-mri contract, but the regul have kept this knowledge from the humans. When Duncan encounters a mri warrior in the regul government building on Kesrith, a series of events begins that will end in disaster for the mri.

Duncan, an orphan without family or roots of any kind, can work alone and survive in fluid situations, and he's trained to survey and assess new environments quickly. Once he and Stavros are on Kesrith, he begins to suspect that the regul aren't telling Stavros everything he needs to know. Having already unexpectedly encountered one mri, Duncan asks Stavros for—and receives—permission to go on an unannounced walking tour of the regul's port facilities. On this scouting expedition he encounters Niun, another mri warrior, who captures him and takes him back to the mri edun, the structure on Kesrith in which the mri live. His military training gives him the ability to adopt alternate perspectives and gain useful insights that keep him alive. The mri do not usually take prisoners, nor do they let themselves be captured if they can still fight; both these "rules" are broken when Niun meets Duncan for the first time.

The rootless Duncan is perfectly positioned to be strongly influenced by a major change in his life. His military experience has made him a maverick by necessity. His lack of rank and lack of knowledge of the humans' plans make him expendable, and he knows it. The regul, who don't write anything down because they remember everything, prize deep knowledge; Duncan is therefore of no use to the regul because of his limited memory. He is also of little strategic value to the humans because of his relatively low rank. His dislike of the regul soon turns to hatred, and his respect for the mri as opponents in war grows into an attachment that his species will condemn as unnatural.

The process by which Duncan grows attached to the mri is necessarily a slow one, given his military training and the fact that the mri were but recently humanity's enemy. Duncan's first long-term experience with the mri is as Niun's prisoner. He learns a little about their ways, their social structure, their beliefs, and sees they aren't the faceless berserkers he was taught to fight.

With their golden hair, gold-toned skin and eyes, the mri are more pleasing to the human eye than the large, awkward and hippo-like regul. Duncan becomes convinced that destroying the mri is a mistake, and that the mri way of life is as meaningful as any human one. He has no family of his own, and the obvious caring and devotion he sees among the mri is too strong to ignore; Duncan is lonely, searching for a home. The mri, in turn, are forced to accept at least his physical presence, and they slowly come to know their one-time enemy through Duncan.

After he saves the lives of the last two mri left in known space from annihiliation by the regul, his growing devotion to them is used against him—and them—when the three are put aboard a ship to follow a mri navigational record. The record leads back to the original mri homeworld, to a life Duncan could barely imagine, and to a choice for Duncan about where he belongs. The mri—brother and sister, warrior and priestess—have to decide whether they can trust this "tsi-mri," this not-mri who chooses to go with them on their journey.

In the end, though, Duncan's choice is almost inevitable. Made obsolete by the end of the war and believing—as the mri do—in a clear-cut form of justice, he aligns himself with them and earns a position among them. He finds a home in the most unlikely of places, and among people he comes to regard as his family. Duncan doesn't so much abandon his humanity as set it aside for a life which suits him better, where he eventually feels welcome and valued. He moves from maverick and orphan to societal and family member, and becomes a liaison between his "biological culture" and his chosen one.

Cuckoo's Egg approaches the human-alien encounter from a different direction.

In this non-Alliance-Union book, a spaceship crewed by humans arrives in the solar system of the shonunin, a species that has just achieved space-flight, with bases on their moon and at least one space station. Surprised and afraid, shonunin ships fire on the human ship, chase it down, and board it.

After the battle to take the human ship, the shonunin make the last human alive a captive, but not before he sends a final message via the human ship's communication system. The shonunin scientists' analysis of the captured ship yields a scientific gold mine, and shonunin technology takes a quantum leap forward as captured human technology is introduced into shonunin culture.

Duun is a shonunin hatani, a member of a kind of philosopher/judge guild. The shonunin government, after the capture of the human ship, brings a question to Duun in his capacity as hatani: what do we do with this new knowledge? Duun's answer is to have more space stations built, and to have a human clone developed and brought to full-term. The human captive died in shonunin custody, but his genetic material was saved and stored. After many mistakes in the cloning process, a male human, Thorn, is born. Duun takes him to his ancestral home and raises him to be hatani, without knowing whether he will succeed, whether Thorn is even capable of becoming hatani. Nine years after the human ship's capture, shonunin listening posts in space begin receiving signals that they recognize as human, although they can't translate them. Duun, receiving this news, decides that when Thorn is old enough, he will learn his own language without being told the purpose for such learning. Duun hopes that Thorn can eventually send a message in return to the humans nine light-years away—if Duun can only keep Thorn alive long enough to do so. Other shonunin interests are bent on preventing Duun's plan from coming to fruition. Not only must Duun push Thorn to his physical and mental limits without even knowing what they might be, he must also keep Thorn from being killed by rival shonunin. Along the way, Duun wants Thorn accepted as hatani as well.

Thorn, lacking human parents, nonetheless exhibits human emotions and reactions. He wants to know who he is, but is afraid of the answers he might find. He wants to be a part of shonunin life, but knows that he is different from shonunin as a race. He wants to please Duun, but he fears he'll never be able to do so.

Being the only human on a planet full of nonhumans automatically makes Thorn a maverick, even though he's raised as shonunin. He cannot change the parts of him that are human hardwiring, and this both frustrates and scares him. But he also wants to be accepted into shonunin culture, despite the difficulty of entering it as the first human hatani and the resulting negative reactions of several shonunin.

When Duun finally reveals what Thorn's purpose is, Thorn wants to turn away from it. And when Duun relates the tally of Thorn's accomplishments in shonunin culture, Thorn's response is: "Do you love me, Duun?" But even this human reaching out is shonunin-tinged, because it's the question a hatani would ask.

Thorn is also a maverick in the sense that his foster-father Duun—and the shonunin as a whole—can't predict what he'll do or of what he's capable. Situated within an alien culture and eventually learning that representatives of his "biological culture" may be on their way to the shonunin homeworld, Thorn is thrust into the role of interpreter and liaison. He eventually accepts the purpose for which Duun has trained him. For Thorn, there is no choice between "going native" and remaining true to his biological species; he must do what Duun asks him to do in order to protect his foster father and prevent potential harm to his adopted species from the approaching human ship.

Unlike McGee and Duncan, Thorn's choices are more closely tied to personal survival than to a moral code. But he has the moral code he learned from Duun, and his belief in this code helps him decide what is best for himself, the shonunin and his own species.

While Elizabeth McGee, Sten Duncan, and Thorn are involved with alien species that are more human than not, *Serpent's Reach* concerns a human alliance with a species that is very alien despite its apparent kinship with earthly creatures.

This Alliance-Union universe novel focuses on the Alpha Hydri system, where the seat of government is Alpha Hydri III (also called Cerdin) and where the majority of human-"native" interaction takes place. The majat of Cerdin are insectoid in physical appearance, hive-mind behavior, and social structure, but the resemblance ends there. Majat are much taller than humans, and their jaws can snap off a human head in an instant. Majat communicate in two ways: in audio mode (using a vibrating, almost buzzing sound) and via chemical exchange ("taste and touch," as it's called in the novel), analogous to one of the major theories of how Earth insects pass information.

After the first human probe's crew were killed by majat, a second probe followed; by the time it arrived, those majat had absorbed knowledge from their initial human contacts.

The majat offered a deal: one "human hive" would be allowed to settle in the Reach (i.e., the entire Alpha Hydri system), but no other humans. That human hive was the Kontrin company. As result of this agreement, the Alliance government declared the Reach a quarantined area, protecting both the majat and their irreplaceable trade items. However, Kontrin-company representatives on the second probe secretly brought millions of human ova to Cerdin, to produce a workforce of azi. To majat, it appeared as though the "human hive" was increasing its numbers as would a majat hive, so they allowed it to continue. The Kontrin "grew" betas, clones that closely resemble born-men, to oversee the production and sale of azi to the majat, who used them to manufacture the "biologicals" (unique organics) that form a vital part of the Reach's commerce.

The four types of majat hives are distinguished by color: red, blue, green and gold. Each majat wears a badge which allows humans to tell to which hive it belongs. As a symbol of their authority and lineage, each Kontrin receives a permanent jewelled mark on the right hand. They are known to the majat by this mark, as it is the only way majat can distinguish them from other humans because it's visible to majat eyes in infrared light. Among the Kontrins and other humans (born or cloned), it acts as currency.

All commerce between human Reach culture and the rest of humanity occurs on a space station orbiting the planet Istra, near the limit of Reach space—an area called the Edge. The Kontrins (aka the Family) are ruled by 27 Houses, each with its Septs and Clans. Over the seven hundred years of human presence in the Reach, Houses have risen and fallen in power and prestige. The majat gave the Kontrins extended lifespans in order to make them more amenable to the majat, whose "hive mind" structure carries both long memory and long life. Majat have difficulty with the concept of death, because the hive mind appears eternal to them, although its individual members can be killed. Since such lifespan extension is vital to continuing human-majat trade, all Kontrins are automatically provided it, but their resulting near-immortality often causes them problems.

Raen a Sul hant Meth-maren is a teen-aged member of the Sept and House which now holds the land where humans and majat first managed to conclude trade agreements and living arrangements. Her ancestors became "hive friends" with the blue majat long ago, and their working relationship flourished over the years. The Family uses assassination as a political tool, and it's wielded most often by those whose ambitions make them impatient. Other Houses hold controlling interests with other majat hives, on Cerdin and on other Reach worlds, but the Meth-marens have held this land for a long time, and other Kontrin are becoming increasingly restless at their long monopoly.

Two less-prominent Houses covet the apparent control the Meth-marens have over the blue hive and its commercial production, and mount a violent joint takeover. Raen emerges from the bloody power struggle as the last Meth-maren alive by escaping the carnage; she asks for and receives sanctuary in the forbidden tunnels of the blue majat, the first born-human ever taken in by majat in such a manner. She is also the first in several hundred years to be allowed into the presence of a hive queen. Other hives learn of this, but do nothing, being concerned with their own human commerce partners. Raen is nursed back to health and as she heals, she contemplates what her mother once told her: "Revenge is next only to winning." Thus, she begins to plan the destruction of the Septs that annihiliated her House.

The orphaned Raen adopts the blue-hive majat as her personal army and second family, thereby proving her ability to change perspective and adapt to survive. She manages to wipe out one of the Septs that murdered her House, but is forced into exile from Cerdin by the Kontrin elders. Her acceptance into the blue hive and into its queen's presence is seen as too radical a change, and she is prohibited from contacting any majat. Nonetheless, both her allies and enemies keep tabs on her. She spends years wandering the system, going from one planet to another. Everywhere she goes, disturbances in the hives follow after her because of what happened to her House. To the majat, she is dangerous but known. To the Family, Raen is a loose cannon. No one in the Family has any definite idea of her agenda, or if she even has one, and that uncertainty makes both her allies and enemies nervous.

When she goes downworld to Istra, beta company executives complain of food shortages, sabotage, and population crisis among the azi. Only a Kontrin can license changes in status or numbers for azi, and the elders on

Cerdin have been silent for nearly 20 years. Without Kontrin direction, the beta-run companies on Istra are at a loss as to what to do. Raen sees the hand of one elder, Moth, in this lack of attention; though she doesn't know Moth's plan, she decides to take on the betas' cause, and draws the attention of the Family closer to herself. Thus, when the opportunity to retake what was stolen from her presents itself, she is prepared to use and be used by the majat as an agent of change. Long life breeds ennui, and Raen sees the Istran situation as a way to break out of her enforced monotony.

Amid plans for a human revolt, Raen discovers that the majat are going through their own revolution. She uses this conjunction to her advantage, and the Reach society and government collapse. When outside contact is finally made again after decades have passed, Raen is still there, and has her own terms for renewed trade. She has gone from being bereft of everything she knew to having everything, and wanting only the reassurance of the majat.

Raen, Thorn, and Duncan are all orphans or become orphaned, which suggests one reason why these characters are uniquely suited to coping with and improving human-alien interactions. Duncan only dimly remembers his family, and Thorn never had a human one, so their behavior patterns were largely set outside a core human-family setting. Raen was ripped from a comfortable, easy existence into a frightening, disorienting solitude, but her family's long association with blue hive gave her an edge. While they conducted commerce with the hives, the Kontrins also studied them. Kontrin elders know a lot about majat, and Raen surreptitiously gleans this knowledge during her space travels through the Reach.

Being an orphan is not a requirement for being a maverick, however. McGee is adept by training and personality at seeing beyond her own culture's borders, and this gives her the ability to see life through the Gehennans' eyes.

Perhaps the ultimate in human-as-Other characters is Bren Cameron, the pivotal human character of the Foreigner series.

Phoenix, a human colony-starship, is on its way to a probe-scouted planetary system of a G5 star, with the aim of constructing and staffing an orbiting station around one of the planets there. But something goes wrong during the transit (something never fully explained), and the ship finds itself in a place without known referents and moving towards a dangerous star. A safer star is located and safely reached, and an Earth-like planet is chosen as the starting point from which a new station will be built.

The planet is not immediately colonized, due to a division in opinion between the pilots and the rest of the crew. For 150 years, the pilots argue against colonization, insisting that the station be built first. Then they insist that the *Phoenix* be repaired. The pilots then separate themselves from the rest of the crew and form the Pilots' Guild, and assume a formal leadership role for all those aboard *Phoenix*. They argue against any human presence on the world around which the station orbits. But the rest of the crew and their descendants have bargaining chips to use, being the ones staffing the station above the world. The Pilots' Guild can't prevent them from building a capsule from spare parts, which they do, and sending down two people in it to explore and begin cataloging the scientific discoveries there. But there's more than plants and interesting animals waiting for the first colonists.

The world is already inhabited by extremely tall, dark and deadly human-oids who call themselves atevi. One human is brought by the first atevi he meets to a nearby village, and from that first contact, a war ensues which forces the humans to be more cautious, and eventually atevi and humans make an arrangement. Humans will live on the island of Mospheira and reveal their advanced technology to the almost-ready-for-space atevi, and a human liaison—the paidhi—will be the only human allowed to live among the atevi. This arrangement becomes a continuously deepening well of treachery, deceit and murder—but that's just the human viewpoint. For the atevi, it's business as usual.

As the current paidhi, Bren Cameron has to understand at a deep level how the atevi mind works in order to retain his job and prevent further violence between humans and atevi. But the atevi mind is a hard nut to crack, and Bren strays dangerously close to death more than once due to misinterpreting what he sees and hears. His constant waffling about whether he's "reading" the atevi right in every situation doesn't help at all; in fact, it would be safe to say that this is this "hero's" fatal flaw.

While Bren absorbs more of the atevi culture and thought process, he becomes more of a stranger to his fellow humans, including those he loves. They try to reach out to him and hold him in the human world, but Bren has little invested in human culture; he finds the atevi too fascinating. Despite his emotional ties to his human intimates, he eventually leaves them behind for the atevi, both as a culture and specifically in the person of the atevi assassin Jago.

Interspecies romance is nothing new to Cherryh. In the Foreigner series, however, it's delineated much more than in any other Cherryh novel to date. But the intimate moments Bren and Jago share have a different meaning to atevi, because they lack the concept of emotion. This is the largest stumbling block in the human-atevi relationship, one that trips Bren up more than once, and gets other humans killed for their misunderstandings. In Bren's world, a little love is a dangerous thing—and this goes against a major human cultural belief.

> At its best, SF is the medium in which our miserable certainty that tomorrow will be different from today in ways we can't predict, can be transmuted to a sense of excitement and anticipation, occasionally evolving into awe. Poised between intransigent scepticism and uncritical credulity, it is par excellence the literature of the open mind.
>
> —John Brunner

The main protagonists in each Cherryh novel must deal with crises both internal and external. In most instances, Cherryh puts the internal crisis in the forefront, to frame and inform the physical action and provide impetus in resolving the story's conflicts. Outsiders and mavericks are far enough along the curve to begin the journey to the Other, and in so doing they provide a stimulus for story that might otherwise not exist.

As a role and as representing the individuals described here, the Other gives readers of these novels a chance to see something new and unfamiliar by offering a unique perspective on human and alien societal norms, a viewpoint often adopted by other SF writers. Hal Clement's *Mission of Gravity* adopts the alien/Other viewpoint, and could be said to take this to the extreme in terms of familiar touchpoints between the human and the alien, but it still works wonderfully well as a story. The Other also resonates in the flamboyant character of Gully Foyle, Alfred Bester's larger-than-life missile of vengeance in *The Stars My Destination*.

With her training and experience in linguistics, classical literature and physical anthropology, Cherryh's repeated use of Others as her viewpoint

THE HUMAN AS OTHER IN THE SCIENCE FICTION NOVELS OF C.J. CHERRYH

characters produces a literary combination that gives readers a highly believable window into worlds and minds outside their own. Her preference for such characters can be seen as a desire to show the value of looking beyond one's own nose—it's a good survival trait. Societal authorities which restrict or prohibit Others, regardless of the reason for their Otherness, risk themselves and their societies being consumed by forces which they cannot fight because they cannot comprehend them. This is an idea Cherryh has dealt with in more detail in other works (*Wave Without A Shore* in particular). Having an open mind is a survival trait; one cannot adapt if one cannot adopt a different perspective, even for a brief time. The ones who See are the ones who prevail.

Storytelling's roots are ancient, and all fiction (regardless of author's purpose or critic's claim) is storytelling. Science fiction has often been slandered as escapist fodder by some claiming to be part of the "literary" perspective in fiction. But all fiction can be called escapist, in that it deals with people and events that never happened specifically as a particular work of fiction portrays them.

Regardless of its tag, any work of fiction carries the potential of bringing a reader to a deeper understanding of self, the world, the spirit, or a combination of these things. This is what art does, and Cherryh sees science fiction as "the purest and truest art in the world," because

> . . . It's the world as it can be, ought to be—must someday, somewhere be, if we can only find enough of the component parts and shove them together. Science fiction is the oldest sort of tale-telling. . . Homer; Sinbad's story; Gilgamesh; Beowulf; and up and up the line of history wherever mankind's scouts encounter the unknown. . . The best tale-telling has always been full of what-if.[8]

147

END NOTES

[1] *Visible Light*, Phantasia Press: West Bloomfield, MI, 1986, p. xiv.

[2] *Myths & Motifs in Modern Literature*, edited by David J. Burrows, Frederick R. Lapides and John T. Shawcross, The Free Press: New York, 1973.

[3] *Forty Thousand in Gehenna*, Phantasia Press: Huntingdon Woods, MI, 1983.

[4] *The Faded Sun: Kesrith*, Nelson Doubleday: Garden City, NY, 1978 (SFBC edition).; *The Faded Sun: Shon'jir*, Nelson Doubleday: Garden City, NY, 1978 (SFBC edition).; *The Faded Sun: Kutath* Nelson Doubleday: Garden City, NY, 1978 (SFBC edition).

[5] *Cuckoo's Egg*, Phantasia Press: Huntingdon Woods, MI, 1985.

[6] *Serpent's Reach*, DAW Books: New York, 1980 (SFBC edition).

[7] *Foreigner*, DAW Books: New York, 1994; *Invader*, DAW Books: New York, 1995; *Inheritor*, DAW Books: New York, 1996 (hb); *Precursor*, DAW Books: New York, 1999; *Defender*, DAW Books: New York, 2001; *Explorer*, DAW Books: New York, 2002.

[8] *Visible Light,* Phantasia Press: West Bloomfield, MI, 1986, p. xiv.

Janice Crosby's piece moves us firmly into academic territory. The formal approach to citations and sources has a purpose—readers can, with the application of basic research skills, follow the chain of evidence Janice uses to make her point about Vanye and Morgaine, two of Cherryh's earliest and yet most memorable characters.

For non-academic readers, here is a tip: ignore the citations. It might require a bit of effort to enjoy the formal tone, but for those who are interested in learning more about Cherryh and her work, the elbow grease is well worth it. Janice is a scholar with a background in popular culture and feminist thought, and her ideas touch on often-discussed aspects of Cherryh's work.

A WOMAN WITH A MISSION; OR, WHY VANYE'S TALE IS MORGAINE'S SAGA

Janice C. Crosby

Although the Morgaine Saga works as both a Middle-Ages re-creation and technological chase drama, and presents many memorable minor characters, the central figures, Morgaine and Vanye, provide interest which grips the reader throughout this tetralogy. Though Vanye's is the consciousness the omniscient narrator chooses to focus on, Morgaine is the linchpin of the series, and compels readers for a variety of reasons. In her one sees Cherryh's landmark technique not just as an emerging SF writer of the late '70's, but also as one with a feminist consciousness who would raise her own questions about female roles and power by using the genre's unique speculative capacity. By examining Morgaine as a feminist character, reviewing her subtle transformations/ revelations of character over the series, the series as a romance, and the relevance of her character to present-day readers, one can better understand the philosophical underpinnings of this cornerstone of Cherryh's oeuvre.

Since the publication of the series' first novel, *Gate of Ivrel*, feminist criticism of speculative fiction [using the term in Barr's sense as including science fiction, utopian fiction, and fantasy (*Alien* xxi)] has come into its own, offering both a better understanding of what feminist authors in SF have achieved, as well as the reasons the genre has such potential for feminist exploration. As Patrick Murphy points out in "Feminism Faces the Fantastic," "Today, the fantastic has become not only a popular genre... but also a genre in which one might use the defamiliarization process inherent in the fantastic to critique contemporary society" (82). In *Lost in Space: Probing Feminist Science Fiction and Beyond*, Barr defines feminist fabulation as a "feminist fiction that offers us a world clearly and radically discontinuous from the patriarchal one we know, yet returns to confront that known patriarchal world in some cognitive way" (11). As early as *The Feminine Eye: Science Fiction and the Women Who Write It* (1982), a land-mark collection of feminist SF criticism, Cherryh was recognized for her challenging of traditional gender roles. Quickly becoming a prolific, award-winning author, Cherryh's work has been recognized in the criticism, but her early novels, such as the Morgaine Saga, merit continued review and analysis, particularly as some of the critical articles such as Brizzi's do not cover the final volume, *Exile's Gate* (1988).

In "Third Person Peculiar: Reading between Academic and SF-Community Positions in (Feminist) SF," Sylvia Kelso describes her discovery of "the pleasure of the feminist or feminist-oriented sf text" which was "more than wonder ... more than aesthetic pleasure; it was a politicized joy. An exciting, empowering glimpse of what women might be" (77). This comment succinctly states why the growing female readership has shaped the genre and the depiction of women in SF, moving the genre past early, stereotypical portrayals of women found in works by male authors, which Joanna Russ outlines in "The Image of Women in Science Fiction." Of the variety of visions of female potential, the warrior (who may appear as an Amazon) provides an image of empowerment often lacking in mainstream fiction. Kathleen Cioffi realizes that stories of women warriors "[mirror] many of the conflicts that contemporary feminists face in their own lives" and they "can be in reality a serious exploration of the nature of a strong woman's role in a society that expects weakness from women" (87). Further, unlike utopian SF, the female warrior allows the author to examine issues of women's capacity for anger and violence.

Marion Zimmer Bradley's own evolution as a writer, partly detailed in

"Responsibilities and Temptations of Women Science Fiction Writers," comments about the initial resistance among forerunners such as herself, C. L. Moore, and Leigh Brackett, who had to write better than men on the same topics (29), when newcomers such as Ursula Le Guin and Joanna Russ openly introduced feminist concepts into science fiction (30-33). Ultimately, finding a female readership large enough to support female writers writing as they wished proved liberating. Thus, Bradley's Darkover series, while including many feisty females who are not the sole focus of the novels, also includes the "Free Amazon" novels, comprised of *The Shatttered Chain* (1976), *Thendara House* (1983), and *City of Sorcery* (1984). In the patriarchal society of Darkover, the Renunciates, or "Free Amazons," renounce all ties which require dependence on males. As the Amazon name suggests, they are all skilled warriors. Another way to include feminist thought was to espouse androgyny, as appears in many of Le Guin's novels, such as *Left Hand of Darkness* (1969), or to propose feminist separatism, such as Sally Gearhart's *The Wanderground* (1978). As will be examined below, Cherryh broke new ground by combining in the character of Morgaine an Amazonian strength with a willingness to bond with a man, rejecting separatism, and acknowledging ruthlessness as a potential female trait.

Among the lineage of fictional heroic femininity, Morgaine stands out as a warrior who goes far beyond the typical Amazonian ideal. For one, Amazons in SF tend to travel with a female partner, clan, or at least friend. There is "female bonding" of platonic or lesbian varieties. For Morgaine, bonds of any kind are an encumbrance. Her partner is the sword Changeling, the soul-devouring weapon that embodies her mission to close the Gates of the qual. So, while Morgaine shares with other feminist characters the common experience of being unheeded or discounted because she is female, such as when 10,000 men are lost to another world when they refuse her orders (*Ivrel* 92), in the Saga the reader does not find her associating with other women, nor young girls who flock in heroine worship. Jhirun, in *Well of Shiuan*, looks more to Vanye as an approachable translator of Morgaine's plans, though she exhibits her own female strength. Morgaine repeatedly tells Vanye that she is ruthless, lies, has no scruples, and no mercy. A warrior who cannot afford the luxury of honor, Morgaine's devotion to her suicide mission allows her no compromises.

While her name evokes the witchery of Morgan le Fey (not yet re-envisioned by Marion Zimmer Bradley), Morgaine's powers are purely techno-logical, yet viewed as magics first by Vanye, then by other human men they encounter. The qual know her weapons as science. Also referred to as the White Queen (*Fires* 407), and a pale rider on a pale horse (*Exile's* 11), she herself admits "men call me Death," titles which imply a Goddess of destruc-tion (*Exile's* 394). Rebecca Beal refers to the analogies to Arthurian legend as "Cherryh's Arthurian humanism" (56), viewing Changeling as similar to Arthur's sword, and the lord-liege relationship between Vanye and Morgaine as that of an Arthurian knight (64-65). Beal argues that "In the Morgaine series, then, Cherryh mitigates the apparent capriciousness of a Morgana-like sorceress by drawing on the resources of a science fiction frame for what is basically a fantasy story, and providing a sympathetic viewpoint—Vanye's—within the fantasy" (66). Mary Brizzi observes that the narrative focus on the "helpful male" is used with other Cherryh hero-ines, in order to emphasize the "emotional strength and control" of the female (34). She also suggests interesting parallels to Grail legend and medi-eval romance in the pairing of Morgaine and Vanye as liege and squire, with the female in the more powerful position. While one can debate whether the story of the Gates grounds the work in the science fiction category, as this reader believes it does, the point that the Morgaine Saga loosely provides one of the first positive reimaginings of Morgan le Fey seems accurate. Morgaine does embody goddess-like destructive powers, which only she (and eventually Vanye) can see as ultimately serving a life-giving purpose: the effort to close the Gates is designed to prevent another "calamity" and prevent the loss of entire worlds. This is why Vanye can ultimately explain throughout the novels, as his understanding increases, that his liege does a good thing, though others cannot perceive it.

In her depiction of Morgaine as a warrior, and her allusions to Arthurian legend, Cherryh's early series draws on two staples of feminist SF: heroic femininity and the re-creation of previously "evil" female characters from male-authored legends into more positive figures. While eschewing utopian fiction for grittier drama, Cherryh clearly aligns herself with the rising femi-nist SF themes of the times.

Brizzi argues that a "keystone to Cherryh's success" is her characteriza-tion, which relies on "her unconventional treatment of male and female personality traits. Her epic heroines are unswerving, rational, godly, dominant; her helpful males are confused, faulted, submissive, and emotional, opposite to traditional roles" (46). Though Vanye initially believes he is following a madwoman, he does so in order to rescue some scrap of honor for himself after having been stripped of it (and his warrior's braid) upon killing his half-brother, then refusing to commit suicide at his father's behest. After he develops an awareness of her mission and what drives her to acts he thinks of as reckless, he continues his devotion to her, even vowing a willingness to take up Changeling and the Gate-closing should she die. This willingness becomes more poignant in *Exile's Gate*, when at a critical moment, Morgaine again calls on his oath to do so, and Vanye reflects "It was not the sort of thing a man wanted to agree to, who loved a woman. It was harder than dying for her, to agree to leave her to die" (386). But he can keep his honorable oath, for Morgaine, a woman, restores to him the honor men stripped of him. At the close of *Fires of Azeroth*, he finally confesses why his braid was taken—for supposed cowardice. Morgaine laughs this off, commenting, "Thee? Braid thy hair, Nhi Vanye. Thee's been too long on this road for that" (223). Vanye, though coming from a patriarchal warrior culture, realizes Morgaine's bravery, and in turn allows her recognition of his strength, bravery, and the honor she cannot afford, to restore his sense of dignity.

In fact, not only does Vanye come to see that Morgaine's wisdom and experience greatly outweighs his, he happily turns over most of the thinking to her. Of his *liyo* (liege), he remarks " . . . she had thinking to do, and he had none—it was Morgaine chose their way, Morgaine who decided matters, it was Morgaine who told him what he should do . . . . And he was content enough with that arrangement" (*Exile's* 32). Further, Vanye believes that "She was wiser than he—he was accustomed to think so. He missed things, not knowing what he should see, things which Morgaine did not miss" (59). How rare, even in fantasy, for a man to admit a woman to be his superior! Vanye grows so accustomed to her making things work out that by the time of *Exile's Gate*, when by a gesture she conveys that she is not a miracle worker, he finds himself highly disconcerted (72). In the course of that novel, she does listen to him, only to end up with him captured and her having to rescue him (again). Vanye tells her that "half apiece of two good opinions makes one very bad one. . . .If your way is straight down the road, straight we go and I will say no word. My way, to tell the truth, has not fared very well in recent days" (307). Morgaine bears him no grudge, and obviously goes out of her way to restore him to fitness for travel, even though this slows her down. By agreeing that she has the expertise, Vanye yields to her direction without any sense of losing his strength, thereby challenging traditional views of masculinity.

Though Brizzi argues that Cherryh's female characters are rational and not overly emotional, this is only partly true in Morgaine's case. True, Vanye is far more apt to shed tears, but prideful enough not to show them, such as when his wielding of Changeling accidentally kills Bron (*Exile's* 218). Yet Morgaine is plagued by moodiness and her "unreasonable furies" (47). Usually these occur when circumstances or persons slow her down in pursuit of her closing of the Gates, and Vanye faces her wrath whenever his pity for someone such as Jhirun or Chei burdens their journey. The contrast with the traditionally accommodating and nurturing feminine role is highlighted by Cherryh's description:

> She walked off then, in leisurely fashion, up the hill, plucked a twig and stripped it like some village girl walking a country lane, the dragon sword swinging at her side.
>
> She was, he reckoned, on the edge of a black rage. (*Exile's* 48)

Country girls do not bear dragon swords, and Morgaine has no leisure for caretaking, except when it comes to Vanye himself, an indication of his importance.

Vanye, however, takes on the traditionally female role of nurturing. Interestingly, Brizzi describes the ilin-oath ritual, where Vanye's hand is cut and hearth ash rubbed in it, as "a parody of the blood-show of a virginal wedding night" and a "reminder of household duties" (45). In this sense he performs caretaking duties usually associated with women: "[she] took so little care for herself that she would not eat or drink, at times, would forget these things if he were not there to put food into her hand . . ." (*Exile's* 31). For her part, "She refused to be cared for, and she was too often inclined to drive herself when she might have rested, to prove the point" (*Fires* 12). Truly a reversal of "Behind every great man stands a great woman," Vanye's actions reveal an extremely self-reliant woman who must struggle to accept the freely offered care he provides. Toward the end of the Saga, this turns into a subtle game of one-upmanship where there is turn and turn-about—a more egalitarian solution.

Morgaine's largest challenge to patriarchal gender roles comes from the fact that she is a woman with a mission that is more important than any relationship. Translated into everyday life, the closest analogy is with a woman's career (or any lifelong pursuit). While the career woman was becoming somewhat more prevalent by 1976, the idea that a career could eclipse motherhood or other relationships was, frankly, shocking to many. Morgaine's single-mindedness of purpose is depicted as that of a warrior, but is also found in any person devoted to a mission, cause, art, or field of study. For that to be described as the defining characteristic of a female figure, even given the more traditional elements of self-sacrifice that accompany her mission (Brizzi describes her as a "public-spirited heroine" (45)), was and remains provocative. Even at the time of this writing, women are told that the idea of having career, family, and a significant adult relationship is too much, with the implication being that the wise woman will focus on family over career. Magazine articles abound which tell how women can step out of their careers to focus on their children, work at home, or otherwise not devote themselves wholly to the type of achievement which has traditionally been the province of men. While feminists should applaud such choices when they are the honest *choice* of a woman, the sense of an inherent *right* to pursue one's path without deviation remains more alien to most women than any otherworldly existence could be. Though Cherryh never indicates that Morgaine's path is anything but hard, the fact the validity of her quest is never truly challenged is unique. While Vanye occasionally wishes they could stay in some idyllic moment, such as they share in the beginning of *Fires of Azeroth*, once he understands that worlds rely upon her, he never really tries to stop her, instead giving the type of support previously noted. Recalling Kelso's idea of "politicized joy," one can easily imagine the feminist pleasure derived from a text in which women's goals are not only unquestioned but given the concrete support of a "right-hand man" (Crosby, "What Do Women Want?").

Brizzi sees the "movement of the trilogy is from opposing dualities, good and evil, make and female, mad and sane, qual and human, showing that blending or pairing of opposites will result in the best outcome" (45). In the Morgaine Saga, this movement is more of a pairing, and comes about primarily from the nature of both characters, but also as a result of subtle transformations that occur between them as their eventual love takes root and thrives. The romance aspect of the Saga provides an additional textual pleasure for the reader.

As I note in "What Do Women Want?", where I briefly discuss the Morgaine/Vanye relationship in comparison to other types, the cover art of the series reflects the transformation of their relationship. For *Gate of Ivrel*, Morgaine is portrayed in an improbable bikini top, holding Changeling aloft while Vanye crouches at her feet, clearly submissive. Likewise in *Well of Shiuan*, the cover depicts one of Morgaine's rescues of Vanye; he is on foot, at least, but his hands are bound, while she is above him, on horse, Changeling drawn. Though she is also astride and superior for the cover of *Fires of Azeroth*, Vanye is in a protective position as he moves to distance her from the threat of the *harilim*. Though only moments of Gate time have passed when the action of *Exile's Gate* begins, the nearly ten intervening years since the previous publication shown a maturation in both Vanye and Morgaine's relationship and the quality of Whelan's cover art. Morgaine is still to the fore (as the bearer of Changeling she must be, for safety's sake), but now Vanye is mounted and almost equal with her, no longer the kneeling serf.

Their partnership can be read in a number of ways. One inverts the stereotypical idea that women find fulfillment by submission to a man; instead, Vanye clearly finds fulfillment through submission to his *liyo*, his "lady," as has been discussed. Yet before one cries that this just reverses a standard of inequality, note that Morgaine could be considered the hardened, self-sufficient (modern) woman who can only admit her tender, more traditionally feminine qualities through the steadfast love of a good man. If the reader is adamantly against romance, no justification might suffice, put thus baldly. Yet what makes this conclusion palatable, even welcome, is Cherryh's subtle, sometimes humorous, and slow evocation of these changes.

Gate of Ivrel finds the two needing each other, yet uncertain of that need. Vanye's viewpoint shows him to be somewhat superstitious and provincial, with stereotypical views of female behavior. When he is attacked, Vanye wakes to find Morgaine watching him, wearing "men's clothes": "she had a barbaric bent yet unsuspected; and the blade Changeling was hung over her chair, and her other gear propping her feet—most unwomanly" (46). He himself feels unmanned: "He had lost all the face a man could lose, being rescued by his *liyo*, a woman . . ." (47). Later, Vanye notes her beauty, but sees her as a death-dealing serpent, "infinitely beautiful" (57). Yet, as she shows him kindness, begins to admit her need for him, and even shows emotion when traces of tears are seen after the sword kills a companion of theirs, his feelings warm. Though he kills at her direction, he chooses to follow her, and at the close, she hugs him and cries tears of joy when he crosses the Gate to be with her (191). Still ruled by his clan upbringing, he bends enough to know she holds the place for him, and she bends enough to include him.

Well of Shiuan finds him having to prove to her that he belongs at her side, as the conflict with Rho pulls at his conflicted loyalties and spurs her distrust. Subtle hints are given to the reader that his motivation is not just one of duty. When she asks him if it was his oath that caused him to follow her, he cannot answer; "he had left his own land, abandoned everything to follow her. There were some things he did not let himself reason to their logical end" (58). Obviously he is falling in love, but not until he sleeps at her side (with Changeling between them) does he realize "what had drawn him this side of Gates, although he still shuddered to look into her gray and alien eyes, or to lie thus close to her; the shudder melding into quite another feeling . . ." (161). Brought up to think of relationships with qual (which he still suspects her to be) as abomination, Vanye nonetheless finds himself hit with the love whammy. Only when Morgaine thinks they might be forever separated does she allow herself to indicate some reciprocal feelings and kiss him briefly on the lips, enough to leave him "robbed . . . of speech" (233). This prepares the reader for the impending development of their relationship in the final two novels.

Fires of Azeroth shows Vanye beginning to acknowledge his feelings. Early on, he bravely tells her "You are mad if you think it is only my oath that keeps me with you," a statement which leaves her "perplexed" and frowning in thought (14). Gradually, he begins to see other sides of Morgaine, including the sadness she carries at the inevitable destruction she leaves behind her (55). In kind, she tells him how good he is for her (75), an acknowledgement of need that belies the view of Morgaine as totally ruthless. Instead, the reader sees the terrible risk the self-sufficient woman takes when she allows herself to become vulnerable, to have feelings in a world which has shown her how dangerous they are to her path. He also risks himself by telling her of his upbringing and personal life, the painful story of a bastard son and fratricide (179); she tells him she is Halfling, knowing how that scares him—yet neither run, and when she braids his hair in the warrior braid, which only a woman of intimate relationship can do, it offers both a "new beginning" (223). In a true partnership, vulnerability, risk, and trust go hand in hand, very new feelings for both, and a model for non-dominant relationships.

In *Exile's Gate* these feelings come to fulfillment, when Vanye acknowledges Morgaine as the "essential thing" in his life. Chei becomes confused about whether Morgaine and Vanye are lovers, and so does Vanye (86). After being forced to drink powerful liquor around Arunden's campfire, they are just inebriated enough to really kiss, which of course Chei interrupts (146). Vanye is torn between wanting to fulfill their desires and fear that this new aspect of their relationship will complicate things to the point where he is a burden to her. When he finally tells her "I could never leave you. When will you trust me?," her response of "I do not know why thee should love me" indicates an internalization of disgust for the toll Changeling takes on her (149), and is one of the most touching scenes in the Saga. When they finally make love after Vanye's humble, boyish offering of a wildflower to heal a hurt look on her face (259), the reader cheers for that which has been three and a half novels in the making. Though Morgaine makes no avowal never to leave him (nor does Vanye expect one), the subsequent action of the novel indicates that she will do much to keep him with her, to the point of giving him near immortality by storing his pattern within the Gates, because she needs him, "And the road would grow too lonely" (346). At all costs, Morgaine shields herself from as much of the vulnerability love brings as she can by granting, Goddess-like, the promise of eternal life. Having overcome difficulties of trust, they travel on through the Gates, again leaving destruction behind them, for Mante's Gate will not just close, but blow, causing great devastation, and her tears "gave him hope for himself, in such a time, after so many journeys" (414). Committed, heroic, but not as unfeeling as others make her out to be, Morgaine gives meaning and companionship to Vanye, while he grants the understanding and help of a true partner.

Fifteen years after the publication of *Exile's Gate*, the issues of female identity and companionship Cherryh raises are still pertinent. Many men find it hard to take orders from a female, much less acknowledge her skills as superior. When a woman exhibits single-minded devotion to a cause rather than a relationship, she still faces messages that she is unwomanly, less-than. And for the woman who not only exhibits such passion, but would like to have a companion and helpmeet along the way, the only satisfaction she might find of that desire is likely to be in literature of the fantastic, for men like Vanye—friend, defender, aid all-in-one—are rare, the stuff of legends. Thus, while the story, told through Vanye's perspective, does indeed narrate his changes from outcast to partner of a woman with a doomsday sword, the woman herself remains the focus, for Morgaine's Saga speaks to all women who wish to world-hop, wield power, change history, save lives, and maybe even have someone by their side.

WORKS CITED

Barr, Marleen, ed. *Alien to Femininity: Speculative Fiction and Feminist Theory*. New York: Greenwood, 1987.

—. *Lost in Space: Probing Feminist Science Fiction and Beyond*. Chapel Hill: U North Carolina P, 1993.

Beal, Rebecca. "C. J. Cherryh's Arthurian Humanism." *Popular Arthurian Traditions*. Sally Slocum, ed. Bowling Green, OH: Bowling Green State UP, 1992. 56-67.

Bradley, Marion Zimmer. "Responsibilities and Temptations of Women Science Fiction Writers." *Women Worldwalkers: New Dimensions of Science Fiction and Fantasy*. Jane B. Weedman, ed. Lubbock, TX: Texas Tech Press, 1985. 25-41.

Brizzi, Mary T. "C. J. Cherryh and Tomorrow's New Sex Roles." *The Feminine Eye: Science Fiction and the Women Who Write It*. Tom Staicar, ed. New York: Frederick Ungar Publishing, 1982. 32-47.

Cherryh, C. J. *Exile's Gate*. New York: DAW, 1988.

—. *Fires of Azeroth*. New York: DAW, 1979.

—. *Gate of Ivrel*. New York: DAW, 1976.

—. *Well of Shiuan*. New York: DAW, 1978.

Cioffi, Kathleen. "Types of Feminist Fantasy and Science Fiction." *Women Worldwalkers: New Dimensions of Science Fiction and Fantasy*. Jane B. Weedman, ed. Lubbock, TX: Texas Tech Press, 1985. 83-93.

Crosby, Janice. "What Do Women Want? The Positive Male in Fantasy Fiction by Female Authors." *Images of Masculinity in Fantasy Fiction*. Susanne Fendler and Ulrike Horstmann, eds. Lewiston, NY: Mellen, 2003. 125-143.

Kelso, Sylvia. "Third Person Peculiar: Reading between Academic and SF-Community Positions in (Feminist) SF." FEMSPEC 2.1 (2000): 74-82.

Murphy, Patrick D. "Feminism Faces the Fantastic." *Women's Studies* 14 (1987): 81-90.

Russ, Joanna. "The Image of Women in Science Fiction." *Images of Women in Fiction: Feminist Perspectives*. Susan Koppelman Cornillon, ed. Bowling Green, OH: Bowling Green U Popular Press, 1972

Susan Bernardo is another academic who writes about a wide spectrum of issues, ranging from traditional literary subjects to popular culture, matters of gender, and, happily, science fiction.

Cyteen is one of Cherryh's greatest accomplishments. It remains in print (in an all-in-one volume) and given its subject matter, remains a potent work of speculative fiction. As an intensely psychological work, as is most of Cherryh's output, *Cyteen* can be intimidating, especially when viewed as it was intended, a single novel.

While non-academics should avoid the citations and understand the formal language for what it is, a representation of scholarly thought in the field of literary criticism, there is much here to learn about characterization and character development in Cherryh's award-winning novel. In fact, it might be useful to understand that science fiction in this case offers a unique opportunity for a scholar to interrogate these ideas, for in mainstream fiction cloning is not present and the concept of self-creation in that context simply cannot arise.

Read on, and ponder the questions of identity and self-creation that Susan has brought to *The Cherryh Odyssey*.

Note

Cyteen was originally published as three novels in 1988-89: *Cyteen: The Betrayal, Cyteen: The Rebirth* and *Cyteen: The Vindication*. In this essay all page references are to the one-volume version of the trilogy (Warner Books, 1995).

OF EMORYS AND WARRICKS: SELF-CREATION IN CYTEEN

Susan Bernardo

C. J. Cherryh's *Cyteen* presents the reader with an array of power struggles, from personal to geopolitical and potentially interplanetary. Burton Raffel, a prolific scholar and literary commentator, says "The heart and soul of the book is the flawlessly interwoven stream of meaningful story and high-powered insight, of fascinating character and palpitating event." The deepest, most developed struggle in the texts focuses on possible models of identity creation for two of those characters: Ari Emory the second and Justin Warrick. The idea and reality of the autonomous, independent individual coexists uncomfortably alongside notions of varying degrees of the importance of relationships and their fluctuations to the evolution of the person.

Susan Stanford Friedman in *Mappings*, a book that investigates feminism and the role categories play as both boundaries and places of possible exchange, describes an array of dynamics that tend toward self-creation, including one process she calls "relational." The relational process involves the idea that shifting connections to others and varying situations require that the self or subject is ultimately flexible. *Cyteen* exhibits a bias in favor of the relational model of development by showing the reader the problems that arise from the idea of the autonomous self as well as exploring the positive possibilities of human relationships in all their complexity and oscillations. Through the two Ariane Emorys and the continuing struggle of Justin Warrick to navigate the political pitfalls and power plays of Reseune and Novgorod, C.J. Cherryh explores the integral roles of shifting relationships, responsibility and empathy as part of the dynamic of creating active subjects. The subject, or fully developed self, in *Cyteen* can be created only through a complex set of connections, challenges and negotiations with both society and individuals.

Reseune, an independent community of scientists on whose work in cloning society depends, helps shape the powerful, separate status Ariane Emory and Jordan Warrick enjoy. Reseune's laboratories supply Cyteen with people who have particular skill sets and predilections. Without the genetic engineering and creation of psychsets for azi—people whose paths are predetermined by both their genetic makeup and psychological training—Cyteen could not work as a planet with a developed society. Both the first Ariane Emory (Ari 1) and Jordan Warrick, as Specials at Reseune, are in a category set apart from others on Cyteen. This status means that the government and society of Cyteen recognize that they are geniuses and because of this they are so important to society that no one, not even the law, can interfere with them.

Their potential for autonomy and self-direction is all but absolute. Ari 1 does isolate herself from meaningful human contact as she develops. For example, she avoids any entanglements that could limit her. She informs Justin Warrick, who is Jordan Warrick's parental replicate/clone (PR), that sex is simply about physical responses to stimuli and nothing more. Her crass definition stems from her own idea that one must never allow oneself to be manipulated by desire for another or by another's desire for oneself. Power and her own exercise of that power constitute individual freedom for Ariane Emory. Jordan Warrick, too, though he has a PR, becomes physically isolated on Cyteen when he is banished to Planys in order to keep him from getting involved in any political or personal schemes that might get in the way of Reseune's projects and political maneuvering. When Ari 1 is murdered (about a third of the way into the novel) everyone thinks that Jordan killed her, but his Special status keeps anyone from getting at him. In this instance, autonomy leads to death and isolation.

Autonomy, with its attendant sense of isolation, makes for a twisted personality, even for a person as brilliant and powerful as Ariane Emory. One of the most powerful examples of her separateness is her existence after death through her notes in a computer program called Base One. Even the name of the program announces both a sense of dominance and singularity. Ari 1 tells her PR, "*If you survive to reach the power I have had, you will walk a narrow boundary between megalomania and divinity. Or you will let that anger reach humankind; or you will abdicate in cowardice. . .If I have succeeded, there is still work to be done, to keep the hand on the helm. Situations change . . .*" (Cherryh 473). Clearly Ari 1 characterized her own position as godlike, but also recognized the shifting nature of the challenges her successor would face. Ari 1 in one sense is not alone since her thinking extends to all of humankind, but in another way she is a creature who sets herself apart.

Conversely, both Ari's PR (Ari 2) and Justin Warrick see the value of relationships for the healthy development of the self. Early in the book Ari 1 purposely damages Justin by using him sexually and manipulating him psychologically. She wishes both to control Justin and get revenge on his father, who had rejected her. Instead of continuing her predecessor's bent toward control and revenge, Ari 2 builds an array of relationships. Her development, though Denys and Giraud (her uncles) try to model it on Ari 1's experiences because they want Ari 2's intellect to function at as high a level as Ari 1's, has important differences from Ari 1's. For instance, while they deprive Ari 2 of a mother just as Ari 1 had lost her mother, Ari 2 gets another "mother" in her relationship with Ari 1 through Base One. The Base One interface does many of the things a mother would do: it hears her, answers her questions and maintains a structured set of rules. For example, when Ari 2 is a precocious 10-year-old she gets curious about sex and turns to Base One for some answers. Ari 1's dead voice tells her that when a person thinks about sex, it is hard to focus on other areas:

> If I asked you to do a complicated math you'd probably make a mistake right now. That's the important lesson, sweet. Biology interferes with logic. There's two ways to deal with it—do it and get it out of your head, because that feeling explodes like a soap bubble once you've done sex—or if it's somebody you really like, or somebody you don't like, who upsets you and makes you feel very, very strong reactions, you'd

better think a whole lot about doing it, because that kind explodes all right, but it keeps coming back and bothering you. When you get into bed with somebody, you're not going to be thinking with your brain, sweet, you'll be thinking with the part of you that doesn't have anything but feeling, and that's damned dangerous. (387)

Ari 2 can ask any question she wants and she gets answers based on her level of access. Though Ari 1 claims that Base One and she are different entities, this idea breaks down in passages that clearly use Ari's voice, as in the passage quoted above. Ari 1 wrote the program to allow increasing access for Ari 2 based on her own intellectual and emotional development. As Ari 2's scores on various measures improve, so does her level of access to information. Ari 2 understands this manipulation, but plays the game willingly to increase her levels of access.

Ari 2 owes her legal personhood, furthermore, to her predecessor's status and the fact that Ari 2 is a parental replicate (318). A parental replicate is more than a simple clone in the case of Ari 2. When Jordan Warrick tells Ari 1's political enemies (prior to her murder) that she is working on psychogenesis he refers to it as "mind cloning" and adds, " 'if the program does what Dr. Emory hopes, we can recover the ability in the same field.' " (17). In other words, Ari 1 has come up with a way to replicate both the physical attributes and intellectual talents of a parent. Ari 2's interactions with Base One are actually part of that process. The more access Ari 2 gets to the capacities of Base One, the subtler her own understanding of key issues becomes. For instance, she learns about power and its nature from Ari 1. Ari 2 writes about power in her personal journal: "It's not territory. It's equilibrium. An equilibrated system has tensions in balance, like girders, like trusses in a building. Rigid systems are vulnerable. Ari said that. Equilibrated systems can flex under stress" (497). The idea of flexibility and working with stress aligns with an idea of Friedman's about the nature of identity: "Identity depends upon a point of reference; as that point moves nomadically, so do the contours of identity, particularly as they relate to the structures of power" (Friedman 22). This flexibility in response to the influence of her parent becomes a key characteristic of Ari 2. In the midst of this growing link to Ari 1, Ari 2 carves out her own space, her own presence. Initially, her difference from her parent concerns her uncles Denys and Giraud: ". . .they had an anomaly; they had a child far less serious than the first Ari, far more capricious and more restrained in temper" (Cherryh 288).

According to Jean Pfaelzer in her article "Subjectivity as Feminist Utopia," "A girl's sense of herself is profoundly anchored in relationship, connection and identification with her mother" (99). As a parental replicate who is undergoing psychogenesis, Ari 2 is a case of extreme identification with the mother. She even wonders at one point "'Can I get away from her—and still be me?'" (Cherryh 419). Her concern is the opposite of her uncles', who want a repeat of the first Ari. Jenny Wolmark, who sees the key role identity plays in *Cyteen*, says "the creation of multiple selves [is]. . . both liberatory and repressive" (78). Ari does manage a degree of subjectivity as she builds family relationships with Amy Carnath, Maddy Strassen and Sam Whitely, for example. She also genuinely likes Justin without, at least initially, all the Machiavellian complications her genetic mother loaded into that connection. Of course, her question about her ability to be herself and potentially other is key. As Pfaelzer astutely observes, intersubjectivity is integral to subjectivity:

> This concept [intersubjectivity] designates both an individual capacity and a social space. It resists absolutes and permanence on the one hand, and, most likely, androgyny, on the other. Intersubjectivity posits a tension between sameness and difference. Empathy and difference exist simultaneously. Together, they evolve through an active exchange with another person, usually, in the first place, the mother. (106)

Ari 2's relationship with a mother has two manifestations: Jane Strassen, the mother who is removed in order to replicate Ari 1's experience, and Ari 1 as she represents herself in Base One.

It is through Ari 2's access to Ari 1's most private files that we learn that the hateful, manipulative Ariane Emory was also a brilliant and creative thinker. Her idea of socio-genesis reaches beyond the personal notion of autonomy. The idea of reformulating society reveals an Ariane Emory with utopian leanings despite her personal bents toward sadism and cynicism. Ari 1, in going along with the defense project labeled Gehenna, gave the azi who were to be placed on the planet a basic instruction in their deepsets. As Ari 2 tells the Council, "'she told the azi it was their planet and they had to take care of it and survive and teach their children what was important, that was all'" (Cherryh 476). Ari 1's plan was actually nothing less than an attempt to improve human society. She also, as it turns out, had seeded many azi (not just Gehennans) with deepsets that she hoped would improve society. Ari 1's only fear in doing all this was for the azi—the fear that should citizens (CITs—humans who are not psychologically programmed and manipulated as part of their early development and subsequent training) find out what she had done, that some azi were different, would lead to pogroms against those azi. In other words, even the apparently isolated, power-hungry Ari 1 contained within herself the essential tension between self-interest and empathy.

Ari 2 certainly shows both her individual survival instinct and a capacity to connect with and care about others in her reaction to the bomb attack aimed at her in Novgorod. The violence of the bomb attack helps jolt the new Ari into her more complete personhood. As Friedman would say, Ari responds to a shifting landscape of power. Her statement to the press after the attack emphasizes freedoms as she announces her intent to run for a seat on the Council. She says:

"Every time the Council sits to debate honest differences, everybody wins, precisely because civilization is working and the majority and the minority are trying to work out a fair compromise that protects the people they represent. That's why these types who want their own way above all have to destroy that; and that's precisely why the best answer is a consensus of all the elected bodies that ideas are valuable, peaceful voices deserve serious consideration, human needs have to be dealt with in a wise distribution of resources. . .Whoever did this, from whatever misguided notion of right above the law, he hasn't scared me into retreat, he's made me know how important the law is; and I will run for office, someday; I'll run, and I'll respect the vote in my electorate, whatever the outcome, because an honest contest is one thing, but creating chaos to undermine the people's chosen representative isn't dissent, it's sabotage of the process, the same as the bombers are trying, and I'll have no part of that either"(661).

Law is certainly something that Ari 1 had used to advantage as she worked for her goals and the goals of Reseune in Council. Ari 2 is certainly aware of all the deal making and power plays that normally characterize the workings of the Council. She also clearly understands the importance of the relationship between dominant (majority) and different (minority) ideas. Her speech, though it states a pure version of the importance of the place of order as against chaos, also privileges science—"ideas are valuable"—and speaks of compromise as a way of getting results. This speech also acts an announcement of Ari 2 as a subject who focuses on both herself and others as she refers to "human needs" that "have to be dealt with in a wise distribution of resources." The statement becomes even more interesting when she and Justin return to Reseune after the tribulations of Novgorod and Ari's people (especially Florian and Catlin, her azi) use lethal force against her uncle Denys. Denys, it turns out, had set the bomb plot in motion because he began to see that he would not be able to control Ari 2 as he had hoped, in part because she is becoming as powerful as her parent. Ari 2, like her predecessor, sees the webs of deceit that surround most of the workings at Reseune, but when she and others are attacked, she also rises above the political fray long enough to care about what is happening to others.

Ari 2 falls into a pattern of female leaders in C.J. Cherryh's fiction that Lynn Williams identifies, though her article does not refer to *Cyteen* explicitly. In making her case, Williams refers to a number of C.J. Cherryh's characters: for example, Djan from *Brothers of Earth*, Chimele from *Hunters of Worlds*, Elai of *Forty Thousand in Gehenna* and Signy Mallory of *Downbelow Station*. Williams says: "In Cherryh's politically conservative view, aristocratic power is not in itself evil as long as it is used well, and preservation of the status quo is preferable to violent change. Her women characters recognize their duty to take care of their dependents, not exploit them. [They are] distinctly feminine leaders who believe that power and responsibility go together, and that reform rather than revolution is the best solution to political problems" (91). Ari 2's first idea upon returning to Reseune after the Novgorod trip is to talk with Uncle Denys, accept his offer of retirement and seclusion and carry on with her own plans. As she tells Justin, " 'I hope we can do this without a shot' "(Cherryh 677). It is, as Florian tells Ari, unfortunately, impossible to take the peaceful path: "'Denys is dead. . . I'm sorry, sera. It was a set-up'" (679). Ari 2's views of her own situation and the position of Reseune in the larger political landscape show the reader that she is the responsible power broker who cares about others. She treats Justin differently than her predecessor had, for instance. It is she who has Jordan Warrick brought back to Reseune from his exile at Planys. Her use of people appears to continue where the first Ari left off, but she takes the level of intelligence and insight she has into the personalities and likely actions of others and sees that knowledge as a pathway to the link of potential friendships and allegiances as well as part of political maneuvers.

She understands how others feel and has a degree of empathy. As Pfaelzer points out "Empathy is not merger. Empathy requires an articulated and differentiated image of the other" (99). Ari has the capacity to allow others to be subjects as she claims her own selfhood by the end of *Cyteen*. She announces to her Uncle Denys that it is her time, that she is in the ascendancy. The deal she tries to come to with him would allow him all that is most important to him: the continuation of the PR of his brother Giraud Nye, his research wing, his azi and his books. It is Denys who blows the deal by taking the old violent way and setting an assassin's trap for Ari at Reseune as he had used Abban (the dead Giraud's azi) to do in Novgorod. Even though Ari later figures out that Denys must have done something to trigger Abban to set the bomb attack in motion in Novgorod, she has compassion for Abban. Ari thinks of what Abban must be going through as an azi who has lost his Supervisor when she sees him in Novgorod. Ari asks Abban if he is all right and thinks:

> Abban was well above a hundred himself, having had one Supervisor for most of his life. He was very lost now, she thought, with Denys focused now on Giraud-to-come. Somebody had to take him—or give him Final tape and a CIT-number, which Abban was ill-suited for. All Abban had gotten since Giraud had died seemed to be snubs from the Family and responsibility for all the details, precious little grace for what he was suffering, and it made her mad. (Cherryh 651)

Given Ari's bent toward empathy, it seems natural that she and Justin Warrick should join forces by the end of *Cyteen*.

Throughout *Cyteen* he is the sensitive character whose capacity for caring about others lands him squarely in the well-constructed traps of the first Ari. For example, his concern for Grant leads Justin to send Grant away in an attempt to escape the manipulations of Ari 1. Justin thinks he can successfully get Grant away from the evil influence of Ariane Emory by sending Grant down river to freedom. Grant's capture by abolitionist extremists and the Reseune force's subsequent slaughter of them as they rescue Grant and return him to Reseune unravels Justin's imagined idea that freedom from the influence of power is possible. Everyone—from the abolitionists to the first Ariane—wants to use Grant to political advantage. He is the quintessential hostage: Ariane can keep Justin and Jordan in line by using her power over Grant and the abolitionists want to use him to expose practices at Reseune that they believe are unethical. Grant's azi status both helps and hurts him as he tries to maneuver around these forces. On the one hand, he is reliable because of his psych sets, and on the other hand he has little capacity for independent judgment when he is in a situation that is new and perhaps dangerous. When he is supposed to be heading down river toward freedom, Grant runs into trouble. The abolitionist extremists, who want to stop the creation of azi altogether, get him instead of the people (Kruger and Merild) who would have helped him. Grant is unsure who the abolitionists are, whether this is part of Justin's plan for him or whether he's made a mistake and not followed his instructions properly. Justin tries to give Grant physical freedom even though Grant cannot have true psychological independence. Grant's return to Reseune where he undergoes various psychological interventions illustrates how fragile, yet consistent he is. Justin's ongoing concern for Grant provides an example of empathy that actually links him with Ari 2 who, along with her growing political prowess, keeps in sight the situations of others.

Justin initially sees Ari 2 as someone to avoid and suspect because he has been warned not to interfere with her and because her predecessor's manipulations of him still cause him to have terrible flashbacks. His fear keeps him from truly working with Ari 2 until very late in *Cyteen*. When he and Ari 2 are on the plane back to Reseune from Novgorod and it becomes clear that she is telling him all she knows of their current situation and the situation at Reseune, Justin says: " 'Why are you trusting me?' " (671). As she goes on to claim her difference from the first Ari it becomes obvious that Justin needs to shift his view of her and reassess what the link of friendship between them will mean to both Grant and his father. He shows himself capable of making the shift as he thinks through the likely dangers they face and those she faces in particular, as they return to Reseune. His flexibility in this situation links to Friedman's notions of the dynamic self.

Though Justin and Ari 2 arguably have different paths as they grow up, they have much in common beyond their PR status. Their research interests and talents link, for instance, and their care for azi and the place of loyalties in a shifting political landscape also provide them with common ground. Through Ari 2 pointing out that Justin would care more for Grant than his father, Jordan, should he be forced to choose between them, the novel also shows that Justin does not put himself before others (since Jordan is, in effect, an older version of Justin). Justin also acts as an example for Ari 2 as she struggles with the question of differentiating herself from Ari 1. Justin has found a separate sense of identity while remaining connected to his father. Justin, like Ari 2, announces both his selfhood and his concern for his father in Novgorod when he tells the Council that he is troubled by current events that are dredging up the whole investigation into the murder of Ari 1 and the suspicions everyone had about Jordan: " 'maybe just that people are taking this up that had absolutely nothing to say to help him twenty years ago and all of a sudden everyone's interested, *not* because they know whether he's guilty or innocent, but because it's a political lever in things my father's not in touch with . . .' "(649). He sees the situation as a part of a larger landscape and shows his ability to analyze the potential moves of others. Even Ari 2 thinks, *"They'll find out they're dealing with a Special, after he's made off with their keys and their cred-slips—damn, he's good when he cuts loose . . ."*(653). She clearly sees Justin as a person who is on her intellectual level. His speech before Council, his ideas about the design of psych sets and his conversations with Grant and both Aris show the reader someone who is aware of manipulations and tries to find a path through them. His approach goes from a mostly passive one during the time of Ari 1, to one that calculates consequences in advance. When he analyzes the situation, finds a voice and sees how his and Ari 2's interests link, Justin begins to have hope.

The novel has many passages that focus on the use of voice as a way to explore the shifting nature of the self. There is Ari 1's dead/alive voice in Base One, Ari 2's journal and her interactions with Base One, Justin and Ari 2's internal ideas, which we get at length, and even notes on various azi and CIT types that are under development. Cherryh layers these voices to create an array of situations and characters who are almost maddeningly intelligent and analytical, but at the same time maintain a capacity for influential actions and words. Her creation of two Aris and two Warricks works to create odd displacements of identity since both sets of parent /PRs are genetically identical, but personally different. Friedman points out that "Identity often requires some form of displacement—literal or figurative—to come to consciousness" (151). Cherryh sets up the conditions for the development of her main characters and complicates that process by doubling and then removing the parent part of each set from the action, but never from the deepest workings of the plot and the PR characters' awareness. Presence and absence almost become interchangeable through Ari 1's living voice in Base One and through Jordan's political influence. The tension that this process of doubling and displacement creates is just the complicated set of contradictions, doubts, reversals and brilliant insights it takes to create the Specials of *Cyteen*. For the reader, the intricate world that Cherryh creates in the novel makes for a sense of psychological realism, intense power struggles and fascinating scientific possibilities that lead to a reassessment of our understanding of both individuals and society. From the god-like, replicable Specials to the deep machinations of political intrigue, *Cyteen* is a work of brilliance that could only have come from the mind of the master-writer, the non-replicable C.J. Cherryh.

WORKS CITED

Cherryh, C.J. *Cyteen: Complete in One Volume*. New York: Warner Books, 1988, 1995.

Friedman, Susan Stanford. *Mappings: Feminism and the Cultural Geographies of Encounters.* Princeton: Princeton University Press, 1998.

Pfaelzer, Jean. "Subjectivity as Feminist Utopia." in Jane L. Donawerth and Carol A. Kolmerten, Eds. *Utopian and Science Fiction by Women*. Syracuse, NY: Syracuse University Press, 1994.

Raffel, Burton. "C.J. Cherryh's Fiction." *The Literary Review* 44, 3 (Spring 2001) 24 July 2003 *Infotrac*.

Williams, Lynn F. "Women and Power in C.J. Cherryh's Novels." *Extrapolation* 27, 2(1986): 85-92.

Wolmark, Jenny. "Destabilising Gender and Genre." *Aliens and Others: Feminism and Post-Modernism*. Iowa City: University of Iowa Press, 1994. 54-80.

Fortune passes everywhere. How else to explain the strange friend of a friend process by which Elizabeth Romey became aware of this project—how else to explain the good fortune for this text and thereby readers alike? A student of politics, law, and society, Elizabeth's main scholarly work has been in the field of psychology. How lucky, then, that she is a fan of Cherryh's work and can speak knowledgeably about the psychological aspects of *Cyteen*.

This she does in detail, with appropriate cautions concerning real-world practice of such ideas. All too necessary, as while a physicist can discuss faster-than-light space travel, there is no need to fear such ideas being put into practice, something that is not quite so true with psychological manipulation.

And if this amount of good fortune isn't enough, Elizabeth is also a novelist, which adds another layer of complexity and depth to her discussion of Cherryh's work.

DR. ARIANE EMORY, SR.:
PSYCHOPATH—OR SAVIOR?

Elizabeth Romey

The measure of the brilliance of C.J. Cherryh's masterwork *Cyteen* is that attentive and willing readers can learn something new from and about the book every time they read it. At the same time that brilliance sometimes gets overlooked precisely because of the subtlety and complexity of its handling of matter not only technically rich but emotionally loaded.

Cyteen was published in 1988 and won the Hugo for best novel in that year. It's a story in which psychology is taken to its height, in which people can be programmed like computers, in which humans conceived and reared in traditional fashion—called CITs, short for citizens—coexist with and sometimes act as protectors of the azi, humans genetically engineered and conditioned to fulfill certain tasks, often as servants or soldiers. But people are not computers, and with these immense advances in psychology come an equally immense threat to the survival of humanity—a threat that only one character has the ability and perspective to recognize.

I first came to *Cyteen* as I was beginning a master's degree in educational psychology with an emphasis on gifted and creative studies, and it is fair to say that it completely changed my outlook on the field. Four and a half years and many soul-searching discussions later, I still find it has things to teach me. As both a student of intelligence and a writer of fiction who tries in her own work to deal with some of the same complex themes of talent development and the nature of intelligence, I had, as it were, a vested interest in interpreting this fictional portrayal of genius as it related to both my professions. As a psychologist myself, I warmed to Dr. Ariane Emory, Sr., in the first pages of the novel—and on first reading, was deeply shocked as both a psychologist and a human being by her treatment of Justin Warrick. Yet that very shock galvanized me to pay attention, and by the end of the novel I was fully persuaded that Ari Emory Sr. is not only a genius, but a savior—not only of the younger geniuses whose talent she has molded, but also of her entire society and possibly humanity as a whole.

At this point, and speaking as a student of psychology, I cannot emphasize enough: Kids, don't try this at home. What Ari Sr. is doing would be not only impossible but highly unethical in our time, and no ethical psychologist would even consider attempting it. Period. Even the sex-therapy techniques developed by Master and Johnson in the seventies and Wilhelm Reich's research into the therapeutic value of the human orgasm are at best looked on with skepticism or suspicion by the majority of psychologists—to say nothing of ethics committees and licensing boards. (For more on the subject of the current state of ethics in psychology, see for example Koocher and Keith-Spiegel's *Ethics in Psychology*—not to mention the APA Code of Conduct.) We simply don't have the know-how—and we know enough to know that we don't, or we should.

At the same time, it is a reflection of Cherryh's brilliance that she is able to create a world which so eloquently addresses the possible future state of psychology as a science—to enable us to think the unthinkable. What Ari Sr. does could certainly not be done in our world—and it is a mark of Cherryh's subtlety and perhaps her own sense of ethics as an author that it is likely far easier for the reader to judge the good doctor by the current standards of psychology than to assume that a modern psychologist could safely and in good conscience emulate Ari Sr.'s techniques. Yet to do so casts a negative light not only on Cherryh's work and the brilliance with which *Cyteen* as a novel is infused, but also on the discipline of psychology as a whole. As a student of psychology, I am certainly ethically obligated to make clear that Ari Sr.'s world and standards are not our own; but this cuts two ways. We cannot do what Ari Sr.

did, but that is precisely the measure of her genius—and more to the point the genius of her creator.

Dr. Emory's genius is one of the givens of the novel; Cherryh makes this point as crystalline as possible through her development of the concept of "Special Persons"—individuals not only highly intelligent but capable of such unique high-level thinking in a discipline and such brilliant insights that their intellects and by extension they themselves are legally protected national treasures—and by her designation of Dr. Emory as one such. But in order to truly appreciate the magnitude and importance of the speculation Cherryh makes in her creation of Dr. Emory and the rest of the cast of *Cyteen*, it is also necessary to appreciate Emory's genius as a positive force on both the micro and macro levels.

1. Getting Rid of the -1: Impossibility and Willing Suspension of Disbelief

For humans to go faster than the speed of light is impossible according to the laws of physics—at least as we now understand them. I have occasionally heard this described as "the problem of the negative one" in the equation that describes the speed of light. But that hasn't stopped science fiction writers—many of them with backgrounds in the hard sciencs—from speculating about it, much less from using it in their novels, with only mild objections from the more scientifically literate critics.

That is the nature of the leap that Ari Sr. as a character demands of us—but a leap relative to the human psyche, and to psychology as a discipline, rather than physics.

In the field of psychology at present—especially my own area of psychology, the study of high intelligence or mental giftedness—the subject of the nature of intelligence and creativity, the origins of mental talents and the processes that contribute to or hinder their development, and even the very definition of what intelligence as a construct is and how to measure it are subjects of intense debate. By contrast, in Ari Sr.'s time it is clearly possible, as with the azi, not only to predict the basic range of an individual's talents at the genetic level, but also to micromanage the backgrounds and environments of these individuals to optimize their potential in particular areas. Likewise, the development of Special Person status—and, by implication, the fact that a governing body could come to a consensus on what constitutes extraordinary ability, evaluate individuals to determine if they

179

possess it, and agree to protect its possessors—indicates a far greater and more objectively based understanding of human talent and its development than is the case at present. To put it plainly, they have intelligence testing and talent development down to a science—which we at present do not.

Ari Sr. goes a step further—beyond the impossible into the unthinkable.

Let me emphasize this point again: the nature of the intervention that Ari Sr. runs on both Jordan and Justin—specifically, the psychosexual acts she performs or causes to be performed on them—is not something that could be done at our current level of psychological knowledge. At the present time, we do not know enough about human psychology for any therapist to run such an intervention. Further, the current zeitgeist in the profession is such that no ethical therapist would even consider it.

But this fact—the very impossibility of doing what Ari Sr. does—is what makes *Cyteen* so remarkable. It is unfortunately all too easy to impose current standards of behavior in general and psychological ethics in particular on a character who is operating in a time and culture in which the discipline of psychology has advanced as far beyond its present standards as the present, modern-day discipline of physical medicine has done relative to the Elizabethan era. But to do so, and to dismiss Ari Sr. as a mere megalomaniac is to blind oneself to the genius of Cherryh—and to the very mind-stretching nature of speculative fiction in general. Just as writers who use FTL "bend" the laws of physics in order to speculate, so Cherryh bends the existing understanding of psychology for the same purpose—she creates a world in which Emory and to some extent her colleagues have gotten rid of their discipline's -1.

2. That Which Does Not Destroy Us: Justin Warrick and Ariane Emory, Jr.

The sticking point, of course, for most readers of *Cyteen*—the point which nearly derailed me on my first reading of the book—is generally Ari Sr.'s treatment of Justin Warrick, her student and protégé. I use both the word "treatment" and the word "protégé" in two senses: Ari Sr. "treats" Justin in the psychological sense, and she also protects him, sometimes from threats that no one else would understand as such. No one would deny that Justin initially suffers at her hands—but then, few psychologists would deny that sometimes the therapeutic process involves pain. But is this pain constructive, therapeutic—or merely the result of Ari Sr.'s desire for personal and highly unethical gratification of her own needs? And was this the only treatment possible, or even the best one? I make the case that Ari Sr.'s approach to treating Justin is not only not gratuitous or purely self-serving, but was in fact optimal, if not perhaps altogether necessary.

The nature of the treatment itself is the first question: did Ari Sr. *really* need to subject Justin to the unspecified but apparently highly disturbing sexual acts she has her azi perform on him? Or was there another, "better" way to achieve the same result?

Given my previous remarks on the subject of the nature of psychology as a discipline in Ari's time as opposed to our own, I must admit that it is impossible to evaluate her methods with much certainty. And I do not attempt to judge Ari Sr. by the standards of ethics and understanding that govern contemporary psychologists. To do so would be like judging a modern surgeon by the standards imposed on the profession during the Civil War—a particularly apt comparison, given that Emory and her colleagues are called "psychsurgeons."

First, the simple fact that Ari Sr., who is acknowledged by her own contemporaries, even those with whom she is at odds, as one of the foremost, if not *the* foremost, experts in her field, chooses this technique is potentially an argument in its favor. However, more rigorous methods of evaluation are available, even at the current level of psychology as a discipline relative to that in Ari Sr.'s time.

The opinion of her own colleagues is certainly a factor, and one of the strongest indicators that Ari Sr. is in fact engaging in an intervention with Justin—as opposed to merely indulging her own appetites at the expense of a vulnerable underage lab assistant—comes from Justin's own father, Jordan. On viewing the tape of the acts performed on Justin, he immediately recognizes that Ari is running an intervention on Justin—a fact not revealed to the reader until late in the novel. According to the psychosocial "givens" of the novel, Jordan, as a Special Person in a field similar to Ari's, is one of the only people competent to judge her work on a professional level—and he recognizes the science behind the sex.

However, the fact that Ari Sr.'s treatment is scientifically based and/or carried out using psychological techniques does not make it ethical. Even in our own time, one of the reasons why psychologists are ethically forbidden to have sexual relations with clients is precisely because they can—and some unscrupulous ones do—use their knowledge of counseling techniques to manipulate their clients against the clients' best interests. The fact that this is apparently a scientifically sound intervention, as judged by a contemporaneous colleague, does not make it an ethically sound one.

The very degree of advancement of the discipline makes it difficult if not impossible to know what other options were actually available to Ari Sr.; Cherryh does not give us a window into the processes the good doctor used to decide on and develop this intervention, except that she had done something apparently similar to Jordan and that it had failed to produce the desired effect. All we have to go on is the results of the intervention that Air Sr. did perform—results we can reasonably assume she intended.

Chronologically first is the insight into himself that Justin gains—the unwelcome but perhaps necessary awareness of his own sadistic or power-hungry streak that surfaces the morning after. It is an awareness that disgusts him, not least because his conscience, his values, hold that such sadistic behavior is wrong. He recognizes that before Ari Sr.'s intervention, he might well have acted cruelly toward others in revenge, but he would not have understood why he wanted to. Thus, the intervention had the effect of making him aware of impulses or desires that run contrary to his own sense of right and wrong—and thus enable him to stop himself from acting on those impulses. This can certainly be considered a benefit to him personally.

Additionally, when one considers the delicate nature of his relationship to Grant ALX, his azi, another benefit surfaces. It is unclear from the book whether Grant and Justin had become sexually involved before the intervention; however, Jordan and his own azi Paul, who were father figures and role models to both boys, were a couple, and this modeling is the first reason Justin cites as an adult when asked about his own relationship with Grant. Justin's awareness and rejection of impulses based on sadistic or power-seeking tendencies would undeniably be of benefit in keeping the relationship between himself and Grant from becoming unhealthy—or more unhealthy, depending on your sense of ethics.

The rest of the benefits to Justin come in the area of his talent development, his relationship with Ari Jr., and their work in the area of sociogenesis, and it is difficult if not impossible to separate them from each other; indeed, even the question of Justin's awareness of impulses toward cruelty and the rejection thereof are significant. Therefore, we will now introduce the next of Ari Sr.'s protégés—again, I use the word in both senses.

Ariane Emory, Jr. is not merely a clone of her predecessor; she is a replicate, a psychological near-duplicate of the first Ari. But she is not an exact copy, and this is where Ari Sr.'s conscience shows itself.

Ari Jr. is "Ariane Emory, version 2.0"—that is, with at least some of the bugs worked out. Specifically, she is a version 2.0 made to the specifications of her predecessor, which indicates or at least suggests the possibility that Ari Sr. intended the differences between them as well as the similarities. In effect, Ari Sr. engaged in a plan of "self-improvement": a creation of a self without those traits she perceived as flaws.

And what are the differences—the flaws that Ari Sr. debugged in her replicate? Arguably they are the traits that get Ari Sr. into trouble with her readers. The sadistic streak that Ari Sr. warns her replicate about seems less evident in the second version—even when she does something impulsive and selfish, as when she takes her own azi Florian to bed, she takes corrective action almost immediately. While her initial relationships with her peers are often fraught with tension, some of this is clearly the result of the stressors imposed by her "uncles," who regularly remove from her social circle any playmates who might compromise the replication program, in the process depriving little Ari Jr. of at least one favorite playmate and making many of the other children scared of her. Additionally, her later seeming callousness with age-mates, as when she threatens Amy Carnath and later 'Stasi Ramirez, derives from this situation and a need to inform herself or protect her friends. Likewise, still another source of tension between Ari and her peers will be familiar to anyone in gifted education—the simple differences in ability and the stress they can place on interpersonal relationships; Miraca Gross, for example, has done some fascinating research on the differences in friendship patterns and expectations between highly gifted and average or moderately gifted children. Ari Jr.'s reactions to Justin are also more empathetic—if sometimes calculatedly so.

Ari Sr. may well have tipped her hand here: her replicate's higher level of empathy also enables her to work even more effectively with people than her predecessor, and possibly to do a better job of endearing herself to the general public. Both are essential factors in enabling the young Ari Jr. to survive to maturity and to fulfill the purpose for which her predecessor intended her, which will be discussed further. In a sense, Ari Sr. thus protects her replicate, by enabling her to be "likeable"—a strategy not unfamiliar to many parents of gifted students, as Stephanie Tolan, for example, discusses in her oft-quoted essay "Is It A Cheetah?"

But Ari Sr.'s protection of her replicate may not stop there. Ari Jr. is put into the care of Denys Nye, who is apparently a satisfactory surrogate for Ari Sr.'s own childhood caregiver, Geoffrey Carnath—with a difference: Geoffrey Carnath apparently sexually abused the first Ari and possibly her azi, while Denys keeps his hands to himself. The second Ari's comments on the subject of Denys' brother Giraud and his attitude toward young girls suggest that he might have been a more perfect surrogate in this respect than his brother. Yet Ari Jr. goes to Denys.

Why? A reasonable assumption is that Ari Sr., herself a victim of her uncle's abuse, would have recognized that some of her own lack of empathy probably derived from that experience, and determined that her replicate would be better served by retaining that empathy. Likewise, if we look at Justin's reaction to his abuse at Ari Sr.'s hands, we can speculate that Ari Sr. herself may have had a similar self-realization, regarding the nature of her own sadistic impulses and their ethicality, either as a direct result of the abuse she suffered or as a result of her own attempts to cope with and recover from it, and that she determined that Justin needed a similar education into his own impulses.

Again, why? Setting aside broader moral concerns, Justin's own consciousness, both of his own sadistic and or power-hungry impulses and especially of the potential vulnerability of a cocky and brilliant student, are significant in his relationship with Ari Jr., who comes to him first as a friend, then as a student, and eventually attempts to initiate a sexual relationship with him. This is another place where Ari Sr. protects her replicate: a Justin unaware of his own impulses toward cruelty or domination might well have played them out on Ari Jr.—perhaps not with intent or malice, but certainly resulting in damage. Likewise, his prior "abusive" relationship with Ari Sr. actually makes him more sympathetic toward her replicate, both in a general sense and specifically when she herself tries to initiate a sexual relationship between them.

This dynamic also protects Justin from Ari Jr.—from an Ari Jr. whose sexual advances he might well have rebuffed anyway since his sexual tastes don't run to females: from a brilliant, powerful, and in some ways spoiled young woman who is also capable of the petulance of any adolescent in the face of rejection. Ari Jr. might well have reacted with impulsive cruelty when faced with Justin's rejection—a rejection and reaction which could have destroyed both their friendship and their professional relationship—except that she learns about his relationship with her predecessor, even to the point of viewing the tapes of his sexual interactions with Ari Sr. This revelation has the effect of arousing her empathy for Justin, such that she no longer resents his rejection of her and even seems to regret her unknowing overtures, or rather the pain she understands she caused him.

The positive and even protective effects of the nature of Ari Sr.'s intervention on Justin do not stop with his relationship to her replicate. Late in the novel it is made clear that Ari Sr. recognized Justin's talent—not only its existence but the nature of the insights he was capable of having—and the attentive reader will recognize that her intervention specifically tended toward producing conditions under which Justin could actually have those insights.

One of her comments to Justin is to the effect that he could do better work—really significant work—if he could get over his worship of his father and his father's ideas. While it is never made clear just how much of the circumstances surrounding her death were under her control, it is undeniable that the result of Ari Sr.'s death and the conditions under which it happened led to a result she could not have considered other than desirable: Jordan and Justin are separated from each other, under conditions which make it impossible for them to discuss their work for many years—thus giving Justin a chance to develop his talent independent of his father's influence.

Indeed, independent of any influence—and this factor can be seen to be a predictable and likely therefore deliberate result of Ari Sr.'s intervention on Justin. The simple fact of their sexual involvement causes most of the other practitioners at Reseune to discount the theories that Justin promulgated and that brought him to Ari Sr.'s attention, because they believe that her only interest in him was sexual. This gives Justin his equivalent of what Einstein called the "job in a lighthouse" that every young scientist needs in order to develop his work creatively and independently. On the other hand, the nature of his involvement with Ari Sr., which was both traumatic and sexual, had the effect of causing him to "fix" on that period of his life and on the work he did then, so that he would find it personally necessary to pursue his research down a line of analysis which only Ari Sr. recognized as significant, despite the discouragement of other knowledgeable individuals in the field.

Other knowledgeable individuals—but not Grant, "his" azi, who often finds himself in the role of caretaker to his ostensible Supervisor. This, too, is part of Ari Sr.'s design—as, indeed, is Grant himself, an azi designed and "programmed" by her to be Justin's companion . . . and to realize his own innate talents as a psychologist. The general nature of Justin and Grant's relationship, and especially their professional discussion, clearly have a significant impact on his work: he finds himself relying on Grant so often, because of Grant's own general competence and talent—not to mention the fact that Grant considers azi superior to CITs in many ways and sometimes decries the fact that azi are legally subordinated to CITs, even chafing when Justin tries to assume the role of Supervisor. This influences Justin's attitude toward the azi, so that he not only has greater evident empathy for them, as witness his inability to do realtime work, but also greater respect—which in turn feeds back into his work.

And what is the nature of that work? The same as the purpose for which Ari Jr. was created—sociogenesis: the deliberate creation of a social structure.

3. The Big Picture: Sociogenesis and Pivotal Talents

As discussed above, Ari Sr.'s intervention with Justin, her development of her replicate and of Grant ALX have had a positive impact on all three young people. But the reach of Ari Sr.'s ambition and compassion—her science and her conscience—goes beyond enabling three talented young people to realize the full potential of their gifts.

Put simply, Ari Sr.'s "client" is her entire civilization. The nature of her unique and formidable talent is such that she can perceive a flaw in the structure of human society that no one else does—that no one else even realizes is a flaw.

In the world of Cyteen, the azi are for the most part taken for granted as a part of the population—and specifically a subordinate part. Azi can only exercise citizenship rights after undergoing a process of "deconditioning"—which Grant describes as "proving we're as crazy as CITs are." They are considered wards of the state, and the attitude of their

Supervisors, CITs specially trained in handling azi, is primarily paternalistic. Some political groups make a problem out of the azi, but these are mostly seen as lunatic fringe elements. More to the point, these groups also see the azi as inferior—their solution to the problem would be to have all humans, however created, reared as CITs. Ari Sr. herself, however, takes the next step intellectually, and recognizes the true nature of the flaw in society and its possible consequences.

The flaw is this: not only are the azi in danger of being institutionalized as a slave race, but their very real advantages in terms of their thought processes and stability are in danger of being overlooked or marginalized, not only because of a legal system that makes them wards of their Supervisors, but because their basic design orients them to extrinsic rather than intrinsic motivation: their motivation and self-esteem are tied to the approval of their Supervisors and superiors and to reward-tape given or at least authorized by these CITs. The laws outlining azi-Super relationships are an effect of the dependence, even psychological enslavement, of azi to CIT, rather than a cause.

Ari Sr. apparently perceived this problem some time before the start of the novel—certainly around the time of the Gehenna mission, mentioned in *Cyteen* and discussed in *Forty Thousand in Gehenna* in more detail. In the latter novel, we see that the children of azi who are not azi themselves rebel against the automatic enslavement to CITs that their azi parents try to teach them—yet they retain some of the virtues, the cooler pragmatism and logic of the azi, as a result of their upbringing. The culture of Gehenna is, as Ari Jr. describes it, an azi culture.

In *Cyteen*, we learn that this was Ari Sr.'s design from the first—she describes Gehenna as an alarm system: a microcosm which appears to indicate that azi and their descendants are better equipped to survive in hostile environments than CITs—and that unless action is taken, it is all too likely that the human race will dwindle to primitive tribes of azi-descendants, who relive their race's distant history unawares.

Although the reports from Gehenna do not come back until late in the novel, it is clear from the notes she leaves for her replicate that Ari Sr. perceived this imminent disaster—and the means of fixing it. All she needed was another century of active working life, and someone to adapt the azi's motivation patterns from extrinsic to intrinsic.

She gets both—the first in her replicate, who is able to pick up where she left off, and the second in Justin, the possibility of whom she saw in his father. It is through her encouragement, even manipulation, that Jordan is persuaded to raise a clone of himself and to take on the rearing of Grant—a pair of geniuses who serve as further experiments into the possibility of replication of extraordinary individuals. Both of them are reared under different conditions from their parents—but environments that are calculated to enable them to actualize their talents to the same extent but in different ways.

But the possibility of replicating geniuses is only a means to Ari Sr.'s end—literally, saving humanity. It is for this purpose that she ran the intervention on Justin, with the results described above. All those results, but especially the ones that impact most directly on his work, are intended to facilitate not only his work on motivation, but as importantly, his partnership with Ari Jr.

As discussed, both Justin's isolation and his relationship with Grant have a significant impact on his work—specifically, the development of a training-structure that will orient the azi to be motivated not by a Supervisor's approval, but by love of their work for its own sake, regardless of the nature of that work. As anyone familiar with motivation theory understands, intrinsic motivation is generally preferable to extrinsic motivation, but in this case it has an even more significant effect—it will liberate the azi from their dependence on their Supervisors.

Justin's work, however, though vital, is not the whole of the project; simply liberating the azi is not enough. The true work of Ari Emory, both the original and her replicate, is to create a human society which will survive the social crisis she sees as imminent. The process began before the start of the novel—when Ari Sr. embedded programming into the psychsets of many azi that would cause them to have children and teach them—laying the groundwork for a population which absorbs the rational values of their azi parents while lacking their dependence and subservience. The role of Ari Jr. is to monitor this process—she is simply the only person fully capable of comprehending her predecessor's work to the extent necessary and adjusting the direction of the intervention Ari Sr. began.

So—in the end, Ari Sr.'s superficially selfish and callous act is in fact merely part of a large and vitally necessary plan for the most ethical of goals possible: the preservation of the human race.

4. Sitting in Judgement: Ethics Committees, Human Subjects Research, and the Role of Deception

All discussion of sociogenesis and talent development aside, at the simplest level, the question of Ari Sr.'s ethics (or lack thereof) is one of sexual conduct—and sexual abuse. On that level, the world of *Cyteen* appears in many respects to adhere to looser standards of sexual conduct than our own. This fits with other evidence regarding their cultural and biotechnological development: these are people who have apparently harnessed human procreative drives, such that children need not be conceived, let alone born, unless wanted, and those at Reseune, at least, are trained in an understanding of human psychology that would seem to render obsolete many of the rules or controls on sexuality in our society.

Yet in some respects, their rules are strikingly similar. Ari Sr.'s abuse of Justin is condemned. Likewise, even among the "inner circle" who come to appreciate the nature of her work there is recognition that an ethics board even in their world would have rejected this particular intervention on its face—though it is debatable whether someone with Ari Sr.'s status as both a political power and a Special Person would have been required to account for her research before such a "jury of her peers."

Ari Sr. appears to have justified her intervention with Justin on the grounds that it was necessary for a larger goal. But this only moves the question back a stage—for how can Ari Sr.'s larger work, her sociogenesis project, itself be justified? She worked alone, without controls and without open consultation with colleagues—both of which are significant elements of sound ethical research practice. And her work itself was designed to alter the entire structure of society.

It is in the nature of the discipline of psychology and of science in general in our time—to say nothing of the egalitarian ethics of modern society as a whole—to ask, how could she?

But it is in the nature of Ari Sr.'s time—the evolution of science and also of society as a whole—to answer us, How could she not?

For a psychologist in today's world to attempt even the tenth, even the hundredth part of what Ari Sr. did would be unconscionable. But Ari Sr. does not live in our world. The world of Cyteen—and of *Cyteen* as a novel—is one in which the creation of azi, humans whose psyches are constructed from the ground up, is considered ethical, in which it is legal though perhaps frowned upon for a researcher to terminate azi test subjects when she is finished experimenting on them. It is a world in which scientists set political policy. It is, most of all, a world in which certain individuals are identified by their government as having a talent so significant that they are effectively beyond the reach of law.

Ariane Emory is one of those individuals.

Jordan Warrick could not even be tried for murder—because his mind was deemed more valuable than the potential subversion of the legal process. With such power comes responsibility—the responsibility to use the talent for which you were given that power, that freedom.

And that is exactly what Ari Sr. did.

In effect, she is doing no more, and no less, than carrying out the duty entrusted to her by her government when she was accorded Special Person status. That is what it means to be a Special—someone recognized to have a talent so far beyond the ordinary, so far beyond the ability of others to evaluate, that it is to the advantage of society as a whole to give them the freedom to do their work in their own way.

The reason for the relative secrecy with which she carried out her plans, then, becomes threefold—and no element involves any question of guilt or prosecution. First, the simple fact is that by definition most people would not have understood what she was doing—that is why she was a Special Person. In the second place, as Ari Sr. states clearly, the possibility of retaliation by CITs against azi if they learned of her work approached certainty.

The third element is one which should be familiar to researchers—that of necessary deception. Even today, Institutional Review Boards permit researchers to deceive their subjects if they can show that the degree of deception involved is necessary for the research.

Even discounting the safety of the azi, Ari Sr.'s deception was necessary for her work—the very nature of the change she meant to make in her society required that the members of that society not know it was taking place. Attitudes had to be shifted at an unconscious level. As such, the nature of the research could not be revealed except to a very trusted few who were part of the project.

Not even to an ethics committee.

One of the most difficult, dangerous—and ultimately most rewarding—tasks a writer can undertake is to challenge not just our most basic ideas of what is real, but our deepest understanding of what is right—and what is not. Cherryh's genius lies in her ability to take the reader with her on a journey that explores some of the most fundamental truths, not just of our world, but of ourselves.

It is in some ways a harder task than that which Ari Sr. undertook. She, after all, had the advantage of working in a world in which, as I have discussed, her ideas and actions were tenable, were supported by data. Cherryh's task in creating that world and its mistress must have been far more difficult—to imagine so far beyond the existing knowledge in a given discipline, and to create a world in which that leap could comfortably be taken for granted.

To appreciate the nature of Cherryh's speculations, it may be instructive to look at the state of what might be called intelligence psychology at the time she was writing and researching *Cyteen*. Fortunately, there is a book which does just that: Robert Sternberg's *Conceptions of Giftedness* anthology (second edition), published in 1985, which surveyed the research and theory of the most respected thinkers in the field of gifted education at the time. The title itself is suggestive: *conceptions*, plural—and while many of the authors' ideas do dovetail, there also exist clear differences among them as to what constitutes "giftedness"—a marked departure from the state of the art in Ari Sr.'s world as conceived by Cherryh.

By the same token, the conceptions propounded by a number of these writers, including Renzulli, Gruber, Csikzsentmihalyi, and Sternberg himself, also fit beautifully into the "conception of giftedness" used in *Cyteen*. Renzulli's "three-ring" model of talent development—above-average intelligence, creativity, and task commitment—finds an echo in Ari Sr.'s self-described monomania; she has not only the talent but the desire or commitment to her work. Likewise, her creation of situations which would require her replicate to "work real-time" and solve day-to-day problems might reflect the influence of Sternberg's triarchic theory, which breaks intelligence into analytic, creative, and practical abilities. Csikszentmihalyi's exploration of the role of culture (in the sense of zeitgeist and social valuation of certain gifts) and time (in an almost Nietzschean sense of "rumination," or less politically, incubation) in the development of gifts also finds its echo in the very nature of Ari Sr.'s replication experiments. And Gruber's conception of giftedness as "the self-construction of the extraordinary" takes on a whole new meaning when applied to psychogenesis and the replication of one's talent!

By the same token, the aforementioned work of Masters and Johnson in sex therapy was at its height in the seventies; while my own research does not tend in this direction, Ari Sr.'s use of Catlin and Florian bears at least a super-ficial similarity to the use of "sexual surrogates" in sex therapy—though I strongly doubt that any sex therapist ever tried her degree of intervention (at least I hope not).

Without knowing the extent and nature of Cherryh's research into the state of psychology at the time of her writing, I can say that as a student of psychology I certainly found that her speculation resonates with the field as it existed at the time of her writing. Far more significantly, *Cyteen* strikes to the heart of some of the most significant questions, theories, and develop-ments in the field at the time: the role of nature and nurture in the develop-ment of talent and personality; the role of sex in psychotherapy and what constitutes ethical behavior for a therapist. These are questions which are still being asked in one form or another today, and again as a student of psychology I found that *Cyteen* still has things to say to our profession, even a quarter-century later. The discipline may have changed, our knowledge base and ethical culture may have shifted, but *Cyteen* still speaks to ques-tions we ask ourselves—not just as psychologists but as human beings.

But isn't that just what science fiction writers do? How is that different from creating a world in which FTL is possible?

It's different because the nature of the discipline is different—because psychology as a science is, far more than the hard sciences, subject to the prevailing zeitgeist, the mores of the time. It is a human science, a social science, and therefore much more embedded in its cultural context in terms of what can be perceived and understood as "knowledge" than are the phys-ical sciences—that very lack of "objectivity" is one of the chief complaints of "hard" scientists as regards the social sciences.

It is also therefore a discipline far more subject to moral or ethical constraints. Very few people, and almost no physicists, would argue that there is something immoral about a fictional scientist who works with FTL technology—or that an author is herself immoral to write about it. Yet in the social sciences, readers, even some with background in relevant fields, feel free to do just that.

But despite these constraints, these restrictions, Cherryh has succeeded—succeeded on two levels: succeeded in imagining a world in which psychology as a discipline has advanced as far as physics has—and done it in such a way that it is tenable to a psychologist, that it does make sense as a possibility. In *Cyteen*, Cherryh does more than encouraging her readers to imagine the impossible—she dares us to consider the unthinkable. At our current level of understanding, Ari Sr.'s actions would be both impossible scientifically and unthinkable ethically—but Cherryh creates a world in which they are not only acceptable but actually an ethical necessity.

Her subtlety is also a measure of her brilliance. The role of speculative fiction is to use the extreme cases as an invitation to readers to consider the possibilities inherent in our world and in the human spirit—and it is this that Cherryh does brilliantly. A lesser writer would bludgeon the reader with the point; it is a mark of her genius, a genius at least equal to her character's, that a careless interpretation of the novel might indeed take Ari Sr. as a mere psychopath. It is the reader's decision to join Cherryh and her Dr. Emory on their journey into the nature of humanity, or not; the choice, and its consequences, are theirs.

Like Ari Sr., then, Cherryh engages in a kind of sociogenesis—worldbuilding. Unlike Ari Sr., though, she accomplished her masterpiece without the support of a world in which it is possible. And that is a true work of genius.

To provide as much breathing space as possible for contributors, this piece started life during the planning stages of this project as a hefty interview. As articles rolled in and *The Cherryh Odyssey* filled with the ideas and concepts of others, I realized there was more than enough intellectual room left over for me to explore the odyssey I've been avidly following for nearly 30 years. While the long-planned interview took place, it serves here as one of half a dozen sources for my contribution.

One of the goals of these introductory statements prior to each article is to help frame the author's perspective and the textual format for readers who might be unfamiliar with purely academic traditions. In my case, I am both fiction writer and scholar. This MLA format article is intended to be literate yet readable at many levels. The references are intended to document sources, not to confuse—all material is designed to stand upon its own legs. If one is not concerned about the source of quoted materials, it should be possible to ignore the references and nevertheless receive the intended message.

THE LITERARY ODYSSEY
OF C.J. CHERRYH

Edward Carmien

Carolyn Janice Cherry, born 1942 in St. Louis, Missouri, became "C. J. Cherryh" in 1976, a slight alteration of name that had two functions: to obfuscate her gender, in a male-dominated field, and to provide for a unique moniker which to this day, nearly three decades of her literary odyssey later, makes C. J. Cherryh the only Cherryh there is.

In between those two dates Cherryh grew up in Missouri and later in Oklahoma, attended the University of Oklahoma (graduating with a Bachelor of Arts in Latin in 1964) and Johns Hopkins University in Maryland (Master of Arts in Classics, 1965), and became a high-school teacher in her home state. Early in her teaching career she studied computer science at Oklahoma University.

Cherryh's path to writing began in the adventure-oriented television shows of her youth. Disturbed when one favorite show went off the air, she started writing her own yarns. A self-taught fiction writer, Cherryh devoted herself to the study of narrative from a young age, building concepts and skills she would later put to use in her professional writing.

These and other details are available from many sources, as Cherryh's frequent convention visits and published interviews have provided hundreds if not thousands of opportunities for these and other biographical details to see print over the years. Her decision in 1976 to leave teaching was at the suggestion of Donald A. Wollheim of DAW Books, a key figure in Cherryh's literary development.

"I quit teaching at about the time I was working on *The Faded Sun*; Don told me 'quit the job' and gave me a three-book contract with no due date and no specifications. I figured since it amounted to more than a year's income as a teacher, I could take the risk, if I started in September," says Cherryh (Cherryh). Following on the heels of her success with her first novel, *Gate of Ivrel*, Cherryh's move to write full time led to the beginning of an extremely prolific literary career that has led to 60+ titles as of 2004.

Donald A. Wollheim's DAW Books began publishing science fiction and fantasy novels in 1972. First seen as a "pulp" publisher, Wollheim made a point of putting into print authors who were newcomers to the field. Previously, science fiction novelists made their way through the strong magazine market of the time (Gunn 3: xxii). Cherryh and other writers of the era fueled a dramatic rise in the number of science fiction / fantasy titles seeing print every year. This increase was accompanied by higher literary expectations. Cherryh is part of "what would later be called 'the New Wave,' which would attract a group of bright young writers more interested in literature" (Gunn, 3: xxv).

It is no accident that it was Cherryh's *Downbelow Station* that helped erase DAW's pulp reputation. The critical and popular success of that book was due in part to Cherryh's development as a prose stylist, something Donald A. Wollheim encouraged with his acceptance and publication of what Betsy Wollheim calls "magic cookie books," novels with little commercial potential but which possess great artistic merit—or at the very least, great artistic experimentation.

A true literary odyssey requires a hero of intellectual scale. As readers of Cherryh's fiction know, she is a woman of vast intellectual appetite. An avid student of the human condition, Cherryh has applied her keen eye to countless topics: languages, anthropology, animal husbandry, technology, the sciences, the martial arts, history, and this is but an overview. What she does not practice, she imagines; what she does not visit first hand, she devours second hand via television and books.

Add to this devouring hunger a spirit of optimism common in writers of fantastic literature and one begins to approximate Cherryh as a living and creative mind. Even the events of 9/11 have not brought her spirits low. Humanity still has a future, she asserts: this rough spot, too, shall pass. "The question isn't what outsiders do to us, rather what we do to ourselves in the name of security—that's the bigger danger" (Cherryh). Many of her novels present a sense of awareness of this issue. It is part and parcel of her intense scrutiny of and speculation about the human condition as it might be in space, in alien environments, under the influence of extraordinarily different technology than what we are familiar with today.

Space travel is one of Cherryh's many specific abiding interests. When asked about the current efforts to win the Ansari X Prize (ten million dollars for the first team to achieve certain spaceflight goals, such as flying to 100km altitude), Cherryh's optimism was expressed through a solid grasp of the physical challenges faced by the various teams attempting to win the prize. "Private enterprise may get into orbit and launch satellites, or even tourism, but doing the exploratory projects requires more than companies can do—unless the government follows the Greek model and gives them a tax rebate for doing it" (Cherryh).

Dick Rutan's SpaceShipOne project, as of this writing the closest to winning the Ansari X Prize, is a good case in point: it is not a "heavy lift" project (though one might conceivably be grown out of the technology Rutan's company, Scaled Composites, is developing) but rather a small, passenger-oriented space craft appropriate and useful for a quick visit to low orbit.

It may be many years before spaceflight is commercially viable for ordinary working folks, but Cherryh is certain it will eventually happen. And if America doesn't do it? "The Chinese . . . may well beat us, and then we'll run from behind" (Cherryh).

The Business of Writing

Cherryh is a successful, commercially viable writer. She is not, however, Stephen King. Writing and selling books is for many a workaday career—often a passion that serves as a second job, sometimes a living, and rarely a career that enriches (often via movie deals and tie-ins) beyond common understanding.

Cherryh could achieve such success, or at least provide for a greater chance of such success. "To have a breakout commercial success," she notes, "you have to hit it lucky, or write shorter sentences. I don't expect it" (Cherryh). The key signal here is a denial of, or more likely the absence of, an overriding commercial expectation about her craft. Much of science fiction and fantasy literature is highly commercial—pulp, in one manner of speaking, or hack work: product for the hungry popular culture.

This is one of the key charges against the genre, that it is "sub-literature" or in some way of a different nature than so-called mainstream literature, the kind without fantastic elements. That Cherryh has so consistently through her long career written prose that is thoughtful and at times experimental is a sign of her strong commitment to the literary aspect of her writing.

Donald A. Wollheim, by publishing Cherryh's "magic cookie" novels, gave voice to a serious prose stylist who influenced a generation of writers. Her use of language and representation of alien speech and thought was in her early work new and shocking. By presenting and then regularly using "alien" words in *Hunter of Worlds* (rather than presenting an alien idea, then assigning and using an English or close to English equivalent), Cherryh raised the bar, linguistically speaking, on an area of science fiction she did not invent but to which she has added considerably (Clute and Nichols 723-25). Digesting and understanding this prose is more difficult than it could have been, had she failed to give such speech artistic expression. Had she written more simply she would ultimately have communicated less to her readers, and the results would not have been nearly so fascinating (although such novels might have found a broader audience).

While she explored linguistics in *Hunter of Worlds* and other "magic cookie" novels, books Cherryh says are "pretty serious . . . they're idea heavy, and more allegorical than most of my writing," she has successfully carried forward many of the lessons she learned by the publication of these essentially non-commercial texts into later, more commercially successful novels (Cherryh). For example, today, Cherryh's more seasoned approach to speculative language is successful and thought-provoking in her Foreigner series. Concepts such as "man'chi" are fundamentally alien and not expressible using human terms. Readers are required to learn such key vocabulary terms, but their use immeasurably enriches the series.

Writers during the past several decades have in general become more adventurous with their use of language. Elizabeth A. Lynn, Jo Clayton, Iain M. Banks and many others write with an awareness of linguistic issues, a reflection of Cherryh's influence on science fiction and fantasy's approach to linguistics in general during the past several decades.

Any examination of Cherryh's work from a business perspective must take into account her publications in, by common definition, two genres—science fiction and fantasy. Many fans have felt over the years a fondness for one or the other but less frequently both of these types of Cherryh novel.

One explanation for this dichotomy of reception lies within Cherryh's fondness for realism and a consistent grounding of her work in the practical world. This statement may appear to be at odds when used about an author who writes about faster than light space travel, cloning, human programming, nanotechnology, and magic, but throughout her career Cherryh has insisted on getting the details right. Horses are not sports cars: one cannot ride them pell-mell through the leafy wood, then leap off at the end of a hard day's ride with a blithe expectation of doing so again the next day, and the next. The velocity, mass, and vector of spacecraft are real variables, no matter what speculative science provides the motive force, and these variables have real-world consequences that must be taken into account in order to maintain a sense of the "real" in Cherryh's works.

Perhaps it is the difficulty of nailing down to reality the vicissitudes of magic that makes her fantasy less palatable to those who favor Cherryh's science fiction. "Science fiction succeeds best for me," says Cherryh. "That's always been true. When I write fantasy, I tend to get into historical exactitudes, at least as far as the technology goes; perhaps some day fantasy realism will come into fashion . . . . " leading, possibly, to greater commercial success for her fantasy (Cherryh).

Cherryh's prose is less commercial than it might be, but commercial success is not a primary motivator for this literary author. Nevertheless, she is successful enough to have produced 60+ titles in less than 30 years. By any standard, she is a success, both as a writer and as an important voice in American literature. Commerce, of course, is the least important of the measures of such relevance. Of greater importance is her impact on her readers, an impact she accentuates with a busy schedule of science fiction and fantasy conventions, where she is seen and heard by thousands of fans every year.

Conventions, Fans, and Sundries

Early in her writing career, Cherryh devoted herself to the convention circuit. For readers not familiar with such conventions, some description is in order. Where Stein held forth in her salon in Paris to the literary lights of her era, writers of fantastic literature are called forth to serve as guests (and singularly, as Guests of Honor) at gatherings of fans of the genre.

Ranging in size from dozens, to hundreds, to even thousands of participants, these conventions are held throughout the United States and around the world. On almost every weekend of the year one or more conventions are being held, typically in hotels known for more ordinary conferences. Guest writers hold forth as panelists and speakers, sign autographs, and participate in various other activities. Naturally, books are sold at such events, too.

Not a salon gathering, exactly, yet the very same activities occur—deep thought about the direction of the genre, comparisons between authors and their works, and for working writers, a chance not only to speak with fans but to network with other writers and professionals in their field. Cherry would like to see such conventions regain what she sees as a vital place in the intellectual process that is science fiction:

> The field has also suffered from the decline of literary sf conventions in favor of bigger and more tracks of programming, which have done nothing to stimulate a flow of ideas, or give convention-goers something in common to talk about—like the fact that almost everyone had been to the same panel. Too many tracks, too much green ichor in the marketplace (well, call it icons of any sort) and not enough promotion from the publishers or the conventions. (Cherryh)

Cherryh commits an unusual amount of time to such salon-style activities, and she has done so since the very beginning of her writing career. There is not much direct commercial benefit to be had from such visits. In fact, when discussing her writing schedule, such visits are described as obstacles.

Cherryh spends time creating the lyrics to songs sung by fans at such gatherings. Filk songs, as they are called, are generally quite funny and sometimes poke good-natured fun at luminaries in the field. She once wrote a considerable amount of background information about the imaginary history and culture behind her "company wars" novels for a game of the same name. Her written advice to writers is extensive and thoughtful. What benefit does accrue from all of these activities?

"I'm never going to get rich," from such visits with fans, she says, "but I do enjoy their company and conversation. I find it stimulating" (Cherryh). Ultimately, what appear to be important to Cherryh are the human interactions she shares as a result of her work. Hers is not a literature of exclusion, written for an elite, but a popular literature—living and breathing work meant to be shared and enjoyed, in person when possible.

Writing the Good Stuff

One way of thinking about the history of science fiction is to divide it into two piles: the "good stuff," and the "other stuff." Generally this view is informed by an assessment of both quality and purpose—the "good stuff" is, well, good. Readable, engaging, high quality, imaginative and thoughtful are adjectives that go along with this definition. The good stuff is of course commercial to some degree—otherwise it wouldn't have seen print—but on a cost/benefit basis, it may or may not be an activity that leads one to a safe and secure retirement at the end of a working life.

The "other stuff" is typically not so good, by at least some measures. Hack work, trash, pulp, imitative, and dull are adjectives that go along with this definition. The "other stuff" is commercial by definition, product intended to sell quickly and end up in someone's pocket or to be returned, resold, or recycled.

Of course, part of appreciating science fiction and fantasy is appreciating the "other stuff" for what it is. If nothing else, reading it leads one to many fascinating revelations about popular culture, and what such works say about the culture that produces and supports such material. In short, it can't all be good—*if it were, how would we know the difference?*

When asked about trends in the field, Cherryh said:

> There are a number of writers who innovate, who attack the problems of human reaction to scientific advance, who talk about the human condition in a technological world, and who have the long view. These are the carriers of the torch. The ones who content themselves with a tiny bit of 'sense of wonder' are within the fold, but they're

the same sorts who were always writing the 'gave a mighty whack and green ichor flowed. . .' sort of yarn. Now, unfortunately, they're touted to the skies and given slick covers, while the real books languish in the niches and don't get much promotion. That's where sf conventions ought to come in—rather than spending their time and effort talking about the latest tv creation and trying to up their numbers . . . The torch is still burning, but it's been passed with far less publicity than it deserves (Cherryh).

Cherryh's devotion to the craft she practices is clear. Trends do not define her work, as one might expect of someone who transcends or at the very least pushes at the confines of the genres in which she writes. The New Wave, as a movement, does not exactly fit, as part of Gunn's definition includes such writers being "disposed to disregard, resent, or react against the kind of science fiction that had been published earlier" (Gunn 3: xxv). Cyberpunk, for example, came and went during the confines of her writing career to date. None of her work is representative of that energetic and enjoyable subset of science fiction.

Instead, all of her work is serious, in the way of what is usually called "mainstream" literature. It demands to be taken seriously. Understanding and enjoying it is work. As "good stuff" is in many if not all ways in the eye of the beholder, not every reader agrees that Cherryh's work is "good stuff." That, in a paradoxical sense, might be a good thing—*if everyone liked it, would it be as good?*

Literature

In other venues I've argued for a redefinition of not only science fiction and fantasy literature but also detective, horror, romance, and thriller fiction from being "genre" (or more pejoratively from the literary camp "sub-literature") to being various sorts of Romantic Literature, in the tradition of Keats and Byron and Shelley. While this article is not the proper venue to fully present this idea, the concept is one supported by the ideas of James Gunn and others—including C.J. Cherryh: "Personally, I view genre as 'the old stuff' and mainstream as an antiromantic bastard child that came along when 20th century philosophy could no longer maintain optimism in a machine age" (Cherryh).

Gunn's definition of science fiction as the "literature of change" is useful here, and he notes, as does Cherryh, that the ancients wrote science fiction, tales about traveling to the moon, as in Lucian of Samosata's "A True Story" (Gunn 1: 3). Here the definition of science fiction is clearly not one rooted in the American movement of the past century. Definitions, of which there are many, rooted in that tradition cannot sensibly be applied here.

It is not surprising that Cherryh links herself not only with the ongoing American science fiction tradition but also to Romantic Literature. It is a surprise that relatively few mainstream scholars do so, making Burton Raffel's "C.J. Cherryh's Fiction" significant in that it discusses the literary qualities of Cherryh's prose using terms and methods familiar to mainstream critics and readers.

In an age where the effects of industrialization are so rooted in our past it is hard to recognize them without conscious effort, and where developments in electronic communication have spawned new opportunities and problems for society, a literature that on the one hand removes us from the cares of our mechanical world and thereby reminds us of what, in an idealized sense, came before, is valuable. In this sense, fantasy is "a kind of strange modern stepchild of SF . . . optimistic, but more internal than SF, more a voyage of the spirit" (Cherryh).

Equally necessary, in our machine and electronic age, is a literature that discusses hope amidst all the change we experience. The law of unintended consequences touches us all: internal combustion engines bring us unbridled freedom of movement, at a cost unknowable 100 years past, a cost of pollution, illness, and tens of thousands of deaths a year due to accidents. On an even more basic level, as Jared Diamond notes, just living in large groups creates unintended biological consequences of contagion and immunity that historically have brought massive change around the world (195-214). Our philosophy must reconcile such stresses, Cherryh says, noting that "SF has caught particular flak because it's optimistic and about machines, which would seem to some philosophers to be insane" (Cherryh).

Women Characters

Thirty years ago, science fiction and fantasy was dominated, numerically at least, by male writers. Women were the apparent exception—"apparent," given James Tiptree/Alice Sheldon, and a number of authors who used initials as first names on their books. In such an environment of apparent exclusion from the market, issues of gender and character are bound to arise, as they should.

Into this environment stepped C.J. Cherryh and *Gate of Ivrel*. Sold with an apparently stereotypical cover denoting a sword-wielding woman, the book presented Morgaine, a hard-hearted woman on an epic quest to close Gates that allowed travel between worlds. She is the hero, and a real bastard to boot.

Absent from the story are arguments about woman's place in society. Morgaine, one discovers over several novels, was raised in a society that treated men and women equally. Though she often visits feudal, low-technology cultures that treat women as they were treated historically in western Europe, Cherryh makes little effort to cast a critical eye on the arrangement.

Readers of Marion Zimmer Bradley's work of the 1970's find little of the gender politics of those novels in Cherryh's work until her Chanur novels of the 1980's. In these novels, five star-faring races live uncomfortably but successfully in a trading compact. The newest race to see the stars is a lion-like feline race: culturally feudal, in some respects, they crew their merchant vessels with relatives who represent a single family or clan on their home planet.

What makes this remarkable is that the feline crew who takes in this sole human character, a male, is entirely female. Their men are not suitable for space travel, being prone to the usual male failings of unpredictable violence and low intelligence. The male human suffers throughout the Chanur novels from the attitudes his fellow travelers share about men. He does eventually emancipate himself to some degree, and in the later novels so does a feline male, these events constituting some of the only text Cherryh intentionally devotes to the question of gender politics. It is here Cherryh acknowledges addressing the question of unequal treatment due to gender: "My only comment on the battle of the sexes is the discrimination against the young fellow in the Chanur novels" (Cherryh). By addressing the issue using a reverse example, Cherryh deliberately focuses on the issue itself rather than tying the question to contemporary discussions of the topic.

Cherryh's optimism about the future of our human society extends into this realm as well. "I have a view of a future in which what you do matters, not where, how, or what you were born" (Cherryh). Her reaction to those who make polemical statements about such issues is unequivocal: "I particularly detest people getting so caught up in their cause that they deal as much hurt as the people whose behavior they oppose. I was a teacher. I can't put down any of the kids, gender be hanged" (Cherryh).

Science fiction is often thought of as being a literature of ideas. Experimentation, extrapolation, and speculation are all activities that are welcomed in the field. Social commentary is common: Wells' *The Time Machine* comments about war in a way that seems prescient to us today, while Le Guin, Russ, Tepper, and many others discuss gender in challenging and thoughtful ways.

Cherryh does not directly discuss gender issues. For her, the story is the thing, and the characters who populate her stories are relentlessly well-placed, given the cultural context from which they spring. Morgaine pursues her quest with monomaniacal focus and drive. Her gender is less important than her essential character, and how she relates to other characters as her story unfolds over several novels. Time and time again, Cherryh focuses upon *story* rather than *politics*, a fascinating choice, given that her novels are famously detailed, often taking place in highly charged political environments, as does her new novel *Forge of Heaven*. "Look not at these characters' gender, but at these characters' actions toward other genders for my personal statement on gender politics," she says (Cherryh).

In short, Cherryh's focus is more upon the literary questions of character, character motivation, plot, and narration than on an experiment, an extrapolation, or a speculation about a social issue. This is not to say that science fiction novels that do focus on such issues aren't themselves worthy, readable, or of quality. Nor do I suggest that Cherryh's work can't be mined for statements about social issues—the material is there, but it is not the focus of her intent as a storyteller. Rather, Cherryh's novels are vehicles for engaging stories, unsurprising if one recalls what prompted her to begin writing at the age of ten: the sudden absence of a beloved adventure serial from television.

Journeys

The journey Cherryh began as a (very young) writer in 1952 has been echoed throughout her life by many real-life journeys. Cherryh came close once to Odysseus's homeward journey on a "ramshackle car ferry lucky to make it to port in Olympia" (Cherryh). She passed Ithaca, and she slept on deck, warmed both by the exhaust and the thought of avoiding cabin mates of dubious character.

This sea journey was related to Cherryh's tracing, in reverse, of a march by Caesar. This and other journeys clearly play a role in sustaining and informing her literary imagination. Though the sea journey was on a vessel of questionable quality, she "wouldn't have missed it for the world—including the sea serpent, when we ran into the dredge in the dark; you can see where the old folk got their yarns" (Cherryh).

These journeys expose Cherryh's keen eye and tremendous intellect to the world; this engages a process of assessment of formal knowledge in comparison to the real thing. The ultimate result is food for her imagination. Is it possible her preference for telling stories using fantastic elements makes it more necessary for her to ground her work in the vivid cloth of the real? Or are these journeys, and the observations that spring from them, an ineluctable element of her character, an aspect of Cherryh that would exist no matter what her chosen profession?

Cherryh notes that "I'd always be the one tourist to volunteer to ride the camel (elephant, fill in the blank) . . . but what I do for a living makes it morally essential to try anything that won't foreseeably be fatal, innately injurious to self or other living things, or downright stupid." Not all experiences have been hers to experience—yet. She hasn't tried downhill skiing, but "ice skating has turned out wonderfully" (Cherryh).

Her wandering character provides a strong basis for the verisimilitude of her writing, and for that readers of Cherryh's work should be thankful.

Classical or Romantic?

This divide is one way of examining the differing literary philosophies of our European cultural heritage. The classical, springing from ideas such as Aristotle's dramatic unities (from *The Poetics*) and a subsequent desire to emulate such classic ideals, contrasts usefully with the romantic urge of freedom of expression, of giving life to passion in whatever artistic way seems best to the artist.

These summaries are far from complete, but they give an idea of the philosophical split. Using them as lenses through which to view Cherryh's work provides an opportunity to examine the fundamental underpinnings of her intellect.

Lynn F. Williams, in her 1986 article "Women and Power in C. J. Cherryh's Novels" suggests Cherryh writes about worlds in which authoritarian governments are common, in which caste systems are prevalent, and that her powerful women characters are concerned with the "creative preservation of society" (85, 85, 91). This classical tendency would appear to contrast with Cherryh's avowal that the root of her storytelling lies in the romantic realm. Unlike much science fiction in which toppling authority (or at least rebelling against it) is the underlying theme, such as in much of William Gibson and Steven Brust, Cherryh's work does indeed emphasize maintenance of the continuity of authority. But does this represent a classical tendency?

When presented with this idea, Cherryh said:

> A space station is necessarily not a democracy, for some purposes: safety requires rules. I don't do too many successful dictatorships; even Cyteen is an elected democracy, in spite of the autocratic control in the labs, and the Alliance [Downbelow Station—ed.] is a democracy, a council of captains. But you can't run a ship by vote. (Cherryh)

Cherryh here returns to the practical, to the real. While Williams has a point, in that Cherryh does consistently use such cultural environments as settings in much of her work, time has outstripped Williams' statement about it being only powerful women characters that are concerned with the creative preservation of society. Bren Cameron of the Foreigner series is male, and his character is devoted to the preservation of the current system of authority (which in turn keeps a human colony on an alien planet safe, among many other benefits).

It could be argued that Bren himself is a feminized character, however. He wears his hair long, as is the custom among the aliens he lives with (a unique human in this regard), and ultimately his love interest is an alien woman with many masculine traits, at least when measured by human standards—she is taller and stronger than Bren, is trained in the martial and military arts, and possesses an icy demeanor commonly attributed to men with stunted emotional lives (although again, one must recall what is alien is not human). These potential counter-arguments aside, Bren remains male, and in the end is not the only character from Cherryh's novels that acts to preserve the status quo.

In fact, for Cherryh, the real question is one of environment:

> I view physical environment as more apt to produce certain specific kinds of cultures, certain sizes of territory as apt to produce more conformity than others. I think of it more as a problem in—well, anthropology is a kind of a misnomer, but at least land and environment, climate and relation to other territories is something I spend a lot more time on than I do on who is what gender . . . . (Cherryh).

What if one removes the question of gender from the equation? Are we left with an assessment of Cherryh's imaginary cultures as being largely classical in construction? Yes. Cherryh's consistent use of caste systems (that go largely unchallenged or changed in the course of her novels—any change is gradual and necessary for the continuation of the system) is incontrovertible, and points clearly to what can be called a classical tendency in her creative expression.

Cherryh sees not an adherence to a philosophical stance or view, but opportunity. "I write about caste systems because there are so many of them, of one sort or another, and because certain kinds of conflicts arise most naturally in caste systems . . . [such as that of] the Mri" (Cherryh). Again, she finds fertile ground in which to plant conflict out of which to spin tales of resolution. While she does not commonly tell the tale of authority vanquished, or even the tale of authority criminally suborned, the environments she constructs are rigorously real, intensively informed by her highly educated observations of the human societies worldwide and down through history.

Whether one accepts Cherryh's claim of romantic tendencies or whether one sees Cherryh as essentially classical in nature is, in the end, not important. Understanding the dramatic consequences of her choice of setting, of what's called in the business "world building," is more relevant to appreciating where Cherryh has been during these past three decades. Where will she travel next?

What's Ahead?

"I haven't done anything on dinosaurs yet—one of my passions; and I haven't done any historical [novels] yet—I bog down packing in historical detail; so I suppose I'll just get along as always, absorbing everything that interests me and coughing it up as SF stories" (Cherryh). How long might it take for Cherryh to fulfill one or more of these interests? Her current project list is daunting, leaving little time for expression of these ideas. In short: fans, don't hold your breath.

Historically, Cherryh has rarely ventured outside of traditional text as a means of expression. *Gate of Ivrel* was made, in part, into a graphic novel. She and business partner Jane Fancher toy with the possibility of finishing that project for online distribution—but there are always book projects waiting for attention. Once a game manufacturer created a board game out of the strategic situation presented in her company war novels, and Cherryh contributed background material for the rules set. Of other ventures, such as cinematic versions of any of her work, there is not a word.

The internet might serve as a venue for new "magic cookie" fiction, but "alas, the age of the magic cookie book is pretty well past, unless I write something strictly for the internet—which I've thought of doing, but again, never have the time for" (Cherryh).

One thing is certain: barring unforeseen circumstances, this prolific author, who publishes better than two books a year on average, will continue to contribute to the world of fiction for some time to come.

Cherryh's Odyssey

Like Odysseus, who traveled home from the Trojan war in a seemingly endless journey, finding adventure (and considerable romance) along the way, Cherryh's literary life has and continues to be an often difficult but ultimately rewarding trip for her readers.

Just as Odysseus and his crew braved many dangers and sailed many interesting seas, Cherryh has taken her readers into dangerous territories of the mind, something the best science fiction can do, as well as into perilous places of the spirit, as does the best fantasy. At times, she does both.

Like any successful author, Cherryh has both fans and detractors. Her fans devour her books the minute they are available, and many gather in online communities to sip virtual (but safe?) tea and to discuss the details of books old and new in the Cherryh firmament. Detractors note the difficulty inherent in comprehending Cherryh's use of language. She doesn't water down her text or write in any way to a language-impaired audience. Her use of an intense third-person perspective also draws fire from some, as does Cherryh's focus upon interior crisis and resolution, to the detriment, it is sometimes said, of the external elements of her adventure narratives.

All of these views are signs of Cherryh's competence as a writer and her mastery of prose fiction. That she has an adoring fan base signals she can successfully tell compelling stories, stories that incorporate various kinds of the fantastic. That readers more used to a different kind of prose in their science fiction and fantasy texts find Cherryh hard to digest is a sign, paradoxically, of the literary qualities her prose possesses.

Too much movement in one direction or the other would not benefit Cherryh's work, though indeed some of her most recent work shows signs she is leavening the intensely internal narrative style of the early Foreigner novels of the mid 1990's, leaving her more recent work lighter, airier, and more effective than ever. *Forge of Heaven* and the most recent Foreigner novels are easier reads than their predecessors, showing that Cherryh, like any artist, recursively examines her art and evolves as a result.

This odyssey is far from over, and I suggest to readers who have yet to do so: sign on board for the journey forward into the unknown. There is plenty of reading on the shelf for those who need to catch up, and plenty more waiting on unknown shores, somewhere ahead, somewhere beyond this day.

WORKS CITED

Cherryh, C.J. Personal interview. 25 May 2004.

Clute, John and Peter Nicholls. *The Encyclopedia of Science Fiction*. New York, St. Martin's Griffin, 1995.

Diamond, Jared. *Guns, Germs, and Steel*. New York, W. W. Norton & Company, 1999.

Gunn, James. *The Road to Science Fiction*. 6 vols. Lanham, MD, Scarecrow Press, 2003.

Williams, Lynn F. "Women and Power in C. J. Cherryh's Novels" *Extrapolation* Vol. 27 No. 2 (1986): 85-92.

Of the many goals of this text the most specific was for it to include what you are about to read—or at least leaf past, as it is a reference work—a selected bibliography of works by and about C.J. Cherryh. As editor it was my feeling that the utility of *The Cherryh Odyssey* would be less than it should be without such a resource. Stan Szalewicz is a colleague here at Rider University. After advertising my editorial desire for such a bibliography far and wide and receiving no offers, Stan stepped forward to assist.

He has done an admirable job, and increased my already strong respect for my colleagues who are members of our library faculty. There is no obvious story here, no well-supported statement about Cherryh's use of imagery, no breakdown of a major character's behavioral elements.

Look deeper to find the story, a story represented by sundry publications and publishers, authors and editors, a story that spans decades and shows every sign of continuing on into the future. The story is one of impact and meaning, influence and relevance. Stan has looked high and low, near and far, and collected together nearly all of what is relevant to this subject. If not read, then remember this tool, this instrument of research, and put it to good use.

SELECTED BIBLIOGRAPHY OF C. J. CHERRYH

compiled by Stan Szalewicz

This bibliography is selective rather than comprehensive. It features resources one is likely to find in a typical public and/or academic library. I have deliberately included many similar general science fiction and fantasy reference resources because it is common for any one library to possess only a portion of these works. More importantly, while most general reference guides within a discipline duplicate information, the scope, accuracy, and completeness of that information can differ significantly from one source to another. With so many titles to choose from, researchers should be able to find at least a handful of reliable resources in any library.

Because science fiction and fantasy are a subset genre of popular fiction, they are central to the core collection of the typical public library. Therefore, I focused my initial search on public libraries of various sizes. During four months of investigation, I also visited academic libraries at teaching and research universities alike, both in person and via the Internet. Onsite visits enabled me to examine pertinent electronic resources available only within the institution. Naturally, I also explored—albeit rudimentarily—the staggering number of sites dedicated to science fiction and fantasy on the World Wide Web.

This bibliography comprises five sections: 1) General Resources, 2) Internet Resources, 3) Novels, Novellas, and Short Stories, 4) Other Writings by Cherryh, and 5) Reviews. The citations herein are as complete as I could make them without having the opportunity to examine personally all works cited. I suggest that researchers use this bibliography as a means to the means, not a means to an end. At the very least, this is a launching point from which to conduct research about C. J. Cherryh.

GENERAL BIBLIOGRAPHIC RESOURCES,

INTERVIEWS, ESSAYS, AND CRITICISM

Abbey, Lynn. "C. J. Cherryh." *Bucconeer* 2 (Sept. 1997): 22-23.

Adams, John. "Linkages: Science Fiction and Science Fantasy." *School Library Journal* 26 (May 1980): 23-28.

Antièeviæ, Neven. "C. J. Cherryh, najviši sopran space opere." Delo 27:3 (Mar. 1981): 91-102.

Ashley, Mike, and William G. Contento. "Cherryh, C. J." *The Supernatural Index: A Listing of Fantasy, Supernatural, Occult, Weird, and Horror Anthologies.* Bibliographies and Indexes in Science Fiction, Fantasy, and Horror. 5. Westport, CT: Greenwood Press, 1995. 166.

Bacon-Smith, Camille. "Military Command in Women's Science Fiction: C. J. Cherryh's Signy Mallory." *The Swan: Online Newsmagazine for Discussion of Fantastic Fiction* 3 (2002). 17 May 2004 <www.dm.net/~theswan/baconsmith.html>

—. *Science Fiction Culture.* Feminist Cultural Studies, the Media, and Political Culture [Series]. Philadelphia: Univ. of Pennsylvania Press, 2000. 100+.

Bailey, K. V. "Alien Gifties: The Reflective Perspectives." *Foundation* 49 (Summer 1990): 23-34.

Bainbridge, William Sims. "Women in Science Fiction." *Dimensions of Science Fiction*. Cambridge, MA: Harvard University Press, 1986. 172-96.

Balter, Gerri. "Interview with C. J. Cherryh." *Rune* 61 (Fall 1980): 5-10.

Barron, Neil, ed. *What Do I Read Next?: A Reader's Guide to Current Genre Fiction*. New York: Gale, 1995. 252, 385.

—. *What Fantastic Fiction Do I Read Next?: A Reader's Guide to Recent Fantasy, Horror and Science Fiction*. Detroit: Gale, 1998. 5+.

Bartholomew, Barbara. "C. J. Cherryh: A Corrupter of Minds." *Lan's Lantern* 10 (June 1980): 34-36.

Beal, Rebecca S. "C. J. Cherryh's Arthurian Humanism." *Popular Arthurian Traditions*. Ed. Sally K. Slocum. Bowling Green, OH: Popular Press, 1992. 56-67.

Bell, M. S. "Sheer Joy of Storytelling: An Interview with C. J. Cherryh." *Leading Edge* 8 (Fall 1984): 11-23.

Berry, John D. "Cherryh's Complex Cultures." *Science Fiction Commentary* 62 (June 1981): 66-67.

Bleiler, Richard, ed. *Science Fiction Writers: Critical Studies of the Major Authors from the Early Nineteenth Century to the Present Day*. 2nd ed. New York: C. Scribner's Sons, 1999.

Bonner, Frances. "From the Female Man to the Virtual Girl: Whatever Happened to Feminist SF?" *Hecate* 22:1 (1996): 104-19.

Brizzi, Mary T. "C. J. Cherryh and Tomorrow's New Sex Roles." *The Feminine Eye: Science Fiction and the Women Who Write It.* Ed. Tom Staicar. Recognitions [Series]. New York: F. Ungar, 1982. 32-47.

Brown, Rachel Manija. *Elven Blades and Zero-G Ki: The Evolution of Marital Arts in SF and Fantasy.* 9 Sept. 2002. 17 May 2004 <www.strangehorizons.com/2002/20020902/martial_arts.shtml>.

—. *The Golden Age of Fantasy Is Twelve: SF and the Young Adult Novel.* 8 July 2002. 17 May 2004 <www.strangehorizons.com/2002/20020708/twelve.shtml>.

Brunsdale, Mitzi M. "C. J. Cherryh: Carolyn Janice Cherry, 1942." *Beacham's Popular Fiction in America.* Ed. Walton Beacham and Suzanne Niemeyer. Vol. 1. Washington, DC: Beacham Publishing/Research Publishing, 1986. 258-66. 4 vols.

Buker, Derek M. *The Science Fiction and Fantasy Readers' Advisory: The Librarian's Guide to Cyborgs, Aliens, and Sorcerers.* Chicago: American Library Association, 2002. 4+.

Burgess, Michael, and Lisa R. Bartle. *Reference Guide to Science Fiction, Fantasy, and Horror.* 2nd ed. Reference Sources in the Humanities Series. Westport, CT: Libraries Unlimited, 2002.

Burnick, Gale. "An Interview with C. J. Cherryh." *Science Fiction Review* 29 (Nov. 1978): 14-18.

Carmien, Edward, ed. *The Cherryh Odyssey.* Holicong, PA: Wildside Press, 2004.

Chernaik, Laura. "Spatial Displacements: Transnationalism and the New Social Movements." *Gender Place & Culture: A Journal of Feminist Geography* 3:3 (Sept. 1996): 251-75.

"C. J. Cherryh: Adjusting the Language." *Locus* 30:1 (Jan. 1993): 5, 66.

"C. J. Cherryh: Asking the Hard Questions." *Locus* 23:4 (Oct. 1989): 7, 64.

"C. J. Cherryh." *Authors & Artists for Young Adults*. Ed. Thomas McMahon. Vol. 24. Detroit: Gale, 1998. 54 vols. to date.

"C. J. Cherryh." *Contemporary Literary Criticism*. Ed. Daniel G. Marowski, Roger Matuz, and Jane E. Neidhardt. Vol. 35. Detroit: Gale, 1985. 102-15. 183 vols. to date.

"C. J. Cherryh Interview." SFFWorld.com (Jan. 2000). 17 May 2004 <http://www.sffworld.com/authos/c/cherryh_cj/inter-views/20001.html>.

"C. J. Cherryh: Lightning Strikes." *Locus* 36:1 (Jan. 1996): 5, 72.

"C. J. Cherryh." *The Sound of Wonder: Interviews from The Science Fiction Radio Show*. Ed. Daryl Lane, William Vernon, and David Carson. Vol. 1. Phoenix: Oryx Press, 1985. 22-51. 2 vols.

"C. J. Cherryh (Update)." *Beacham's Popular Fiction 1991 Update*. Ed. Walton Beacham, et al. Washington, DC: Beacham, 1991. 225-32.

"Cherryh, C. J." *Science Fiction and Fantasy Book Review Index, 1980-1984*. Ed. H. W. Hall. Detroit: Gale Research, 1985. 51-52.

"C. J. Cherryh." *Science Fiction Book Review Index, 1974-1979*. Ed. H. W. Hall. Detroit: Gale Research, 1981. 59-60.

"Cherryh, C. J." *The Science Fiction Source Book*. Ed. David Wingrove. New York: Van Nostrand Reinhold, 1984. 121.

"Cherryh, C. J." *Something about the Author: Facts and Pictures about Authors and Illustrators of Books for Young People*. Ed. Alan Hedblad. Vol. 93. Detroit: Gale, 1997. 38-42. 146 vols. to date.

"Cherryh, C. J." *Who's Who of American Women, 1999-2000.* 21st ed. New Providence, NJ: Marquis Who's Who, 1998. 174.

"Cherryh, Willis, Effinger, Resnick Win Hugo Awards." *Locus* 23 (Oct. 1989): 1, 36-42, 60-62.

Clute, John. "Cherryh, C. J." *The Encyclopedia of Fantasy.* Ed. John Clute and John Grant. New York: St. Martin's Press, 1997. 180.

—. "Cherryh, C. J." *The Encyclopedia of Science Fiction.* Ed. John Clute, Peter Nicholls, and Brian Stableford. New York: St. Martin's Griffin, 1995. 180-81.

—. "C. J. Cherryh." *Science Fiction: The Illustrated Encyclopedia.* 1st American ed. London: Dorling Kindersley, 1995. 187.

Colby, Vineta, ed. *World Authors, 1985-1990.* Wilson Authors Series. New York: H. W. Wilson, 1995. 141-43.

Cottrill, Tim, Martin H. Greenburg, and Charles G. Waugh. *Science Fiction and Fantasy Series and Sequels: A Bibliograpy.* Vol. 1: Books. Garland Reference Library of the Humanities. 611. New York: Garland, 1986. 47.

Creasey, Ian. *Travel by Jargon.* 19 May 2003. 17 May 2004 <www.strangehorizons.com/2003/20030519/jargon.shtml>.

del Rey, Lester. *The World of Science Fiction, 1926-1976: The History of a Subculture.* New York: Garland, 1980. 282+.

Donawerth, Jane. *Frankenstein's Daughters: Women Writing Science Fiction.* 1st ed. Syracuse: Syracuse Univ. Press, 1997. 18+.

—. "Utopian Science: Contemporary Feminist Science Theory and Science Fiction by Women." *NWSA Journal* 2:4 (Autumn 1990): 535-557.

Dunn, Thomas P. "Cherryh, C. J." *Twentieth-Century Science-Fiction Writers*. 3rd ed. Ed. Noelle Watson and Paul E. Schellinger. Twentieth-Century Writers Series. Chicago: St. James Press, 1991. 135-36.

Eagen, Tim. *C. J. Cherryh: The Outcast and the Uncertain Mind*. Sept. 1997. 17 May 2004
<www.stmoroky.com/reviews/authors/cherryh.htm>.

Eisenhour, Susan J. "A Subversive in Hyperspace: C. J. Cherryh's Feminist Transformation of Space Opera." M.A. thesis. Eastern Illinois Univ., 1996.

Falc, Emilie Oline. "An Analysis and Critique of the Vernacular Discourse in Selected Feminist Science Fiction Novels (Octavia Butler, C. J. Cherryh, Vonda McIntyre, Anne McCaffrey, Elizabeth Ann Scarborough)." Diss. Ohio Univ., 1997.

Fancher, Jane. "So, Who Is This CJC and Why Is She GoH [i.e., Guest of Honor] of Bucconeer?" *Bucconeer* 4 (June 1998): 27-28, 31.

Ferrell, Keith, and Dugald Stermer. "How to Build an Alien." *Omni* 15:1 (Oct. 1992): 50-55.

Fogelberg, Heidi. "Gender, Power and Identity in the Chanur Series." B.A. thesis, Arizona State Univ., 1988.

"Fragen on C. J. Cherryh." *Science Fiction Times: Magazin für Science Fiction* 25:6 (June 1983): 5-8.

Gannon, Charles. "*Downbelow Station*." *Magill's Guide to Science Fiction and Fantasy Literature*. Ed. T. A. Shippey and A. J. Sobczak. Vol. 1. Pasadena: Salem Press, 1996. 243-45. 4 vols.

Genefort, Laurent. *Architecture du livre-univers dans la science-fiction à travers cinq œuvres: Noô de Stefan Wul, Dune de Frank Herbert,*

La compagnie des glaces de G.-J. Arnaud, Helliconia de Brian Aldiss, et Hypérion de Dan Simmons. Diss. Université de Nice-Sophia Antipolis, 1997. Villeneuve d'Ascq, France: Presses universitaires du Septentrion, [2001]. 11+.

Gould, Karen J. "Cherryh, C. J." *Twentieth-Century Young Adult Writers.* 1ˢᵗ ed. Ed. Laura Standley Berger. Detroit: St. James Press, 1994. 113-15.

Grothey, Mina Jane. "Cherryh, C. J." *Reader's Guide to Twentieth-Century Science Fiction.* Comp. and ed. Marilyn P. Fletcher, ed. James L. Thorson. Chicago: American Library Association, 1989. 139-43.

Hall, Hal W., comp. *Science Fiction and Fantasy Research Database* (June 2000-). College Station, TX: Cushing Library, Texas A&M Univ. 17 May 2004 <www.library.tamu.edu/cushing/sffrd>.

Harvey, Jessica Georgina. "Are We Not Men Too? Women and the Sex-Gender Role Reversal Motif in Science Fiction." M.A. thesis. Acadia Univ., 1993.

Hayles, N. Katherine. "The Life Cycle of Cyborgs: Writing the Posthuman." *A Question of Identity: Women, Science, and Literature.* Ed. Marina Benjamin. New Brunswick, NJ: Rutgers Univ. Press, 1993.

—. "The Life Cycle of Cyborgs: Writing the Posthuman." *The Cyborg Handbook.* Ed. Chris Hables Gray. New York: Routledge, 1995.

Heidkamp, Bernie. "Responses to the Alien Mother in Post-Maternal Cultures: C. J. Cherryh and Orson Scott Card." *Science-Fiction Studies* 23:3 (Nov. 1996): 339-54.

Herald, Diana Tixier. *Fluent in Fantasy: A Guide to Reading Interests.* Genreflecting Advisory Series. Englewood, CO: Libraries Unlimited, 1999. 31+.

Herald, Diana Tixier, and Bonnie Kunzel. *Strictly Science Fiction: A Guide to Reading Interests*. Genreflecting Advisory Series. Englewood, CO: Libraries Unlimited, 2002. 4+.

Hopper, Jeannette M. "Sexist Stereotypes and Archetypes: What To Do with Them/What the Writing Woman Can Hope for." *How to Write Tales of Horror, Fantasy & Science Fiction*. Ed. J. N. Williamson. Cincinnati: Writer's Digest Books, 1987. 112-20.

Howlett-West, Stephanie. "Hooked on Cherryh: On the Trail of the High-Priestess of Sci-Fi." *Biblio* 2:10 (1997): 52-54.

"Hugo Award Winners." *Science Fiction Chronicle* 11:1 (Oct. 1989): 5.

Husband, Janet G., and Jonathan F. Husband. *Sequels: An Annotated Guide to Novels in Series*. 3rd ed. Chicago: American Library Association, 1997. 78-80.

Hyde, Paul Nolan. "Dances with Dusei: A Personal Response to C. J. Cherryh's *The Faded Sun*." *Mythlore* 18:2 (Spring 1992): 45-53.

"Interview: C. J. Cherryh." *American Fantasy* (Winter 1988): n. pag.

Jaffery, Sheldon. *Future and Fantastic Worlds: A Bibliographic Retrospective of DAW Books (1972-1987)*. Starmont Reference Guide. 4. Mercer Island, WA: Starmont House, 1987. 66+.

Jakubowski, Maxim, and Malcolm Edwards. *The Science Fiction Book of Lists: A Totally Biased and Delightfully Irreverent Reference Guide to 100 Years of Science Fiction and Fantasy*. New York: Berkley Books, 1983. 8+.

James, Edward, and Farah Mendlesohn, eds. *The Cambridge Companion to Science Fiction*. Cambridge Companions to Literature. Cambridge: Cambridge Univ. Press, 2003. 66+.

Jones, Gwyneth. "Consider Her Ways: The Fiction of C. J. Cherryh." *Deconstructing the Starships: Science, Fiction and Reality.* Liverpool Science Fiction Texts and Studies. 16. Liverpool: Liverpool Univ. Press, 1999.

Jones, Neil. "Cherryh, C(arolyn) J(anice)." *St. James Guide to Fantasy Writers.* 1ˢᵗ ed. Ed. David Pringle. St. James Guide to Writers Series. New York: St. James Press, 1996. 108-10.

—. "C. J. Cherryh: An Annotated Bibliography." *Interzone 55* (Jan. 1992): 47-49.

Keller, Ken. "Checking in with C. J. Cherryh." *Shayol: Science Fiction Fantasy 5* (Winter 1982): 36-48.

Kelso, Sylvia. "Tales of Earth: Terraforming in Recent Women's SF." *Foundation 78* (Spring 2000): 34-43.

Kennaway, Richard, comp. *Some Internet Resources Relating to Constructed Languages.* 26 May 2004 [sic]. 17 May 2004 <www2.cmp.uea.ac.uk/~jrk/conlang.html>. Path: Particular Constructed Languages; H[ani]; and, K[iffish].

Kennedy, Samuel H. "Aspects of Linguistics and Communication in Selected Works of C. J. Cherryh." M.A. thesis. Texas Tech Univ., 1990.

King, Betty. *Women of the Future: The Female Main Character in Science Fiction.* Metuchen, NJ: Scarecrow Press, 1984. 188+.

Kunzel, Bonnie. *First Contact: A Reader's Selection of Science Fiction and Fantasy.* Lanham, MD: Scarecrow Press, 2001. 1+.

Lee, Tony. "Conflict and Culture under Foreign Stars." *Strange Adventures* 41 (1992). Rev. and published in *The Zone* 1 (Summer 1994): 21-23.

Lev, Peter. "Whose Future?: *Star Wars, Alien*, and *Blade Runner*." *Literature Film Quarterly* 26:1 (1998): 30-37.

Levy, Michael M. "The Year in Science Fiction." *What Do I Read Next?: A Reader's Guide to Current Genre Fiction*. Neil Barron, et al. New York: Gale, 1995. 365-72.

Levy, Michael M., and Brian Stableford. "The New Wave, Cyberpunk, and Beyond: 1963-1994." *Anatomy of Wonder 4: A Critical Guide to Science Fiction*. Ed. Neil Barron. New Providence, NJ: R. R. Bowker, 1995. 241-42.

L'Hoest, Christian. *Littérature de science-fiction et bibliothèques publiques*. Liège: Editions du C.L.P.C.F., 1988. 64+.

Liebermann, Paula. "*Tripoint*: A Rebuttal." *New York Review of Science Fiction* 10: 2 (Oct. 1997): 18-22.

Mahlow, Rene. "Ein Gesprach mit Caroline Janice Cherryh." *Das Science Fiction Jahr*. Ed. Wolfgang Jeschke. München: W. Heyne, 1987. 13-57.

Marchesani, Joseph J. "*Cyteen*." *Magill's Guide to Science Fiction and Fantasy Literature*. Ed. T. A. Shippey and A. J. Sobczak. Vol. 1. Pasadena: Salem Press, 1996. 186-87. 4 vols.

Markowitz, John. "SFC Interview: C. J. Cherryh." *Science Fiction Chronicle* 19 (July-Aug. 1998): 6, 37-39.

McGuire, Patrick L. "Cherryh, C. J." *Twentieth-Century Science Fiction Writers*. 2nd ed. Ed. Curtis C. Smith. Twentieth-Century Writers Series. Chicago: St. James Press, 1986. 133-35.

—. "Water into Wine: The Novels of C. J. Cherryh." *Starship* 16:2 (Spring 1979): 47-49.

Meher, Anita. "Bi-Fi." *Sciences* 37 (May-June 1997): 8.

Miller, Ron, illus. *Firebrands: The Heroines of Science Fiction and Fantasy.* Text by Pamela Sargent. New York: Thunder's Mouth Press, 1998. 50+.

Monk, Patricia. "Gulf of Other Minds: Alien Contact in the Science Fiction of C. J. Cherryh." *Foundation* 37 (Autumn 1986): 5-21.

Murray, Terry A. *Science Fiction Magazine Story Index, 1926-1995.* Jefferson, NC: McFarland, 1999. 12+.

Nicholls, Stan. "C. J. Cherryh Interview." *Interzone* 31 (Sept.-Oct. 1989): 24-26, 36.

—. *Wordsmiths of Wonder: Fifty Interviews with Writers of the Fantastic.* London: Orbit, 1993. 43-54.

O'Brien, Mary Margaret. "The Female Hero in the Speculative Literature of the Twentieth Century: An Evolution of Adamic Eve." Diss. St. Louis Univ., 1986.

Pederson, Jay P., ed. *St. James Guide to Science Fiction Writers.* 4th ed. St. James Guide to Writers Series. New York: St. James Press, 1996. 181-82.

Pendergast, Sara, and Tom Pendergast. *St. James Guide to Young Adult Writers.* 2nd ed. St. James Guide to Writers Series. Detroit: St. James Press, 1999.

Pergameno, Sandro. "L'avventura revisitata da Carolyn J. Cherryh." *Cosmo informatore* 14 (Summer 1985): 10-12.

Pierce, John J. "Cherryh, C(arolyn) J(anice) (1942-)." *The New Encyclopedia of Science Fiction.* Ed. James Gunn. New York: Viking, 1988. 90-91.

—. *Foundations of Science Fiction: A Study in Imagination and Evolution.* Fwd. Frederik Pohl. Contributions to the Study of Science Fiction and Fantasy. 25. New York: Greenwood Press, 1987. 15+.

—. "The History of the Future." *Great Themes of Science Fiction: A Study in Imagination and Evolution.* Fwd. Thomas J. Roberts. Contributions to the Study of Science Fiction and Fantasy. 29. New York: Greenwood Press, 1987. 201-24.

—. *Odd Genre: A Study in Imagination and Evolution.* Contributions to the Study of Science Fiction and Fantasy. 60. Westport, CT: Greenwood Press, 1994. 6+.

Pringle, David, ed. *St. James Guide to Fantasy Writers.* 1st ed. St. James Guide to Writers Series. New York: St. James Press, 1996.

—. *The Ultimate Guide to Science Fiction: An A-Z of Science-Fiction Books by Title.* 2nd ed. Hants, Eng.: Scolar Press; Brookfield, VT: Ashgate Publishing, 1995. 14+.

Raffel, Burton. "C. J. Cherryh's Fiction." *Literary Review: An International Journal of Contemporary Writing* 44:3 (Apr. 1, 2001): 578-91.

Rand, Ken. "Interview: C. J. Cherryh." *Talebones* (Fall 1996): n. pag.

Reginald, Robert. *Science Fiction and Fantasy Literature, 1975-1991: A Bibliography of Science Fiction, Fantasy, and Horror Fantasy Books, and Nonfiction Monographs.* Detroit: Gale Research, 1992. 174-76.

Roberts, Robin. "Feminist Science Fiction." *A New Species: Gender and Science in Science Fiction.* Urbana: Univ. of Illinois Press, 1993. 90-116.

Russell, W. M. S. "Life and Afterlife on Other Worlds." *Foundation* 28 (1983): 34-56.

Sabella, Robert. "C. J. Cherryh." *Who Shaped Science Fiction?* Commack, NY: Kroshka Books, 2002. 181-82.

Sadoul, Jacques. *Histoire de la science-fiction moderne (1911-1984)*. Ed. rév. et complétée. Ailleurs et demain: essais. Paris: R. Laffont, 1984. 317+.

Sargent, Pamela. "Women [Authors]." *The New Encyclopedia of Science Fiction*. Ed. James Gunn. New York: Viking, 1988. 510-14.

Schlobin, Roger C. "Farsighted Females: A Selective Checklist of Modern Women Writers of Science Fiction through 1980." *Extrapolation* 23:1 (Spring 1982): 91-107.

—. *Urania's Daughters: A Checklist of Women Science-Fiction Writers, 1692-1982*. 1ˢᵗ ed. Starmont Reference Guide. 1. Mercer Island, WA: Starmont House, 1983. 12-13.

Schweitzer, Darrell. "Boskone XXIV Honors Cherryh, Shaw, Clareson, Hosts a Real Wedding." *Fantasy Review* 10 (Apr. 1987): 11.

—. "Interview: C. J. Cherryh." *Thrust* 11 (Fall 1978): 29-31.

Sellars, Nigel. "Interview with C. J. Cherryh." *Pirate Writings: Tales of Fantasy, Mystery, and Science Fiction* 4 (Fall 1996): 11-13.

Shinn, Thelma J. *Worlds within Women: Myth and Mythmaking in Fantastic Literature by Women*. Contributions to the Study of Science Fiction and Fantasy. 22. New York: Greenwood Press, 1986. 14+.

Smith, Jeannette C. "The Role of Women in Contemporary Arthurian Fantasy." *Extrapolation* 35:2 (Summer 1994): 130-44.

Stableford, Brian. *The Dictionary of Science Fiction Places*. Illus. Jeff White. New York: Wonderland Press, 1999. 75+.

—. "The Modern Period: 1964-1986." *Anatomy of Wonder: A Critical Guide to Science Fiction.* 3rd ed. Ed. Neil Barron. New York: R. R. Bowker, 1987. 241-42.

Stephensen-Payne, Phil. *C. J. Cherryh, Citizen of the Universe: A Working Bibliography.* Bibliographies for the Avid Reader. 43. Leeds: Galactic Publications, 1992.

Stern, J. L. "Creating a Credible Alien." *Writer* 104:4 (Apr. 1991): 12-15.

Stinson, J. G. "Going Native: The Human as Other in Selected Works of C. J. Cherryh." *Strange Horizons* (Mar. 2002): 26-41.

Thompson, Raymond H. "Science Fiction and Science Fantasy." *The Return from Avalon: A Study of the Arthurian Legend in Modern Fiction.* Contributions to the Study of Science Fiction and Fantasy. 14. Westport, CT: Greenwood Press, 1985. 77-86.

Tymn, Marshall B., Kenneth J. Zahorski, and Robert H. Boyer. *Fantasy Literature: A Core Collection and Reference Guide.* New York: R.R. Bowker, 1979. 18+.

"The Universe of C. J. Cherryh." *Locus* 17:10 (Oct. 1984): 4, 53.

"The Universe of C. J. Cherryh." *Locus* 20:4 (Apr. 1987): 5.

Vance, Michael. "C. J. Cherryh: Flights of Science Fiction and Fantasy, Part One." *Starlog* 133 (Aug. 1988): 26-28, 71.

—. "C. J. Cherryh, the Quiet Berserker." *Science Fiction & Fantasy Review* 71:65 (Mar. 1984): 9-10, 22.

—. "C. J. Cherryh, the Quiet Berserker: Interview." *Media Sight* 3 (Summer 1984): 22-25.

—. "C. J. Cherryh: Worlds of Science Fiction and Fantasy, Part Two." *Starlog* 134 (Sept. 1988): 42-44, 64.

Walters, Ray. "The Science-Fiction Boom: A Shared Passion for 'What if . . . ?'" *New York Times* (Feb. 5, 1984): BR27.

Watson, Ian, and Stephen H. Goldman. "Language." *The New Encyclopedia of Science Fiction*. Ed. James Gunn. New York: Viking, 1988. 264-67.

Webster, Dan. "Author Enjoys Sci-Fi Writers, Fans." *Spokesman Review* (Sept. 2, 2001): F5.

—. "Sci-Fi Visionary Storytelling Came Early for Spokane's C. J. Cherryh, One of the Science-Fiction World's Biggest Names." *Spokesman Review* (Sept. 6, 2001): D1.

Wells, Susan. "C. J. Cherryh." *Dictionary of Literary Biography: Yearbook 1980*. Detroit: Gale, 1981.

Wells, Tish. "Science Fiction's Starry Future." *USA Today* (Aug. 30, 1989): E1-2.

Westfahl, Gary. "Home on Lagrange." *Islands in the Sky: The Space Station Theme in Science Fiction Literature*. 1st ed. I.O. Evans Studies in the Philosophy and Criticism of Literature. 15. San Bernardino: Borgo Press, 1996. 95-115.

Williams, Lynn F. "Women and Power in C. J. Cherryh's Novels." *Extrapolation* 27:2 (Summer 1986): 85-92.

Wiloch, Thomas. "Cherry, Carolyn Janice 1942- (C. J. Cherryh)." *Contemporary Authors*. New Revision Series. Vol. 10. Detroit: Gale, 1983. 95-96. 125 vols. to date.

Wolf, Barbara Eva. "Universe Makers: Mythology and the Creative Work of Women Writers of Speculative Fiction." Diss. Pacifica Graduate Institute, 2002.

Wolmark, Jenny. "Disruption and Discontinuity in the Narratives of C. J. Cherryh." *Aliens and Others: Science Fiction, Feminism, and Postmodernism.* London: Harester Wheatsheaf, 1993; Iowa City: Univ. of Iowa Press, 1994. 72-80.

Yaakov, Juliette, and John Greenfieldt, eds. *Fiction Catalog.* 14th ed. Standard Catalog Series. New York: H. W. Wilson, 2001. 116-17.

—. *Fiction Catalog: 2001 Supplement to the Fourteenth Edition.* New York: H. W. Wilson, 2002. 16.

Yarrows, Andrew L. "Sci-Fi Fans Meet to Ponder Genre's Present." *New York Times* (Sept. 4, 1989): 13.

Yntema, Sharon K. *More than 100 Women Science Fiction Writers: An Annotated Bibliography.* Updated ed. Freedom, CA: Crossing Press, [1990]. 31-34; "1990 Supplement." 201-02.

THE WORLD WIDE WEB

"C. J. Cherryh: Bibliographic Summary." *Internet Speculative Fiction Database*. 4 Apr. 2004. 17 May 2004 <www.isfdb.org/sfdbase.html>. Path: Fiction Database Search.

"C. J. Cherryh: (Carolyn Janice Cherryh). Fantastic Fiction. 30 Apr. 2004. 17 May 2004 <www.fantasticfiction.co.uk/authors/C_J_Cherryh.htm>.

Cherryh, C. J. Home Page. 12 May 2004. 17 May 2004 <www.cherryh.com>.

Maps of C. J. Cherryh's Fiction. [n.d.]. 17 May 2004 <www.solstation.com/cjc-maps.htm>.

Meetpoint Station. 25 Oct. 1999. 17 May 2004 <www.perrochon.com/cherryh/>.

Science Fiction Weekly. 6 May 1996. 17 May 2004. <www.scifi.com/sfw/>.

Sffworld.com. (1999). Apr. 2004. 17 May 2004. <www.sffworld.com>.

" SFWA Site Search." *Science Fiction and Fantasy Writers of America, Inc.* 8 May 2004. 17 May 2004 <www.sfwa.org/index>.

Shejidan: An Unofficial Cherryh Fan Site. 21 Feb. 2004. 17 May 2004
<www.shejidan.com>.

Tillman, Peter D. "*Interzone's* Guide to SF on the Web." *Interzone* (Mar.
2002): 45-48.

NOVELS, NOVELLAS, AND SHORT STORIES BY C. J. CHERRYH

Abbey, Lynn, C. J. Cherryh, and Janet Morris. *Soul of the City*. New York: Ace Fantasy Books, 1986.

Cherryh, C. J. *Alternate Realities*. New York: DAW Books, 2000.

—. *Angel with the Sword*. New York: DAW Books, 1985.

—. *Arafel's Saga*. New York: DAW Books, 1983.

—. "Armies of the Night." *The Dead of Winter*. Ed. Robert Lynn Asprin and Lynn Abbey. New York: Ace Fantasy Books, 1985.

—. *At the Edge of Space*. New York: DAW Books, 2003.

—. *The Book of Morgaine*. Garden City, NY: N. Doubleday, 1979.

—. *Brothers of Earth*. Garden City, NY: N. Doubleday, 1976.

—. "Cassandra." *Fantasy & Science Fiction* 329 (Oct. 1978): n. pag.

—. "Cassandra." *The Hugo Winners: Volume Four*. Ed. Isaac Asimov. Garden City, NY: N. Doubleday, 1985.

—. "Cassandra." *Nebula Winners Fourteen*. Ed. Frederik Pohl. 1ˢᵗ ed. New York: Harper & Row, 1980.

—. "Cassandra." *The 1979 Annual World's Best SF*. Ed. Donald A. Wolheim. New York: DAW, 1979.

—. "Cassandra." *Women of Wonder, the Contemporary Years: Science Fiction by Women from the 1970s to the 1990s*. Ed. Pamela Sargent. 1ˢᵗ ed. San Diego: Harcourt Brace, 1995.

—. *The Chanur Saga*. New York: DAW Books, 2000.

—. *Chanur's Homecoming*. New York: DAW Books, 1986.

—. *Chanur's Legacy: A Novel of Compact Space*. New York: DAW Books, 1992.

—. *Chanur's Venture*. New York: DAW Books, 1984.

—. *Chernevog*. New York: Ballantine Books, 1990.

—. *Cloud's Rider*. New York: Warner Books, 1996.

—. *The Collected Short Fiction of C. J. Cherryh*. New York: DAW Books, 2004. Brothers – Cassandra – Companions – Dark King – Dreamstone – Endpiece – Frontpiece – General – Gift of Prophecy – Gwydion and the Dragon – Haunted tower – Highliner – Homecoming – Ice – Last Tower – Masks – Mech – Much Briefer History of Time – Nightgame – Of Law and Magic – Only Death in the City – Pots – Sandman, the Tinman, and the Betty B. – Scapegoat – Sea Change – Thief in Korianth – Threads of Time – Unshadowed Land – Willow – Wings

—. "Companions." *The John W. Campbell Awards 5*. Ed. George R. R. Martin. New York: Bluejay, 1984.

—. *Cuckoo's Egg*. New York: DAW Books, 1985.

—. *Cyteen*. New York: Warner Books, 1988.

—. "The Dark King." *The Year's Best Fantasy Stories 3*. Ed. Lin Carter. New York: DAW, 1977.

—. *Defender*. New York: DAW Books, 2002.

—. *Devil to the Belt*. New York: Warner Books, 2000.

—. *Downbelow Station*. New York: DAW Books, 1981.

—. "Downwind." *Cross-Currents*. Ed. Robert Asprin and Lynn Abbey. Garden City, NY: N. Doubleday, 1984.

—. "Downwind." *Storm Season*. Ed. Robert Lynn Asprin. New York: Ace, 1982.

—. *The Dreamstone*. New York: DAW Books, 1983.

—. "The Dreamstone." *Amazons!* Ed. Jessica Amanda Salmonson. New York: DAW Books, 1979.

—. "The Dreamstone." *Margaret Weis & Tracy Hickman Present Treasures of Fantasy*. New York: HarperPrism, 1997.

—. "The Dreamstone." *Strange Dreams: Unforgettable Fantasy Stories*. Comp. Stephen R. Donaldson. New York: Bantam Books, 1993.

—. "The Dreamstone." *Treasures of Fantasy*. Ed. M. Weis and T. Hickman. New York: HarperPrism, 1997.

—. *Ealdwood*. West Kingston, RI: D. M. Grant, 1981.

—. *Endgame*. New York: DAW Books, 1991.

—. *Exile's Gate*. New York: DAW Books, 1988.

—. *Explorer*. New York: DAW Books, 2002.

—. *The Faded Sun*. New York: DAW Books, 2000.

—. *The Faded Sun: Kesrith*. Garden City, NY: N. Doubleday, 1978.

—. "The Faded Sun: Kesrith." *Galaxy Magazine* 244-47 (Feb.-May 1978): n. pag.

—. *The Faded Sun: Kutath*. Garden City, NY: N. Doubleday, 1979.

—. *The Faded Sun: Shon'jir*. Garden City, NY: N. Doubleday, 1978.

—. *Faery in Shadow*. New York: Ballantine Books, 1994.

—. *Fever Season*. New York: DAW Books, 1987.

—. *Finity's End*. New York: Warner Books, 1997.

—. *Foreigner: A Novel of First Contact*. New York: DAW Books, 1994.

—. *Forge of Heaven*. New York: EOS/HarperCollins, 2004.

—. *Fortress in the Eye of Time*. New York: HarperPrism, 1995.

—. *Fortress of Dragons*. New York: EOS, 2000.

—. *Fortress of Eagles*. New York: HarperPrism, 1998.

—. *Fortress of Owls*. New York: HarperPrism, 1999.

—. *Forty Thousand in Gehenna*. Huntington Woods, MI: Phantasia Press, 1983.

—. *Gate of Ivrel*. New York: DAW Books, 1976.

—. *The Goblin Mirror*. New York: Ballantine Books, 1992.

—. "Gwydion and the Dragon." *Once upon a Time: A Treasury of Modern Fairy Tales*. Ed. Lester del Rey and Risa Kessler. 1st ed. New York: Ballantine Books, 1991.

—. "Gwydion and the Dragon." *A Quest Lover's Treasury of the Fantastic*. Ed. Margaret Weis. New York: Warner Books, 2002.

—. "Gwydion and the Dragon." *The Year's Best Fantasy and Horror: Fifth Annual Collection*. Ed. Ellen Datlow and Terri Windling. 1st ed. New York: St. Martin's Press, 1992.

—. *Hammerfall*. New York: EOS, 2001.

—. "The Haunted Tower." *Fantasy Annual V*. Ed. Terry Carr. New York: Pocket Books, 1982.

—. *Heavy Time*. New York: Warner Books, 1991.

—. *Hellburner*. New York: Warner Books, 1992.

—. *Hestia*. New York: DAW Books, 1979.

—. "Highliner." *The 1982 Annual World's Best SF*. Ed. Donald A. Wollheim and Arthur W. Saha. New York: DAW Books, 1982.

—. *Hunter of Worlds*. Garden City, NY: N. Doubleday, 1977.

—. *Inheritor*. New York: DAW Books, 1996.

—. *Invader*. New York: DAW Books, 1995.

—. "Ischade." *Shadows of Sanctuary.* Ed. Robert Lynn Asprin and Lynn Abbey. New York: Ace Books, 1981.

—. *Kesrith.* New York: DAW Books, 1978.

—. *The Kif Strike Back.* New York: DAW Books, 1985.

—. *Kutath.* New York: DAW Books, 1979.

—. *Legions of Hell.* New York: Baen Books, 1987.

—. *Lois & Clark: A Superman Novel.* Rocklin, CA: Prima Publishing, 1996.

—. "Marking Time." *Rebels in Hell.* [Ed.] Janet Morris. New York: Baen Books, 1986.

—. "Mech." *FutureCrime: An Anthology of the Shape of Crime to Come.* Ed. Cynthia Manson and Charles Ardai. New York: Donald I. Fine, 1982.

—. *Merchanter's Luck.* New York: DAW Books, 1982.

—. "Monday Morning." *Rebels in Hell.* [Ed.] Janet Morris. New York: Baen Books, 1986.

—. *The Morgaine Saga.* New York: DAW Books, 2000.

—. "Necromant." *Cross-Currents.* Ed. Robert Asprin and Lynn Abbey. Garden City, NY: N. Doubleday, 1984.

—. "Necromant." *The Face of Chaos.* Ed. Robert Asprin and Lynn Abbey. New York: Ace Books, 1983.

—. "The Only Death in the City." *The Year's Best Fantasy Stories: 8.* Ed. Arthur W. Saha. New York: DAW Books, 1982.

—. *The Paladin*. New York: Baen Books, 1988.

—. *Port Eternity*. New York: DAW Books, 1982.

—. "Pots." *Absolute Magnitude 5* (Summer 1995): n. pag.

—. "Pots." *Afterwar*. [Ed.] Janet Morris. New York: Baen Books, 1985.

—. "Pots." *Future on Ice*. Ed. Orson Scott Card. New York: TOR, 1998.

—. "Pots." *Masterpieces: The Best Science Fiction of the Century*. Ed. Orson Scott Card. New York: Ace Books, 2001. Reprinted 2004.

—. *Precursor*. New York: DAW Books, 1999.

—. *The Pride of Chanur*. New York: DAW Books, 1982.

—. "The Pride of Chanur." *Science Fiction Digest*, 2nd ser. 1 (Oct.-Nov. 1981): n. pag.

—. "The Prince." *Far Frontiers* 4 (Winter 1985): n. pag.

—. "The Prince." *Heroes in Hell*. Ed. Janet Morris. New York: Baen Books, 1986.

—. *Rider at the Gate*. New York: Warner Books, 1995.

—. *Rimrunners*. New York: Warner Books, 1989.

—. "Rook's Move." *War in Hell*. Ed. Janet Morris, et al. New York: Baen Books, 1988.

—. *Rusalka*. New York: Ballantine Books, 1989.

—. "The Sandman, the Tinman, and the Betty B." *Science Fiction: DAW 30th Anniversary*. Ed. Elizabeth R. Wollheim and Sheila E. Gilbert. New York: DAW Books, 2002.

—. "The Scapegoat." *Alien Stars*. Ed. Elizabeth Mitchell. New York: Baen Book/Simon & Schuster, 1985.

—. "The Scapegoat." *Absolute Magnitude* 4 (Spring 1995): n. pag.

—. "The Scapegoat." *The Best Military Science Fiction of the 20th Century*. Ed. Harry Turtledove with Martin H. Greenberg. New York: Ballantine Books, 2001.

—. "The Scapegoat." *Body Armor, 2000*. Ed. Joe Haldeman with Charles G. Waugh and Martin H. Greenberg. New York: Ace Science Fiction Books, 1986.

—. "Sea Change." *Elsewhere*. Ed. Terri Windling and Mark Alan Arnold. New York: Ace Books, 1981.

—. *Serpent's Reach*. Garden City, NY: N. Doubleday, 1980.

—. "The Sibylline Affair." *Prophets in Hell*. [Ed.] Janet Morris. New York: Baen Books, 1989.

—. "Stormbirds." *Four from the Witch World*. Ed. Andre Norton. New York: TOR, 1989.

—. *Sunfall*. New York: DAW Books, 1981. Prologue – The Only Death in the City (Paris) – The Haunted Tower (London) – Ice (Moscow) – Nightgame (Rome) – Highliner (New York) – The General (Peking)

—. "A Thief in Korianth." *Demons and Daggers*. Ed. Lin Carter. Garden City, NY: N. Doubleday, 1981.

—. "A Thief in Korianth." *Flashing Swords! No. 5: Demons and Daggers.* Ed. Lin Carter. Garden City, NY: N. Doubleday, 1981.

—. *The Tree of Swords and Jewels.* New York: DAW Books, 1983.

—. *Tripoint.* New York: Warner Books, 1994.

—. "The Unshadowed Land." *Sword and Sorceress II: An Anthology of Heroic Fantasy.* Ed. Marion Zimmer Bradley. New York: DAW Books, 1985.

—. *Visible Light.* New York: DAW Books, 1986. Cassandra – Threads of Time – Companions – Thief in Korianth – The Last Tower – The Brothers

—. *Voyager in Night.* New York: DAW Books, 1984.

—. *Wave without a Shore.* New York: DAW Books, 1981.

—. *Well of Shiuan.* New York: DAW Books, 1978.

—. "Willow." *Hecate's Cauldron.* Ed. Susan M. Shwartz. New York: DAW Books, 1982.

—. "Willow." *A Magic Lover's Treasury of the Fantastic.* Ed. Margaret Weis. New York: Warner Books, 1998.

—. Witching Hour." *Wings of Omen.* Ed. Robert Lynn Asprin and Lynn Abbey. New York: Berkley Publishing Group, 1984.

—. *Yvgenie.* New York: Ballantine Books, 1991.

Cherryh, C. J., and Janet Morris. "Basileus." *Heroes in Hell.* Ed. Janet Morris. New York: Baen Books, 1986.

—. *The Gates of Hell*. New York: Baen Books, 1986.

—. *Kings in Hell*. New York: Baen Books, 1987.

Cherryh, C. J., and Jane S. Fancher. "Pot of Dreams." *Marion Zimmer Bradley's Fantasy Magazine* 27 (Spring 1995): n. pag.

Cherryh, C. J., et al. *The Sword of Knowledge*. Riverdale, NY: Baen Books, 1995. Bk. 1: *A Dirge for Sabis* – Bk. 2: *Wizard Spawn* – Bk. 3: *Reap the Whirlwind*

Dewees, Christine, and C. J. Cherryh. "The Search." *Wolfsong: The Blood of Ten Chiefs*. Ed. Richard Pini, Robert Asprin, and Lynn Abbey. New York: Tom Doherty, 1988.

Perry, Mark C., and C. J. Cherryh. "Swift-Spear." *The Blood of Ten Chiefs*. Ed. Richard Pini, Robert Asprin, and Lynn Abbey. New York: Tom Doherty, 1986.

MISCELLANEOUS WRITINGS BY C. J. CHERRYH

Cherryh, C. J. "Appreciation." *Return to Avalon: A Celebration of Marion Zimmer Bradley.* Ed. Jennifer Roberson. New York: DAW Books, 1996.

—. "Arms and the Writer." *Writer's Digest* 1979.

—. Rev. of *The Chronicles of Thomas Covenant, the Unbeliever,* by Stephen R. Donaldson. *Galileo* 6 (1978): 100-02.

—. Rev. of *Dying of the Light,* by George R. R. Martin. *Galileo* 8 (1978): 88.

—. Introduction. *Explorer.* Ed. Julie Czerneda. *Tales from the Wonderzone* [Series]. Toronto: Trifolium Books, 2002.

—. "Female Characters in SF and Fantasy." *SFWA Bulletin* 16 (Mar. 1982): 22-29.

—. Forward. *FutureSpeak: A Fan's Guide to the Language of Science Fiction.* By Roberta Rogow. 1ª ed. New York: Paragon Press, 1991.

—. "From Disk to Typesetter." *SFWA Bulletin* 26:3 (Fall 1992): 15-17.

—. *Glass and Amber.* Cambridge, MA: NESFA Press, 1987. Contents: Of Law and Magic – Homecoming – Romantic Science Fiction – The Dark King – Perspectives in SF – Sea Change – The Avoidance Factor – A Gift of Prophecy – The Use of Archaeology in Worldbuilding – Willow – In Alien Tongues – Pots

—. "Goodbye *Star Wars*, Hello *Alley-Oop.*" *Inside Outer Space: Science Fiction Professionals Look at Their Craft.* Ed. Sharon Jarvis. New York: F. Ungar, 1985. 17-26.

—. Introduction. *The Gates to Witch World: Comprising Witch World, Web of the Witch World, and Year of the Unicorn.* By Andre Norton. New York: TOR, 2001.

—. Introduction. *The Lore of the Witch World.* By Andre Norton. New York: DAW, 1980. 7-9.

—. "Linguistic Sexism in SF and Fantasy: A Modest Proposal." *SFWA Bulletin* 15(Spring 1980): 7-9, 26.

—. "On Kipling and Weekday Afternoons." *Heads to the Storm.* New York: Baen Books, 1989.

—. "The Panel Room." *Advice on Writing from Authors.* 17 May 2004 <www.teenwriting.about.com/cs/authorsadvice/index.htm>. Path: C. J. Cherryh: The Panel Room.

—. Rev. of *The Realms of Tartarus,* by Brian M. Stableford. *Galileo* 6 (1978): 94.

—. "Romantic/Science Fiction: The Oldest Form of Literature." *Lan's Lantern* 10 (June 1980): 30-33.

—. "Strong Characters Versus Weak Character." 1996. 17 May 2004 <www.cherryh.com/www/charac.htm>.

—. "Thoughts on the Future of Conflict." [Afterword]. *The Game Beyond*. By Melissa Scott. New York: Baen Books, 1984: 342-50.

—. "To the Rescue." *Cat Fancy* 1977.

—. "The Use of Archaeology in Worldbuilding." *SFWA Bulletin* 13 (Fall 1978): 5-10.

—. "Where Is Science Taking Us?" 2002. 17 May 2004 <www.sffworld.com/authos/c/cherryh_cj/articles/whereisscience1.html>.

—. "Writerisms and Other Sins: A Writer's Shortcut to Stronger Writing." 1995. 17 May 2004 <www.cherryh.com/www/advice.htm>.

Cherryh, Carolyn C. [sic]. "Les sciences socials (et la SF)." *Per Ardua ad Astra* 2 (1987): 1-9.

REVIEWS

Adams, Andrew. Rev. of *Rider at the Gate. Vector* (Dec. 1995): n. pag.

Amies, Chris. Rev. of *Foreigner. Vector* (Sept. 1995): n. pag.

—. Rev. of *Tripoint. Vector* (Summer 1995): n. pag.

Andrews, Graham. Rev. of *Sunfall. Paperback Inferno* (Dec. 1990): n. pag.

Atkin, Julie. Rev. of *Hellburner. Vector* (Oct. 1993): n. pag.

Bailey, K. V. Rev. of *Foreigner. Vector* (Nov. 1994): n. pag.

—. Rev. of *Heavy Time. Vector* (Oct. 1991): n. pag.

Baldry, Cherith. Rev. of *Fortress in the Eye of Time. Vector* (Feb. 1996): n. pag.

—. Rev. of *Fortress of Eagles. Vector* (Mar. 1999): n. pag.

—. Rev. of *Fortress of Owls. Vector* (May 2000): n. pag.

Barbour, Douglas. "What SF Should Be and Seldom Is—A Powerful Narrative: *Cyteen* by C. J. Cherryh." *Toronto Star* (June 4, 1998): M5.

Bird, Colin. Rev. of *The Kif Strike Back*. *Paperback Inferno* (June 1988): n. pag.

Bispham, Lynne. Rev. of *Brothers of Earth*. *Paperback Parlour* (June 1977): n. pag.

—. Rev. of *Ealdwood*. *Paperback Inferno* (June 1991): n. pag.

—. Rev. of *Hestia*. *Paperback Inferno* (Oct.1988): n. pag.

—. Rev. of *Hunter of Worlds*. *Paperback Inferno* (Aug. 1990): n. pag.

—. Rev. of *Port Eternity*. *Paperback Inferno* (Feb.1990): n. pag.

—. Rev. of *Serpent's Reach*. *Paperback Inferno* (Feb.1990): n. pag.

—. Rev. of *Wave without a Shore*. *Paperback Inferno* (June 1989): n. pag.

Bogstad, Janice M. Rev. of *Chernevog*. *Science Fiction & Fantasy Book Review Annual*. Ed. Robert A. Collins and Robert Latham. Westport, CT: Greenwood Press, 1991. 300-01.

Bradley, Wendy. Rev. of *Faery in Shadow*. *Locus* 33:2 (Jan. 1994): 49.

Bredehoft, Thomas A. Rev. of *Finity's End*. *New York Review of Science Fiction* 10:9 (May 1998): 22-23.

Brians, Paul. Rev. of *Afterwar*. *Bulletin of the Atomic Scientists* 42:3 (Mar. 1986): 50-53.

Brizzi, Mary Turzillo. Rev. of *Rimrunners*. *Science Fiction & Fantasy Book Review Annual*. Ed. Robert A. Collins and Robert Latham. New York: Greenwood Press, 1990. 231.

Broome, Terry. Rev. of *Hellburner*. *Vector* (Oct. 1993): n. pag.

Rev. of *Brothers of Earth*. *Publishers Weekly* 210:10 (Sept. 6, 1976): 65-66.

Brown, C. Rev. of *The Faded Sun: Kesrith*. *Isaac Asimov's Science Fiction Magazine* 2:4 (July-Aug. 1978): 17.

—. Rev. of *Gate of Ivrel*. *Locus* (June 30, 1976): n. pag.

—. Rev. of *Well of Shiuan*. *Isaac Asimov's Science Fiction Magazine* 2:4 (July-Aug. 1978): 17.

Brown, Ken. Rev. of *Wave without a Shore*. *Interzone* 29 (May-June 1989): 65.

Brown, Tanya. Rev. of *Faery in Shadow*. *Vector* (Nov. 1994): n. pag.

Budrys, Algis. Rev. of *Chanur's Venture*. *Fantasy and Science Fiction* 69:1 (July 1985): 17-18.

—. Rev. of *Gate of Ivrel*. *Fantasy and Science Fiction* 50:6 (June 1976): 44-46.

—. Rev. of *Hunter of Worlds*. *Fantasy and Science Fiction* 53:6 (Dec. 1977): 26-27.

—. Rev. of *The Pride of Chanur*. *Fantasy and Science Fiction* 63:1 (July 1982): 33-36.

Bunnell, John C. Rev. of *Precursor*. *Amazing Stories* (Spring 2000): n. pag.

Cannon, Peter, and Jeff Zaleski. Rev. of *Defender*. *Publishers Weekly* 248:45 (Nov. 5, 2001): 46-47.

—. Rev. of *Explorer*. *Publishers Weekly* 249:43 (Oct. 28, 2002): 56.

—. Rev. of *Hammerfall*. *Publishers Weekly* 248:23 (June 4, 2001): 63.

Carnall, Jane. Rev. of *Invader. Vector* (Nov. 1996): n. pag.

Carmien, Edward. Rev. of *The Collected Short Fiction of C. J. Cherryh. SFRevu* (Jan. 2004). 18 May 2004 <www.sfrevu.com/ISSUES/2004/0401/The%20Collected%20Short %20Fiction%20of%20CJ%20Cherryh/Review.htm>.

—. Rev. of *Explorer.* SFRevu (Dec. 2003). 18 May 2004 <www.sfrevu.com/ISSUES/2003/0312/Explorer/Review.htm>.

Cassada, Jackie. Rev. of *Angel with the Sword. Library Journal* 110:15 (Sept. 15, 1985): 96.

—. Rev. of *Chanur's Legacy. Library Journal* 117:13 (Aug. 1, 1992): 155.

—. Rev. of *The Collected Short Fiction of C. J. Cherryh. Library Journal* 129:3 (Feb. 15, 2004): 167.

—. Rev. of *The Cuckoo's Egg. Library Journal* 110:9 (May 15, 1985): 82.

—. Rev. of *Cyteen. Library Journal* 113:9 (May 15, 1988): 95.

—. Rev. of *Exile's Gate. Library Journal* 112:20 (Dec. 1, 1987): 131.

—. Rev. of *Explorer. Library Journal* 127:19 (Nov. 15, 2002): 106.

—. Rev. of *Foreigner. Library Journal* 119:3 (Feb. 15, 1994): 188.

—. Rev. of *Fortress in the Eye of Time. Library Journal* 120:9 (May 15, 1995): 99.

—. Rev. of *Goblin Mirror. Library Journal* 117:15 (Sept. 15, 1992): 97.

—. Rev. of *Hammerfall. Library Journal* 126:11 (June 15, 2001): 107.

—. Rev. of *Hellburner. Library Journal* 117:15 (Sept. 15, 1992): 97.

—. Rev. of *Invader. Library Journal* 120:7 (Apr. 15, 1995): 119.

—. Rev. of *Moonsinger's Friends. Library Journal* 110 (Aug. 1985): 121.

—. Rev. of *Precursor. Library Journal* 124:19 (Nov. 15, 1999): 101.

—. Rev. of *Rimrunners. Library Journal* 114:9 (May 15, 1992): 92.

—. Rev. of *Troubled Waters. Library Journal* 113:9 (May 15, 1988): 96.

—. Rev. of *Voyager in Night. Library Journal* 109:7 (Apr. 15, 1984): 825-26.

—. Rev. of *Yvgenie. Library Journal* 116:17 (Oct. 15, 1991): 127.

Cassada, Jackie, and Eric Bryant. Rev. of *Fortress of Owls. Library Journal* 124:1 (Jan. 1, 1999): 166.

Catalano, Frank. Rev. of *The Dreamstone. Amazing Science Fiction* 57:2 (July 1983): 14.

Caywood, Carolyn. Rev. of *Afterwar. Voice of Youth Advocates* 8 (Dec. 1985): 323.

Rev. of *Chanur's Venture. Publishers Weekly* 226:9 (Aug. 31, 1984): 424.

Clareson, Thomas D. "Star Cluster: Silverberg, Disch, and Cherryh Score." Rev. of *Forty Thousand in Gehenna. Extrapolation* 25:3 (Fall 1984): 280-82.

Cleaver, Fred. "Control-Freak Cameron Loses Control: Human Part of Alien Race in *Defender.*" *Denver Post* (Dec. 23, 2001): EE.02.

Clute, John. "A Great Deal in Sand." Rev. of *Hammerfall. Science Fiction Weekly* 7:17 (Apr. 23, 2001). 18 May 2004 <www.scifi.com/sfw/issue209/excess.html>.

Rev. of *The Collected Short Fiction of C. J. Cherryh*. *Publishers Weekly* 251:3 (Jan. 19,2004): 58.

Collier, Ann. Rev. of *Hestia*. *Foundation* 20 (Oct. 1980): 92-94.

—. Rev. of *Well of Shiuan*. *Vector* 106 (Feb. 1982): 30-32.

Coulson, Robert. Rev. of *The Tree of Swords and Jewels*. *Amazing Science Fiction* 57:6 (Mar. 1984): 8, 10.

Coward, Mat. Rev. of *The Goblin Mirror*. *Vector* (Oct. 1993): n. pag.

Cushman, Carolyn. Rev. of *Cloud's Rider*. *Locus* 37:4 (Oct. 1996): 31.

—. Rev. of *Fortress in the Eye of Time*. *Locus* 34:6 (June 1995): 27.

—. Rev. of *Fortress of Dragons*. *Locus* 44:5 (May 2000).

—. Rev. of *Fortress of Eagles*. *Locus* 40:3 (Mar. 1998): 31.

—. Rev. of *Hammerfall*. *Locus* 46:6 (June 2001): 35.

D'Ammassa, Don. Rev. of *Downbelow Station*. *Science Fiction Chronicle* 2:11 (Aug. 1981): 20-21.

—. Rev. of *The Dreamstone*. *Science Fiction Chronicle* 4:9 (June 1983): 29.

—. Rev. of *Inheritor*. *Science Fiction Chronicle* (June 1997): n. pag.

—. Rev. of *Merchanter's Luck*. *Science Fiction Chronicle* 4:2 (Nov. 1982): 29-30.

—. Rev. of *Port Eternity*. *Science Fiction Chronicle* 4:4 (Jan. 1983): 21.

—. Rev. of *The Pride of Chanur*. *Science Fiction Chronicle* 4:11 (Aug. 1983): 30.

—. Rev. of *Wave without a Shore. Science Fiction Chronicle* 3:4 (Jan. 1982): 21-22.

Deal, P. Rev. of *The Tree of Swords and Jewels. Voice of Youth Advocates* 6:6 (Feb. 1984): 342.

Dellamonica, A. M. Rev. of *Defender. Science Fiction Weekly* 7:47 (Nov. 19, 2001). 18 May 2004 <www.scifi.com/sfw/issue239/books.html>.

—. Rev. of *Precursor. Science Fiction Weekly* 5:49 (Dec. 6, 1999). 18 May 2004 <www.scifi.com/sfw/issue138/books.html>.

del Rey, Lester. Rev. of *Brothers of Earth. Analog Science Fiction/Science Fact* 96:12 (Dec. 1976): 164-65.

—. Rev. of *The Faded Sun: Kesrith. Analog Science Fiction/Science Fact* 98:8 (Aug. 1978): 174.

—. Rev. of *Gate of Ivrel. Analog Science Fiction/Science Fact* 96:6 (June 1976): 170.

—. Rev. of *Hunter of Worlds. Analog Science Fiction/Science Fact* 97:8 (Aug. 1977): 172-74.

—. Rev. of *Well of Shiuan. Analog Science Fiction/Science Fact* 98:5 (May 1978): 172-74.

Di Filippo, Paul. Rev. of *The Collected Short Fiction of C. J. Cherryh. Science Fiction Weekly* 10:6 (Feb. 9, 2004). 18 May 2004 <www.scifi.com/sfw/issue355.books.html>.

—. Rev. of *Explorer. Science Fiction Weekly* 8:46 (Nov. 11, 2002). 18 May 2004, < www.scifi.com/sfw/issue290/books.html >.

—. Rev. of *Foreigner. Asimov's Science Fiction* 19:2 (Feb. 1995): n. pag.

Rev. of *The Dreamstone*. *Publishers Weekly* 223:4 (Jan. 28, 1983): 83.

Easton, Tom. Rev. of *Defender*, and *Explorer*. *Analog Science Fiction and Fact* 123:5(May 2003): 132-33.

—. Rev. of *Downbelow Station*. *Analog Science Fiction/Science Fact* 101:10 (Sept. 14, 1981): 168-69.

—. Rev. of *The Faded Sun: Kutath*. *Analog Science Fiction/Science Fact* 100:7 (July 1980): 169-70.

—. Rev. of *Fortress in the Eye of Time*. *Analog Science Fiction and Fact* (Nov. 1995): n. pag.

—. Rev. of *Forty Thousand in Gehenna*. *Analog Science Fiction/Science Fact* 103:11 (Oct. 1983): 163-64.

—. Rev. of *Hammerfall*. *Analog Science Fiction and Fact* 121:10 (Oct. 2001): 132-33.

—. Rev. of *Inheritor*. *Analog Science Fiction and Fact* 116:11 (Sept. 1996): 147-48.

—. Rev. of *Invader*. *Analog Science Fiction and Fact* 115:12 (Oct. 1995): 162-63.

—. Rev. of *Merchanter's Luck*. *Analog Science Fiction and Fact* 103:2 (Feb. 1983): 165-66.

—. Rev. of *Port Eternity*. *Analog Science Fiction/Science Fact* 103:6 (June 1983): 109-10.

—. Rev. of *Precursor*. *Analog Science Fiction and Fact* 120:4 (Apr. 2000): 132-33.

—. Rev. of *The Pride of Chanur. Analog Science Fiction/Science Fact* 102:8 (Aug. 1982): 125-26.

—. Rev. of *Serpent's Reach. Analog Science Fiction/Science Fact* 101:2 (Feb. 2, 1981): 171.

—. Rev. of *Sunfall. Analog Science Fiction/Science Fact* 102:2 (Feb. 1, 1982): 102.

—. Rev. of *Tripoint. Analog Science Fiction and Fact* 115:1&2 (Jan. 1995): 303-04.

—. Rev. of *Voyager in Night. Analog Science Fiction/Science Fact* 104:11 (Nov. 1984): 167.

—. Rev. of *Wave without a Shore. Analog Science Fiction/Science Fact* 102:4 (Mar. 29, 1982): 162-64.

Eisen, Janice M. "Checking in with a Lost Colony." Rev. of *Invader. Washington Post* (May 28, 1995): WBK10.

Estes, Sally. "Books for Youth: Adult Books for Young Adults." Rev. of *Foreigner.* Booklist 90:10 (Jan. 15, 1994): 907.

Rev. of *The Faded Sun: Kutath. Publishers Weekly* 217:1 (Jan. 11, 1990): 86-87.

Rev. of *The Faded Sun: Shon'jir. Publishers Weekly* 215:7 (Feb. 12, 1979): 125.

Feeley, Gregory. "Lost in Space." Rev. of *Heavy Time. Washington Post* (July 28, 1991), final ed: X11.

Rev. of *Fires of Azeroth. Publishers Weekly* 215:17 (Apr. 23, 1979): 78.

Flick, H., Jr. Rev. of *Gate of Ivrel. Kliatt Young Adult Paperback Book Guide* 10:3 (Sept. 1976): 63.

—. Rev. of *Well of Shiuan. Kliatt Young Adult Paperback Book Guide* 12:5 (June 1978): 1.

Rev. of *Foreigner. Publishers Weekly* 241:5 (Jan. 31, 1994): 81.

Rev. of *Forge of Heaven. Kirkus Reviews* 72:5 (Mar. 1, 2004): 205.

Rev. of *Fortress in the Eye of Time. Publishers Weekly* 242:15 (Apr. 10, 1995): 57.

Rev. of *Fortress of Dragons. Kirkus Reviews* 68:7 (Apr. 1, 2000): 432.

Rev. of *Fortress of Dragons. Publishers Weekly* 247:20 (May 15, 2000): 94.

Rev. of *Fortress of Owls. Kirkus Reviews* 66:22 (Nov. 14, 1998): 1638.

Rev. of *Forty Thousand in Gehenna. Extrapolation* 25:3 (Fall 1984): 281.

Rev. of *Forty Thousand in Gehenna. Publishers Weekly* 224:11 (Sept. 9, 1983): 51-52.

Rev. of *Forty Thousand in Gehenna. Washington Post* 108 (Dec. 30, 1984): BW12.

Frane, J. Rev. of *Ealdwood. Locus* 14:6 (July 1981): 11.

—. Rev. of *The Pride of Chanur. Locus* 15:1 (Jan. 1982): 8.

Gardner, C. Rev. of *Brothers of Earth. Kliatt Young Adult Paperback Book Guide* 11 (Spring 1977): 10.

Rev. of *Gate of Ivrel. Publishers Weekly* 209:5 (Feb. 2, 1976): 104.

Gemmel, Ron. Rev. of *Angel with the Sword*. *Paperback Inferno* (Aug. 1987): n. pag.

Gentle, Mary. "Examined Assumptions." Rev. of *Heavy Time*. *Interzone* 54 (Dec. 1991): 62-63.

Glass, B. Rev. of *Gate of Ivrel*. *Delap's F & SF Review* 2:8 (Aug. 1976): 24-25.

Green, Roland. "Cherryh Returns to Old Form." Rev. of *Foreigner*. *Chicago Sun-Times* (Feb. 6, 1994), late sports final ed.: 15.

—. Rev. of *The Collected Short Fiction of C. J. Cherryh*. *Booklist* 100:12 (Feb. 15, 2004): 1047.

—. Rev. of *Downbelow Station*. *Booklist* 77:16 (Apr. 15, 1981): 1138.

—. Rev. of *The Dreamstone*. *Booklist* 79:16 (Apr. 15, 1983): 1075.

—. Rev. of *Exile's Gate*. *Booklist* (Nov. 1, 1987): 417.

—. Rev. of *Explorer*. *Booklist* 99:6 (Nov. 15, 2002): 583.

—. Rev. of *Finity's End*. *Booklist* 93 (Aug. 1997): 1886.

—. Rev. of *The Foreigner*. *Booklist* 90:10 (Jan. 15, 1994): 904.

—. Rev. of *Fortress of Dragons*. *Booklist* 96:17 (Jan. 15, 1994): 904.

—. Rev. of *Fortress of Owls*. *Booklist* 95:8 (Dec. 15, 1998): 730

.—. Rev. of *Inheritor*. *Booklist* 92:16 (Apr. 15, 1996): 1425.

—. Rev. of *Merchanter's Luck*. *Booklist* 79:1 (Sept. 1, 1982): 27.

—. Rev. of *Port Eternity*. *Booklist* 79:9 (Jan. 1, 1983): 600.

—. Rev. of *Precursor. Booklist* 96:6 (Nov. 15, 1999): 608-09.

—. Rev. of *The Pride of Chanur. Booklist* 78:15 (Apr. 1, 1982): 1003.

—. Rev. of *Rider at the Gate. Booklist* 91:22 (Aug. 1995): 1933.

—. Rev. of *Serpent's Reach. Booklist* 77:4 (Oct. 15, 1980): 306.

—. "Their Strengths Are Mightier Than Their Flaws." Rev. of *Rusalka. Chicago Sun-Times* (Jan. 7, 1990), five star sports final ed.: 11.

—. Rev. of *The Tree of Swords and Jewels. Booklist* 80:1 (Sept. 1, 1983): 29.

—. Rev. of *Voyager in Night. Booklist* 80:17 (May 1, 1984): 1225.

—. "Voyages of Starfarers and Time Travelers." Rev. of *Hellburner. Chicago Sun-Times* (Oct. 4, 1992), late sports final ed.: 15.

Green, Roland, et al. Rev. of *Defender. Booklist* 98:6 (Nov. 15, 2001): 560.

Greener, Mark. Rev. of *Cuckoo's Egg. Paperback Inferno* (Feb. 1990): n. pag.

Gregory, Kristiana. Rev. of *The Tree of Swords and Jewels. Los Angeles Times* 102 (Dec. 25, 1983): B6.

Hall Minor, Carla. Rev. of *Foreigner. Magill Book Reviews* (Jan. 1, 1995): n. pag.

Hamburger, Susan. Rev. of *Cloud's Rider. Library Journal* 121:13 (Aug. 1, 1996): 119.

—. Rev. of *Finity's End. Library Journal* 122:15 (Sept. 15, 1997): 105.

—. Rev. of *Inheritor. Library Journal* 121:5 (Mar. 15, 1996): 99.

Rev. of *Hammerfall. Kirkus Reviews* 69:22 (Apr. 15, 2001): 549.

Heck, Peter. Rev. of *Foreigner. Asimov's Science Fiction* 18:11 (Oct. 1994): 163-65.

Herbert, Rosemary. Rev. of *The Dreamstone. Library Journal* 108:6 (Mar. 15, 1983): 603-04.

—. Rev. of *The Faded Sun: Kutath. Library Journal* 105:6 (Mar. 15, 1980): 748.

—. Rev. of *Merchanter's Luck. Library Journal* 107:16 (Sept. 15, 1982): 1772.

—. Rev. of *Sunfall. Library Journal* 106:10 (May 15, 1981): 1102.

Hiilos, Hannu. Rev. of *Rimrunners. Foundation* 50 (Autumn 1990): 122-26.

—. Rev. of *Voyager in Night,* and *Forty Thousand in Gehenna. Foundation* 37 (Autumn 1986): 55-59.

Holstine, Lesa M. Rev. of *Yvgenie. Voice of Youth Advocates* (Apr. 1992): 41.

Rev. of *Hunter of Worlds. Publishers Weekly* 212:1 (July 4, 1977): 74-75.

Hurst, L. J. Rev. of *Chanur's Venture. Paperback Inferno* (Dec. 1986): n. pag.

Rev. of *Invader. Publishers Weekly* 242:15 (Apr. 10, 1995): 57.

James, Edward. Rev. of *Cyteen. Vector* (Dec. 1990): n. pag.

—. Rev. of *Rimrunners. Paperback Inferno* (Aug. 1991): n. pag.

Johnson, Greg L. "The SF Novel as an Alien Art Form: C. J. Cherryh's *Foreigner* Series." *New York Review of Science Fiction* 10:3 (Nov. 1997): 21-22.

Johnson, Mary. Rev. of *Heavy Time. Magill Book Reviews* (Oct. 10. 1991): n. pag.

Jonas, Gerald. Rev. of *Rider at the Gate*, and *Cloud's Rider. New York Times Book Review* 101 (Sept. 15, 1996): 40-51.

—. Rev. of *Voyager in Night. New York Times Book Review* 89 (Nov. 25, 1984): 20.

Jones, Gwyneth. Rev. of *Cyteen. Foundation* 48 (Spring 1990): 70-79.

Jones, Neil. "Big Names." Rev. of *Lois and Clark: A Superman Novel. Interzone* 133 (July 1998): 58-59.

—. "Cherryh Season." Rev. of *Tripoint, Rider at the Gate, Invader*, and *Foreigner. Interzone* 103 (Jan. 1996): 58-60.

—. "History Lesson." Rev. of *Hellburner. Interzone* 66 (Dec. 1992): 61-62.

—. Rev. of *Rusalka. Interzone* 40 (Oct. 1990): 68.

Jones, Neil, and Neil McIntosh. "The Twee and the Dangerous." Rev. of *Gwydion and the Dragon*, by C. J. Cherryh. In *Once upon a Time*. Ed. Lester del Rey and Risa Kessler. *Interzone* 58 (Apr. 1992): 69.

Kaganoff, Penny. Rev. of *Heavy Time. Publishers Weekly* 239:11 (Feb. 24, 1992): 52.

Kaganoff, Penny, and Sybil Steinberg. Rev. of *Yvgenie. Publishers Weekly* 239:42 (Sept. 21, 1992): 92.

Kan, Katharine L. Rev. of *Chanur's Legacy. Voice of Youth Advocates* (Feb. 1993): 345-46.

Kincaid, Paul. Rev. of *Heavy Time. Vector* (Oct. 1992): n. pag.

LaFaille, Gene. Rev. of *Elsewhere. Voices of Youth Advocates* 4 (Dec. 1991): 38.

—. Rev. of *Foreigner. Wilson Library Bulletin* 68:9 (May 1994): 82.

—. Rev. of *Heavy Time. Wilson Library Bulletin* 66:3 (Nov. 1991): 102-03.

Lancaster, Kurt. Rev. of *Invader. Foundation* 67 (Summer 1996): 107-09.

Lawrence, Clinton. Rev. of *Finity's End. Science Fiction Weekly* 3:15 (Aug. 11, 1997).18 May 2004 <www.scifi.com/sfw/issue51/books.html>.

Lerner, Fred. "Science Fiction Multiverse." Rev. of *Tripoint. Wilson Library Bulletin* 69:4 (Dec. 1994): 82.

Letson, Russell. Rev. of *Explorer. Locus* 50:1 (Jan. 2003): 25-26.

—. Rev. of *Finity's End. Locus* 39:5 (Nov. 1997): 21, 61.

—. Rev. of *Foreigner. Locus* 32:3 (Mar. 1994): 19.

—. Rev. of *The Goblin Mirror. Locus* 29:5 (Nov. 1992): 23.

—. Rev. of *Heavy Time. Locus* 26:6 (June 1991): 17.

—. Rev. of *Hellburner. Locus* 28:6 (June 1992): 23.

—. Rev. of *Inheritor. Locus* 36:4 (Apr. 1996): 25.

—. Rev. of *Invader. Locus* 34:5 (May 1995): 25.

—. Rev. of *Precursor. Locus* 44:2 (Feb. 2000): 62.

—. Rev. of *Tripoint. Locus* 32:2 (Aug. 1994): 27, 29.

Leudtke, Paula. Rev. of *Forge of Heaven. Booklist* 100:13 (Mar. 1, 2004): 1146.

—. Rev. of *Hammerfall. Booklist* 97:16 (Apr. 15, 2001): 1539.

Levy, Michael M. Rev. of *Fortress of Owls. New York Review of Science Fiction* 11:12 (Aug. 1999): 22.

Marcus, Robin. Rev. of *Brothers of Earth. Paperback Parlour* 1:3 (June 1977): n. pag.

—. Rev. of *Gate of Ivrel. Paperback Parlour* 1:3 (June 1977): n. pag.

Martin, Sharon E. Rev. of *Rimrunners. Quantum* 36 (1990): 24-25.

Matlock, Trevin. Rev. of *Legions of Hell. Locus* 20:7 (July 1987): n. pag.

McAuley, Paul J. "Lo Tek." Rev. of *Rimrunners. Interzone* 34 (Mar.-Apr. 1990): 62.

McClure, E. J. Rev. of *Finity's End. SFRevu* 1.3 (Sept. 1997). 18 May 2004 <www.sfrevu.com/ISSUES/1997/9709/index.html#FinitysEnd>.

McDonald, Phyllis. Rev. of *The Paladin. Interzone* 37 (July 1990): 67.

McNabb, Helen. Rev. of *The Chronicles of Morgaine. Paperback Inferno* (Oct. 1985): n. pag.

—. Rev. of *Downbelow Station. Vector* 116 (Sept. 1983): 41-42.

—. Rev. of *Invader. Vector* (Sept. 1995): n. pag.

—. Rev. of *The Pride of Chanur. Paperback Inferno* (Aug. 1984): n. pag.

Meacham, B., and T. King. Rev. of *Gate of Ivrel. Science Fiction Review Monthly* 13 (Mar. 1976): 15.

Mead, Dave. Rev. of *Chanur's Homecoming. Science Fiction & Fantasy Book Review Annual.* Ed. Robert A. Collins and Robert Latham. Westport, CT: Meckler, 1988. 128.

Miller, Faren. Rev. of *Angel with a Sword. Locus* 18:8 (Aug. 1985): n. pag.

—. Rev. of *Chanur's Homecoming. Locus* 19:8 (Aug. 1986): n. pag.

—. Rev. of *Chanur's Legacy. Locus* 29:1 (July 1992): 15.

—. Rev. of *Chanur's Venture. Locus* 17:11 (Nov. 1984): 15.

—. Rev. of *Chernevog. Locus* 25:4 (Oct. 1990): 15-16.

—. Rev. of *Cuckoo's Egg. Locus* 18:5 (May 1985): n. pag.

—. Rev. of *Cyteen. Locus* 21:3 (Mar. 1988): n. pag.

—. Rev. of *Faery in Shadow. Locus* 32:1 (Jan. 1994): 49.

—. Rev. of *Forty Thousand in Gehenna. Locus* 16:8 (Aug. 1983): 24-25.

—. Rev. of *Heavy Time. Locus* 26:3 (Mar. 1991): 61.

—. Rev. of *The Kif Strike Back. Locus* 18:6 (June 1985): n. pag.

—. Rev. of *Merchanter's Luck. Locus* 15:8 (Aug. 1982): 9.

—. Rev. of *The Paladin. Locus* 21:5 (May 1988): n. pag.

—. Rev. of *Port Eternity. Locus* 15:11 (Nov. 1982): 8-9.

—. Rev. of *Rimrunners. Locus* 22:4 (Apr. 1988): n. pag.

—. Rev. of *Rusalka. Locus* 23:3 (Sept. 1989): n. pag.

—. Rev. of *Visible Light*. *Locus* 19:3 (Mar. 1986): n. pag.

—. Rev. of *Voyager in Night*. *Locus* 17:3 (Mar. 1984): 11.

—. Rev. of *Yvgenie*. *Locus* 27:4 (Oct. 1991): 17.

Moore, John. Rev. of *Invader*. *Foundation* 67 (Summer 1996): n. pag.

Morton, Nik. Rev. of *Chernevog*. *Vector* (Aug. 1991): n. pag.

—. Rev. of *Rusalka*. *Paperback Inferno* (Dec. 1990): n. pag.

Murphy, Jan. "New Science Fiction: Tri-Sexual Bugaboos and Other Alien Oddities." Rev. of *The Kif Strike Back*. *San Francisco Chronicle* (Feb. 23, 1986): 11.

Nickerson, Susan. Rev. of *The Dreamstone*. *Library Journal* 108:6 (Mar. 15, 1983): 603-04.

—. Rev. of *Merchanter's Luck*. *Library Journal* 107:16 (Sept. 15, 1982): 1772.

—. Rev. of *Port Eternity*. *Library Journal* 107:18 (Oct. 15, 1982): 2007.

—. Rev. of *Pride of Chanur*. *Library Journal* 107:4 (Feb. 15, 1982): 476-77.

—. Rev. of *The Tree of Swords and Jewels*. *Library Journal* 108:14 (Aug. 1983): 1506.

—. Rev. of *The Tree of Swords and Jewels*. *Science Fiction and Fantasy Book Review* 19 (Nov. 1983): 19-20.

—. Rev. of *Wave without a Shore*. *Library Journal* 106:16 (Sept. 15, 1981): 1756.

Notkin, D. Rev. of *The Dreamstone*. *Locus* 16:4 (Apr. 1983): 11, 24.

—. Rev. of *The Tree of Swords and Jewels*. *Locus* 16:8 (Aug. 1983): 9.

Panshin, Alexei, and Cory Panshin. Rev. of *Hunter of Worlds*. *Fantasy and Science Fiction* 54:6 (June 1978): 74-76.

Parks, Richard. Rev. of *Inheritor*. *Science Fiction Age* (May 1996): n. pag.

Penn, David. Rev. of *Serpent's Reach*. *Vector* 110 (Oct. 1982): 36-38.

Pierce, John J. Rev. of *Exile's Gate*. *Science Fiction & Fantasy Book Review Annual*. Ed. Robert A. Collins and Robert Latham. Westport, CT: Meckler, 1989. 218-19.

—. Rev. of *The Paladin*. *Science Fiction & Fantasy Book Review Annual*. Ed. Robert A. Collins and Robert Latham. Westport, CT: Meckler, 1989. 219.

Rev. of *Precursor*. *Kirkus Reviews* 67:19 (Oct. 1, 1999): 1531.

Rev. of *The Pride of Chanur*. *Publishers Weekly* 220:23 (Dec. 4, 1981): 49.

Randall, Marta. "Weird Glass & Three Sexes." Rev. of *Angel with the Sword*. *San Francisco Chronicle* (Aug. 18, 1985): 5.

Rev. of *Rider at the Gate*. *Publishers Weekly* 242:30 (July 24, 1995): 52.

Rieben, Cynthia J. Rev. of *Future on Ice*. *School Library Journal* 45:3 (Mar. 1999): 229.

Robbins, Eric. Rev. of *Future on Ice*. *Booklist* 95:2 (Sept. 15, 1998): 206.

Roberts, Robin. Rev. of *Cyteen*. *Science Fiction & Fantasy Book Review Annual*. Ed. Robert A. Collins and Robert Latham. Westport, CT: Meckler, 1989. 216-18.

Sales, Ian. Rev. of *Cuckoo's Egg*. *Paperback Inferno* (Feb. 1990): n. pag.

—. Rev. of *The Tree of Swords and Jewels*. *Paperback Inferno* (Oct. 1988): n. pag.

Sawicki, Steven. Rev. of *Dirge for Sabis*. *Quantum* 36 (1990): 25.

Sawyer, Andy. Rev. of *The Faded Sun Trilogy*. *Paperback Inferno* (June 1987): n. pag.

Schmidt, Stanley. Rev. of *Finity's End*. *Analog Science Fiction and Fact* (Mar. 1998): n. pag.

Schwartz, S. Rev. of *Serpent's Reach*. *Science Fiction Review* 9:3 (Aug. 1980): 29-30.

—. Rev. of *Sunfall*. *Science Fiction Review* 11:1 (Feb, 1982): 58-59.

Scotford, Laurence. Rev. of *Visible Light*. *Paperback Inferno* (Oct. 1988): n. pag.

Searles, B. Rev. of *The Dreamstone*. *Isaac Asimov's Science Fiction Magazine* 7:8 (Aug. 1983): 170-71.

—. Rev. of *The Faded Sun: Shon'jir*. *Isaac Asimov's Science Fiction Magazine* 3:6 (June 1979): 14-15.

—. Rev. of *Sunfall*. *Isaac Asimov's Science Fiction Magazine* 5:9 (Aug. 31, 1981): 17-18.

—. Rev. of *Voyager in Night*. *Isaac Asimov's Science Fiction Magazine* 8:10 (Oct. 1984): 170-71.

Shorb, Betsy. Rev. of *Angel with the Sword*. *School Library Journal* 32:3 (Nov. 1985): 105.

Smith, Brian. Rev. of *Hunter of Worlds*. *Vector* 99 (Oct. 1980): 21.

Sokoll, Judy. Rev. of *Once upon a Time*. *School Library Journal* 38 (Aug. 1992): 189.

Spice, Martin. "Is This Superman?" Rev. of *Lois & Clark*. *New Straits Times* (Feb. 8, 1998): New Sunday Times—Style: 12.

Stableford, Brian. Rev. of *Precursor*. *New York Review of Science Fiction* 12:11 (July 2000): 23.

Steinberg, Sybil. Rev. of *Chanur's Legacy*. *Publishers Weekly* 239:29 (June 29, 1992): 55.

—. Rev. of *Chernevog*. *Publishers Weekly* 237:36 (Sept. 7, 1990): 79.

—. Rev. of *Cloud's Rider*. *Publishers Weekly* 243:34 (Aug. 19, 1996): 56.

—. Rev. of *Fortress in the Eye of Time*. *Publishers Weekly* 242:15 (Apr. 10, 1995): 57.

—. Rev. of *Fortress of Eagles*. *Publishers Weekly* 244:52 (Dec. 22, 1997): 43.

—. Rev. of *The Goblin Mirror*. *Publishers Weekly* 239:37 (Aug. 17, 1992): 492.

—. Rev. of *Heavy Time*. *Publishers Weekly* 238:20 (May 3, 1991): 66.

—. Rev. of *Hellburner*. *Publishers Weekly* 239:34 (July 27, 1992): 52.

—. Rev. of *Inheritor*. *Publishers Weekly* 243:10 (Mar. 4, 1996): 58.

—. Rev. of *Invader*. *Publishers Weekly* 242:15 (Apr. 10, 1995): 57.

—. Rev. of *Precursor*. *Publishers Weekly* 246:41 (Oct. 11, 1999): 59.

—. Rev. of *Tripoint. Publishers Weekly* 241:35 (Aug. 29, 1994): 65.

—. Rev. of *Yvgenie. Publishers Weekly* 238:42 (Sept. 20, 1991): 124.

Steinberg, Sybil, and Jeff Zaleski. Rev. of *Fortress of Owls. Publishers Weekly* 245:50 (Dec. 14, 1998): 60-61.

Strahan, Jonathan. Rev. of *Finity's End. Locus* 39:2 (Aug. 1997): 31.

—. Rev. of *Hammerfall. Locus* 46:6 (June 2001): 31.

Strain, Paula M. Rev. of *A Dirge for Sabis*, by C. J. Cherryh and Leslie Fish. *Science Fiction & Fantasy Book Review Annual.* Ed. Robert A. Collins and Robert Latham. New York: Greenwood Press, 1990. 232-33.

—. Rev. of *Wizard Spawn*, by C. J. Cherryh and Nancy Asire. *Science Fiction & Fantasy Book Review Annual.* Ed. Robert A. Collins and Robert Latham. New York: Greenwood Press, 1990. 232-33.

—. Rev. of *Reap the Whirlwind*, by C. J. Cherryh and Mercedes Lackey. *Science Fiction & Fantasy Book Review Annual.* Ed. Robert A. Collins and Robert Latham. New York: Greenwood Press, 1990. 232-33.

Taylor, Martyn. Rev. of *Forty Thousand in Gehenna. Paperback Inferno* (Apr. 1986): n. pag.

—. Rev. of *Merchanter's Luck. Paperback Inferno* (Dec. 1984): n. pag.

—. Rev. of *Rusalka. Paperback Inferno* (Feb. 1991): n. pag.

Taylor, R. Rev. of *Downbelow Station. Voice of Youth Advocates* 4:3 (Aug. 1981): 31.

—. Rev. of *Merchanter's Luck*. *Voice of Youth Advocates* 5:6 (Feb. 1983): 43.

—. Rev. of *Serpent's Reach*. *Voice of Youth Advocates* 3:6 (Feb. 1981): 37.

Tiedemann, Mark W. Rev. of *Finity's End*. *Science Fiction Age* (Sept. 1997): n. pag.

Tomason, Sue. Rev. of *Downbelow Station*. *Paperback Inferno* (Dec. 1983): n. pag.

—. Rev. of *Faery in Shadow*. *Vector* (Feb. 1994): n. pag.

Trusesdale, David A. Rev. of *Well of Shiuan*. *Science Fiction Review* 7:3 (July 1978): 39.

Turner, James. "Futuristic Coming-of-Age Stories." Rev. of *Finity's End*. *Christian Science Monitor*, Eastern ed. 89:235 (Oct. 30, 1997): 13.

Underwood, Laura J. "Three Magic Trips Should Please Enjoyers of Fantasy." Rev. of *Faery in Shadow*. *Knoxville News-Sentinel* (Apr. 9, 1995): F6.

Rev. of *Voyager in Night*. *Publishers Weekly* 225:10 (Mar. 9, 1984): 111-12.

Rev. of *Wave Without a Shore*. *Publishers Weekly* 220:2 (July 10, 1981): 90.

Rev. of *Well of Shiuan*. *Publishers Weekly* 213:10 (Mar. 6, 1978): 99-100.

Williams, Lynn F. Rev. of *Rusalka*. *Science Fiction & Fantasy Book Review Annual*. Ed. Robert A. Collins and Robert Latham. New York: Greenwood Press, 1990. 231-32.

Winnett, Scott. Rev. of *Reap the Whirlwind*, by C. J. Cherryh and Mercedes Lackey. *Locus* 23:6 (Dec. 1989): n. pag.

Winters, Dennis. Rev. of *Cloud's Rider. Booklist* 93:2 (Sept. 15, 1996): 226.

Wolansky, T. Rev. of *Fires of Azeroth. Science Fiction and Fantasy Book Review* 1:8 (Sept. 1979): 108.

—. Rev. of *Gate of Ivrel. Science Fiction and Fantasy Book Review* 1:8 (Sept. 1979):108.

—. Rev. of *Well of Shiuan. Science Fiction and Fantasy Book Review* 1:8 (Sept. 1979): 108.

Wooster, Martin Mores. Rev. of *Brothers of Earth. SF Booklog* 12 (1976): 9.

—. Rev. of *The Faded Sun: Shon'jir. Science Fiction and Fantasy Book Review* 1:5 (June 1979): 68.

—. "The Union against the Alliance." Rev. of *The Goblin Mirror. Washington Post* (Oct. 25, 1992): WBK9.

CONTRIBUTOR BIOGRAPHIES

Susan Bernardo

Susan Bernardo is Associate Professor of English at Wagner College. She teaches courses in Victorian Literature, The Romantic Period, Gothic Literature, Fairy Tales and Science Fiction. She has published articles on Mary Shelley, George Eliot and the films of Tim Burton. She is currently co-writing a book on Ursula Le Guin's fiction for Greenwood Press.

Janice Bogstad

Dr. Janice Bogstad is Head of Collection Development for the University of Wisconsin-Eau Claire McIntyre Library, and at Eau Claire since 1990. She is also a member of the faculties of the Graduate and Women's Studies Programs and teaches and supervises M.A. Theses. Her PhD. and MA are in Comparative Literature (U of WI-Madison) for 20th century Anglo-American, French and Chinese Fiction; she also has an MLS in Information Studies. She is an active scholar in the areas of Women's Studies, Medieval Studies, Children's Literature and Science Fiction and Fantasy, presenting in venues such as the Leeds International Medieval Congress and the International Congress for the Fantastic in the Arts. She reviews in a variety of publications, including Publisher's Weekly and the Medieval Feminist Forum, and writes for reference books such as the Oxford University Press Encyclopedia of Children's Literature and the Gale Encyclopedia of Supernatural Fiction Writers. She has been writing about women, science fiction and fantasy since the 1970s.

Edward Carmien

Edward Carmien is a writer and academic with numerous non-fiction titles and a dozen stories in print. An assistant professor at Rider University's Westminster Choir College, he teaches literature, creative writing, and writing to some of the finest singers and musicians in the world. Edward is a member of the Science Fiction Writer's Association, the Science Fiction Research Association, the Modern Language Association, and the Airheads Beemer Club (#7573). He counts himself lucky to have pursued a project that has put him in touch with many talented and creative individuals.

David A. Cherry

David A. Cherry is C.J. Cherryh's brother. He lives in the Dallas, TX area and currently works for Microsoft's Ensemble Studios as an artist, producing ad art and in-game art for PC games. In the 80's and 90's he made a name for himself as a freelance artist and has done numerous book covers, including several covers for his sister's books for various publishers. He is past president and currently vice president of The Association of Science Fiction and Fantasy Artists and is a noted lecturer on art technique and the business of art. Honors and awards include several for best paperback and magazine cover as well as numerous Hugo and Chelsey Award nominations. His main interest in life is being a good Dad to his daughters, Kira and Kasi Shands-Cherry. Art comes second. But he wishes to acknowledge the help, influence, and inspiration provided by his sister, C.J., but for whom David would probably still be a grumpy old lawyer instead of pursuing his dreams as an artist.

John Clute

John Clute was born in Canada in 1940 and raised there. He has since lived in the USA and later in England. He has worked as a reviewer, mostly in the literature of the fantastic, since the early 1960s. Much of this material is assembled in *Strokes: Essays and Reviews 1966-1986* (1988), *Look at the Evidence* (1996) and *Scores: Reviews 1993-2003* (2003). He co-edited *The Encyclopedia of Science Fiction* (second edition 1993) with Peter Nicholls, and *The Encyclopedia of Fantasy* (1997) with John Grant, and wrote *Science Fiction: the Illustrated Encyclopedia* (1995) solo. He publishes fiction infrequently. His two novels are *The Disinheriting Party* (1977) and

Appleseed (2001). The latter is SF. A Third Edition of *The Encyclopedia of Science Fiction* is in the works.

Janice C. Crosby

Janice C. Crosby, Associate Professor of English at Southern University in Baton Rouge, specializes in feminist Science Fiction and Fantasy studies, especially in terms of spirituality, with a number of publications and numerous presentations (especially at PCA) in that area. Occasionally she diverges into Southern fiction and detective writing, and is currently working on an article on James Lee Burke. In her other life, she is Belita Karima, student and teacher of Middle Eastern dance for over fourteen years ("got an article out of that too in *Daughters of the Goddess*").

Jane Fancher

Jane Fancher, a full-time writer, has been C.J. Cherryh's business partner and alpha reader since 1985. A physics/math/astronomy/anthropology major, she never passes up an opportunity to try something new. Over the years, she's paid her bills working with horses, dolphins, airplanes and computers, and currently fills her spare time with painting, stitching, playing with her computer, and watching Mariners baseball. Her mid-life-crisis passion is learning to figure-skate. She lives in Spokane, Washington with her cat, Efanor.

James Gunn

James Gunn, Emeritus Professor of English at the University of Kansas, has had dual careers as a writer and a scholar of science fiction symbolized by his presidencies of both the Science Fiction Writers of America and of the Science Fiction Research Association. His best known novels are *The Joy Makers, The Immortals, The Listeners, Kampus,* and *The Dreamers,* and his best known academic books are *Alternate Worlds: the Illustrated History of Science Fiction, Isaac Asimov: The Foundations of Science Fiction,* and the six-volume *The Road to Science Fiction.*

Burton Raffel

Burton Raffel has been reading sf since about 1939, and writing it since 1952 or so. He has also written a cannibal movie (filmed and exhibited), lots of fiction and poetry, many translations, some critical books and teaching texts and anthologies, and has recently begun a series, for Yale U P, of very fully annotated editions of Shakespeare. He is a member of the Bar of the State of New York, has worked as an editor, a foundation director, and especially as a university teacher. His books for 2004 are *Pure Pagan*, a slender volume of translations from ancient Greek poetry (Modern Library) and vol.# 2 in the Yale Shakespeare series, *Romeo and Juliet.*

Elizabeth A. Romey

Elizabeth A. Romey is currently a doctoral candidate at the University of Connecticut's prestigious gifted-ed psych program with a triple concentration in counseling psychology, gifted-ed psych, and research methodology, and a graduate assistant with the Neag Center for Gifted Education and Talent Development and the Teachers for a New Era Project. In her (purely hypothetical) spare time, she writes science fiction (with an emphasis on political science, behavioral genetics, and psychology) and fantasy. Her first two novels, *Lera of Tymoria: The Dragonmage* and *DragonMagic*, are available from Royal Fireworks Press, while the third book in the series, tentatively titled *The Arkanus*, is in progress.

Bradley H. Sinor

Not too long ago a friend of Brad's commented that Brad wrote family stories. "Yeah," Brad told him, "If you're related to the Addams Family or one of Dracula's relatives."

Be that as it may, Brad has seen more than his short stories published in the last few years in such anthologies as *Warrior Fantastic, Knight Fantastic, Dracula in London, Bubbas of the Apocalypse, Merlin, Lord of the Fantastic, Men Writing SF as Women,* and *Four Bubbas of the Apocalypse.* In 2004 he will have new and reprint stories escaping into the world in anthologies such as *Haunted Holidays, The Magic Shop,* and *Rotten Relations* (written in collaboration with his wife Sue). Two collections of his short fiction have been released by Yard Dog Press, *Dark and Stormy Nights* and *In the Shadows.*

He has also seen his non-fiction appear in *Dark Zones, Starlog, Personal Demons, Enterprise, California Highway Patrolman, Top Deck,* and *Long Island Monthly* among many, many others. He will have a new essay appearing in the anthology *Walking Through the Stargate* as well as *The Cherryh Odyssey*.

Heather Stark

"I was drawn to the idea of writing a piece on C.J. Cherry for this book because I have been reading her work for over twenty years, and, even after all this time, I still find it both puzzling and wonderful. Work that is merely puzzling or merely wonderful doesn't inspire quite the same curiosity. One reason that I find her work puzzling is because it constantly resists my attempts to put it in a box. This isn't just because there is so much of it, and an unusually big box would be required. It's the diversity of the work that is the real puzzle: many *different* boxes would be required. But which boxes? Why? That's the mystery that I keep coming back to. At home, I have taken a totally pragmatic approach to the issue: I put all her work together, on a shelf of its very own—a very *big* shelf. Probably quite correctly, this places it all in a category of its very own. In [my] essay, I try other approaches to puzzling out why I find it wonderful—and why I find it puzzling."

J.G. Stinson

J.G. Stinson is a freelance proofreader, copy editor and writer who lives in Michigan with her son. She says she was first exposed to SF in 7th grade, when she found the *Masterpieces of Science Fiction* anthology (in particular, Alfred Bester's T*he Stars My Destination*) and Andre Norton's *Moon of Three Rings* in her school library. She bought her first Cherryh novel (the paperback edition of *Gate of Ivrel*) in 1976, based solely on the introduction written for it by Andre Norton. Her reviews, interviews and essays have been published in *Strange Horizons, Tangent, The New York Review of Science Fiction, Inscriptions, Speculations* and *SpecFicMe!*

Stan Szalewicz

A native of Oil City, Pennsylvania, Stan Szalewicz was appointed Media Librarian at Talbott Library of Westminster Choir College of Rider University in Princeton, New Jersey, in May 2001. He holds a Master of Arts degree in organ performance from Indiana University of Pennsylvania, and a Master of Library Science degree with specialization in music librarianship from Indiana University, Bloomington. Prior to coming to Rider University,

Stan worked as a music cataloger at Indiana University's Archives of Traditional Music, the OCLC Online Computer Library Center, Inc. in Dublin, Ohio, and at the Public Library of Cincinnati and Hamilton County.

Betsy Wollheim

Elizabeth R. Wollheim, known by everyone as Betsy, is the daughter of veteran paperback science fiction editor Donald A. Wollheim. She got her editorial start at the tender age of fifteen as a freelance copyeditor for Ace Books, working under the highly critical, ever-constant gaze of her father. She worked almost exclusively on Westerns which she still believes to be the dullest of all genres. After graduating college with a BA in English Lit, and simultaneously attending art school majoring in photography, she worked in magazine printing for two years which proved an invaluable experience. Returning to New York City in 1975, she began working for her parents at DAW Books, the first publishing company devoted exclusively to science fiction and fantasy, beginning ten of the most difficult years of her life. Betsy took control of DAW in April 1985, and has been running the company with her business partner, Sheila Gilbert, since then. At DAW she is the Publisher, Editor-in-Chief and Co-Art Director and is involved in virtually all other departments, including marketing, royalties, contracts, and finance. After 33 years, DAW is still an independent company with 100% of its corporate stock privately held by Betsy and Sheila. Betsy lives in Manhattan with her husband, musician Peter Stampfel, and their two daughters.